HORIZONS

BOOK 2

ELECTIVE 5
OPTIONS 7 & 8

Access your eBook

New eBook users

1. Scratch the foil below to reveal your unique licence code
2. Register on www.folenshive.ie with your code
3. A parent or legal guardian will have to give their consent for you to access our eBooks
4. Download the FolensHIVE app to your device or use the web platform
5. Login to access your eBook

Current FolensHIVE users can redeem additional eBooks through the app.

Teachers please go to FolensHIVE to login or register

FolensHIVE

First published in 2016 by Folens Publishers

Hibernian Industrial Estate, Greenhills Road, Tallaght, Dublin 24

© Tara Fitzharris, Brian Daly 2016

Illustrations: Peter Bull Art Studio

ISBN 978-1-78090-644-7

Acknowledgements

The authors would like to thank Amanda Harman and Mike Harman, as well as Conor Walker, Alycia Kearney, Karen Hoey and all the staff at Folens for all their help and support while working on this project.

Tara Fitzharris: I would like to dedicate this book to Lily and Ruby. I would also like to thank my family and friends for their support and encouragement over the years.

Brian Daly: I would like to dedicate this book to my parents; without their encouragement I might never have studied Geography. I would also like to thank my family for all their support and patience, and the staff and students of Adamstown Community College for their input and ideas.

Photograph acknowledgements

The author and publisher would like to thank the following for permission to reproduce photographs: Alamy, Corbis, Getty Images, *The Irish Times*, iStock, Photocall Ireland, Shutterstock, cartoon on p.48 reproduced by permission of CartoonStock, photo on p.102 (bottom) © Jamie Malone. Aerial photographs reproduced by permission of Peter Barrow Photography.

Map acknowledgement

Ordnance Survey maps are reproduced by permission of the following: Ordnance Survey Ireland (Permit No. 9044) © Ordnance Survey Ireland/Government of Ireland

Contents

Introduction

What is this course about?

This is a two-year course that lays the foundations for all areas of Geography. *Horizons 2* covers one Elective unit and two Option units of the course for Leaving Certificate (Ordinary and Higher Level):

- **Elective unit 5:** Patterns and processes in the human environment
- **Option unit 7:** Geoecology (Higher Level only)
- **Option unit 8:** Culture and identity (Higher Level only).

It begins with **human geography**, which examines the distribution, density and movement of population across the globe and throughout history. It looks at the various methods we use to study population, along with detailed case studies. Map work is again further developed in the study of settlement and the location of our towns and cities and how they have changed in size and make-up over time.

After that, we move to study either the **geoecology** Option or **culture and identity** Option for those students hoping to take the Higher Level paper in the exams.

Geoecology examines the development of soil and its soil-forming characteristics. It also examines the impact that both climate and human activity can have on its development. The section also focuses on the desert biome and detailed case studies.

Culture and identity examines how populations can be studied using physical and social indicators such as race, language, religion and nationality. The section also examines the impact of nationality, identity and the nation state on the physical and cultural landscape through the use of case studies.

How to study the course

The key to studying the Leaving Certificate Geography course is to view it as a two-year course, not one to be studied in sixth year. If all exams in both the fifth and sixth year are viewed as important as the Leaving Certificate and if every piece of note-taking and homework is treated as importantly as the GI booklet to be handed in with the exam, then the battle is won. You will be ahead before you have even started. Do not underestimate how little time you have in your senior years – you need to do things well the first time. Start your studying from the beginning of the course, not after Christmas in sixth year. It is a long course, so give it the time it needs and you will achieve good results.

Geoterms: key words and important terms relevant to a topic.

Quick questions: questions that appear in every chapter that encourage students to stop and think about what they have learned. In every set of questions there are **timed activities**, similar to the exam questions asked, that help students to practise the skill of writing **significant relevant points (SRPs),** which can be particularly challenging at the start of fifth year. Students should time themselves while they are completing the activity, as this is the timing that they will need to adhere to in the exams.

Exam hints: tips and hints to help students in their exam preparation.

Exam questions: past paper questions (Ordinary and Higher Level) are included at the end of every chapter.

Hot topics: questions or topics in the chapters that are very popular in the exams.

Case studies: real-world examples of concepts relating to physical and regional geography.

Notes: additional points of information.

Interesting facts: novel points to help support the learning process.

Syllabus links: these indicate what syllabus learning outcomes a chapter relates to.

Chapter links: topics are not always asked in isolation in the exam, which is something students can forget about when they are studying in sixth year. Chapter links show the connection between chapters and how topics could be pooled together in an exam question.

Cross-curricular links: these show where a topic links to other Leaving Certificate subjects.

SRP markers: bold text indicates how much relevant content must be covered per topic.

Mind maps: end-of-chapter mind maps illustrate key summary points.

Skills icons

In the quick questions, the related geography skills being practised are identified:

 Map interpretation skills: reading information from an OS map.

 Map drawing skills: drawing a sketch map of an OS map or an aerial photograph.

 Figure interpretation skills: reading a graph or chart and understanding what the information displayed on it means.

 Figure drawing skills: drawing a well-labelled, clear diagram to explain a process.

 Photograph analysis skills: reading information from an aerial photograph.

 Statistical analysis skills: understanding statistics and using them in your answers.

For teachers

Horizons 2 has supporting resources. There are printable **worksheets** differentiated as Ordinary and Higher Level questions. These can be used to complement the textbook and class work along with the many other **digital resources**, on folensonline.ie.

Teachers' time is precious and an ever-increasing workload is asked of them, so we have tried to lessen that burden a little by providing differentiated class work, lesson plans, digital resources, online resources and self-evaluations in the *Horizons* programme.

Wishing you all the very best,

Tara Fitzharris and Brian Daly

ELECTIVE

5

Patterns and processes
in the
human environment

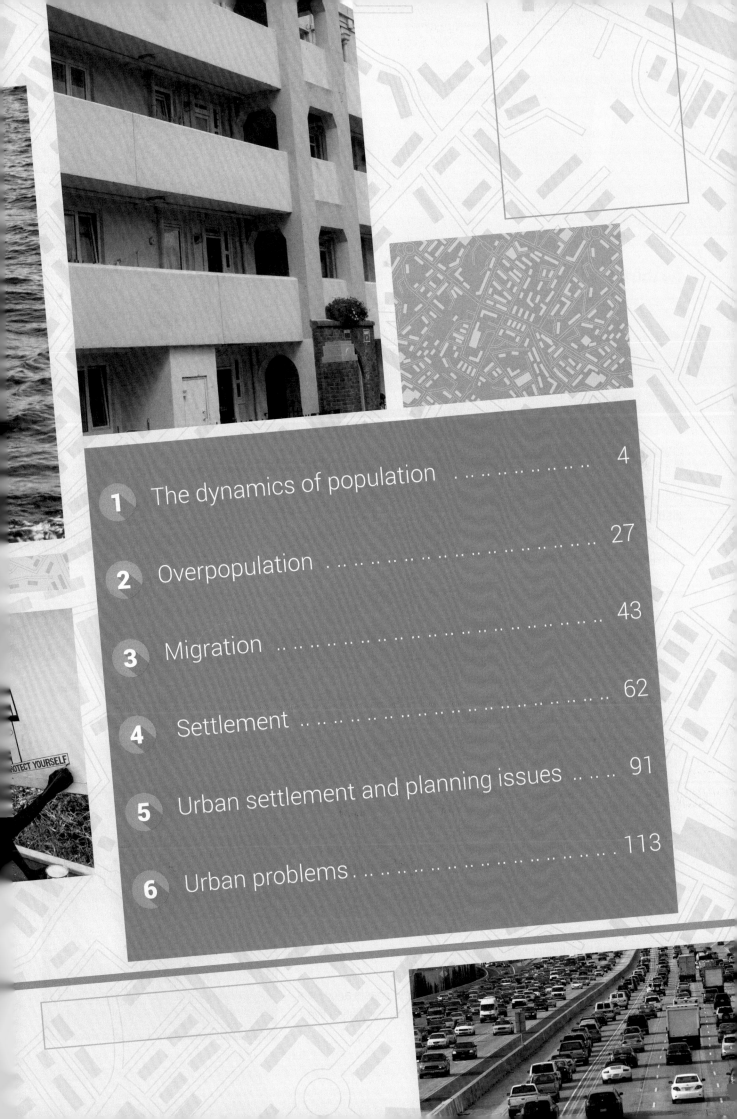

1 The dynamics of population

By the end of this chapter, students will have studied:

○ Population distribution and density
○ The factors that impact on population growth rates and structure
○ The demographic transition model and fertility rates
○ Life expectancy and mortality rates

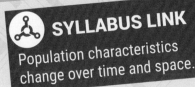 **SYLLABUS LINK**
Population characteristics change over time and space.

NOTE

This section should be allowed at least 11 class periods (40 minutes).

EXAM HINTS

The material in this chapter has appeared on the exam papers every year since 2006.

Introduction

Populations of countries are **dynamic** and change over time in **density**, **distribution** and **structure**. In the developing world populations are growing rapidly, while in the developed world they have started to slow down. The study of population is called **demography**, or **demographic studies**.

Population distribution

Population distribution is the **spread of people across the world**. The distribution of people is affected by many factors, such as landscape, resources, climate, socio-economics and history. The world's population is unevenly distributed, because 80 per cent of the population live on just 10 per cent of the land. Some areas of the world, such as Mali, are sparsely populated, and some areas, such as the Netherlands, are densely populated.

Factors influencing population distribution

Here are some of the factors that can influence population distribution:

- **Altitude:** people prefer to live in locations that are less than 200 m above sea level, as the climate is more favourable and the soils are of good quality. The relief of these lower altitude areas is less extreme, and construction of roads and houses is easier and cheaper.

- **Latitude:** 90 per cent of the world's population live in the Northern Hemisphere, between latitudes 20° and 60° as the climate is more favourable than further north or south. There is also a longer growing season, making farming easier.

- **Water:** population figures for settlements near to coasts and rivers are very high worldwide. Two-thirds of the world's population live within 500 km of the coast.

GEOTERMS

○ A **resource** is anything that can be used by humans. Resources can be divided into renewable and non-renewable.
○ **Dynamic** means 'very active' or 'forceful'.
○ **Relief** is how flat or rugged a landscape is.
○ **Altitude** is the height above a certain point – in this case sea level.

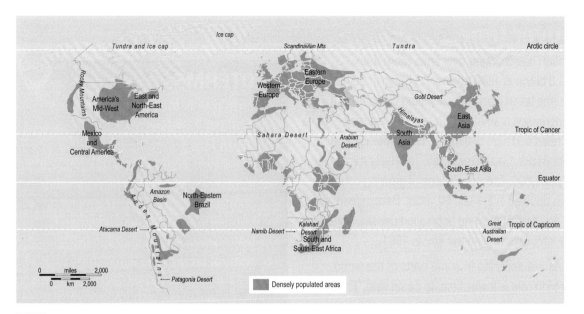

1.1 Distribution of the world's population today

- **Resources:** there are high population densities in Europe, because this was the location of large deposits of coal in the nineteenth century. These deposits were used to fuel the Industrial Revolution, which took place in the region.

- **History:** there are higher population densities along coastal areas of South America, as these are the areas that were colonised by Europeans in the sixteenth century. The plantations brought Scottish and Welsh people to Ireland, and the Great Famine of the 1840s resulted in over a million Irish people moving to the UK and the USA.

- **Urbanisation:** over 50 per cent of the world's population live in urban areas today, up from 30 per cent in 1950. This has mainly been due to rural–urban migration as economies change from agricultural to industrial. Growth rates of urban areas are normally double the pace of the country's population increase.

- **Government:** countries with stable democratic governmental systems attract people, as they bring peace and justice to their citizens. Areas experiencing political conflict often have lower population densities as people are forced to leave quickly for safety.

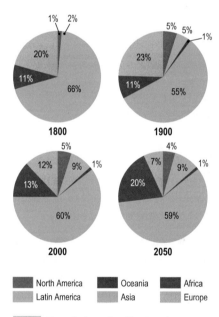

1.2 Population distribution (as a percentage of the world's population) per region from 1800 to 2050 (estimate)

Population density

Population density is described as the **average number of people per square kilometre** (km²). A country is said to be densely populated if it has more than 100 people per km² and sparsely populated if it has fewer than 10 people per km². Ireland has an average population of 65 per km².

Other areas have a high population density, such as Bangladesh with 1,039 per km², or a low population density, such as Mali with 9 people per km². Population density can hide the fact that some areas can have a lot of inhabitants and other areas are inhospitable. For example, Brazil's population density is 20 per km², but in the Amazon Rainforest it is 6 per km² and in the capital, Brasilia, it is 410 per km².

WORKED EXAMPLE

| Ireland's total population | 4,595,000 = 65.4 people per km² |
| Ireland's total area | 70,282 km |

Change over time

The world's population has changed over time, more than quadrupling from 1.6 billion in 1900 to over 7.3 billion in 2015. Most of the growth has taken place in developing countries. Their populations have increased dramatically in recent decades because of declining death rates and high birth rates. **Birth rate** is the number of babies born per 1,000. **Death rate** (mortality rate) is the number of deaths per 1,000. The populations of growing countries such as China have doubled in the last 50 years. Bangladesh has one of the highest and fastest growing population densities of the world, at 1,218 per km², up from 746 per km² in 1991.

Population densities are declining in some parts of the world where a country's birth rate is lower than its death rate. These countries are now experiencing a **natural decrease** (a greater number of deaths than births in a country each year) in their population. For example, the population of Russia has declined from 148 million in 1991 to 143 million in 2014 (9 per km²).

GEOTERMS

- **Birth rate** is the number of babies born per 1,000 per year.
- **Death rate** (mortality rate) is the number of deaths per 1,000 per year.
- **Replacement level** is the number of children born per mother at which population exactly replaces itself from one generation to the next.
- **Natural increase** is when there is a greater number of births than deaths in a country per annum (per year).
- **Natural decrease** is when there is a greater number of deaths than births in a country per annum (per year).

CASE STUDY 1.1
France

Population distribution and density

The population of France is **unevenly distributed** because 50 per cent of the population is located in 10 per cent of the country.

In the past, France was mainly an agricultural society based on **communes** (rural villages), and it was only in the 1930s that urban population figures were higher than rural ones. These figures have continued to increase, and today over 77 per cent of France's population is urban based.

The **Greater Paris area** is one of the main areas in France with a high population density. This area has a population of 11 million people, which accounts for 20 per cent of the French population. Paris is the capital of France and is a **primate city**. It is also the location of the French Government. It provides a vast number of jobs in services, such as tourism and industry. It is the centre of French education, fashion and development. Other densely populated areas include Île-de-France, Nord-Pas-de-Calais and Alsace.

The **'empty diagonal'** is one of the main areas in France to suffer from low population density. This is a vast area of land that stretches from the north-east of France to the south-west. It is an underdeveloped rural region. It suffers from outward migration of young people, as it has been unsuccessful in attracting inward investment. Other more remote areas of France also support low population densities, such as the mountainous regions of the Alps and the drought-ridden region of the Massif Central.

Change over time

France's **population has grown rapidly** in the second half of the twentieth century and first decade of the twenty-first, rising from 19 million to just over 66 million today. This is

1.3 Paris has a high population density

attributed to France being one of the first countries whose death rate significantly reduced during the eighteenth century.

Population growth rates in France are higher than in other countries in Europe. It has the highest **total fertility rate** (TFR) in Europe, at two children per mother, and the death rate has remained stable at less than 10 per thousand.

Persons per sq. km.
- 400 – 914
- 300 – 399
- 150 – 299
- 60 – 149
- 30 – 59

1.4 The population density of France and the 'empty diagonal'

GEOTERMS

- A **primate** city has more than twice the population of the next largest city in the country.
- **Total fertility rate** (TFR) is the average number of babies born to a mother during her reproductive years.
- **Outward migration** occurs when people leave their homeplace and settle in another.

QUICK QUESTIONS

1. Define the term *population distribution*.
2. Name and briefly explain three factors that can influence the location of the world's population. (Timed activity: 6 min; 3 SRPs)
3. Define the term *population density*.
4. Why is population density higher in the developing world than in the developed world?
5. If France's total population is 66 million and its total area is 640,679 km², calculate France's population density per km².

World population growth patterns

World population **growth patterns** have changed dramatically over the last few centuries. During the eighteenth century commentators such as Thomas Malthus were concerned that the world population would vastly outgrow food supplies. They believed a natural disaster was necessary for population figures to return to manageable levels again. Since then, the population of the world has increased six-fold.

The great plagues and wars of earlier centuries wiped out huge numbers of people, but the world's population figures have steadily increased in recent times. These increases have been aided by the **Agricultural Revolution**, which increased food output worldwide with the introduction of crop rotation and other improvements. The **Industrial Revolution** of the nineteenth century absorbed the increasing working population. Finally, the **Medical Revolution** in recent decades has helped to eliminate crippling diseases and improve basic healthcare and sanitation. These have all contributed to the world population more than doubling between 1960 and 2010 and finally reaching over 7 billion in 2011, causing some geographers to label the phenomenon a **population explosion**.

GEOTERMS

- A **growth pattern** is a change in the population growth rate over time.
- During the **Industrial and Agricultural Revolutions** machinery and technology began to be used in farming and manufacturing. During this time many people moved from the countryside to live in towns.
- A **population explosion** is a dramatic increase in the world's population.

Population change

The three main components to determine population change are birth rates, death rates and migration. For the population of the world to remain stable, the average **fertility rate** across the world would have to be 2.1 children per mother. The world fertility rate in 2008 was 2.5 children per mother, causing the population of the world to continue to grow. Most of this growth is taking place in the developing world, where the average fertility rate varies from 2.5 to 3.3 births per mother.

In the developed world the rate has fallen below replacement levels and now stands at 1.56 births per mother. However, life expectancy in countries worldwide is on the increase. In developed world countries, it is set to rise from 75 years today to 82 years by 2050. In developing countries, **life expectancy** is also set to rise from 50 years today to 66 years by 2050.

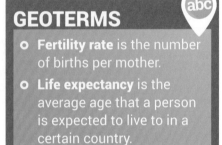

INTERESTING FACTS

People's access to safe drinking water increased from 40 per cent in 1975 to over 80 per cent in 2010.

GEOTERMS

o **Fertility rate** is the number of births per mother.
o **Life expectancy** is the average age that a person is expected to live to in a certain country.

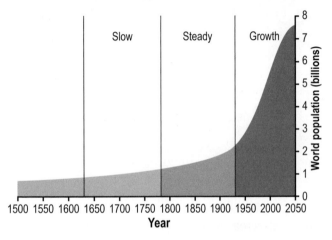

1.5 Global population growth and projected figures for 2050

Changing fertility rates

Factors affecting fertility rates in the developed world

Fertility rates in the developed world are low. As the economy and wealth of a country increases, the birth rate decreases for some of the following reasons:

- **Working mothers:** in Ireland the figure for women working outside the home increased from 28 per cent in 1971 to about 60 per cent in 2014 (it dropped slightly to 55 per cent during the 2008–13 recession due to lack of jobs). The majority of women working in Ireland are of childbearing age. As women have entered the workforce, they tend to have fewer babies. Women can now make informed decisions about their family size since contraception is readily available. They also tend to have smaller families because they do not need large families to support them when they are older. Children may be viewed as an economic liability.

- **Education:** as more women are remaining in education for longer, marriage, and often motherhood, is delayed.

- **Governmental encouragement:** the contribution of women in the workforce has been reinforced by governments with incentives to work, such as paid maternity leave and childcare provisions, and equal pay and promotion opportunities.

- **Increased cost of living:** today most women have to work outside the home to maintain a good quality of life, as living costs continue to rise.

- **Cost of raising a child:** in Ireland the cost of raising a child for five years is estimated at €8,000 per annum. This cost can place people under a lot of economic pressure, which reduces people's desire to have large families.
- **Decline in the influence of the Catholic Church:** this has allowed people to delay marriage and to plan their families.
- **Urbanisation:** this has caused a decrease in population numbers because people have moved to live in cities, so children are no longer needed as farm labour.

The developed world is experiencing a net natural decrease in its population at present because in some countries death rates are higher than birth rates. Inward migration from developing world countries is helping to maintain the population of the developed world. In some countries in Europe, governments are introducing child-friendly policies in order to create sustainable population levels. For example, France has longer maternity leave than other EU states.

Factors affecting fertility rates in the developing world

Fertility rates are still high in the developing world. This causes concern, because if population numbers continue to grow the economies of these countries will be badly affected. This has serious implications for issues such as environment and food supply. Here are some of the main reasons why fertility rates are so high in the developing world:

- **Early marriage:** women in the developing world often start their families at a very young age. For example, in countries such as Mali, 40 per cent of girls have one child before the age of 18. As a result of these early marriages, families are likely to be larger.
- **Traditional roles:** in the developing world only a small (although increasing) percentage of women make up the paid workforce because they are tied to more traditional roles. In countries such as China the figure has increased dramatically, from 7.5 per cent in 1949 to over 49 per cent in 2014.

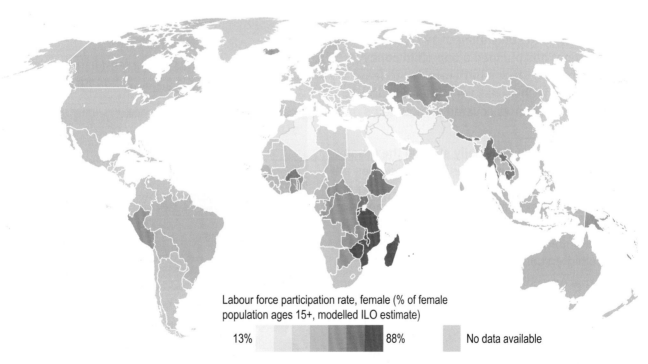

Labour force participation rate, female (% of female population ages 15+, modelled ILO estimate)

13%   88%   No data available

1.6 World map of labour participation rates for women

- **Lack of education:** uneducated women in the developing world tend to have a low social status and lack access to, and correct understanding of, family planning. The trend shows that mothers who have received an education tend to have smaller families. In Brazil a survey of young mothers revealed that those without second level education had an average of 6.5 children. Those who had second level education had an average of 2.5 children.

- **Children viewed as an asset:** in the developing world, children are viewed as an economic advantage because these countries do not have state pensions to provide for elderly people. People rely on their children to support them later in life. Therefore it is important for them to have large families to lessen the burden.

- **Governmental encouragement:** in some countries government policies influence the size of families. On the one hand, in countries such as Romania large families are encouraged because the government wants to ensure large numbers of recruits for the army as well as state workers. On the other hand, the Chinese Government introduced a one-child policy in 1979 with the aim of decreasing the country's huge population growth.

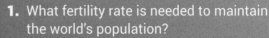

QUICK QUESTIONS

1. What fertility rate is needed to maintain the world's population?
2. Name and explain three factors that can affect fertility rates in the developing world.
3. Name and explain three factors that can affect fertility rates in the developed world.
4. Name one government policy that was introduced that affected a country's population growth.
5. From Figure 1.6 take the percentage rates of women participating in the workforce for three countries and display the information on a bar chart. (Timed activity: 6 min)

CASE STUDY 1.2
China

From 1949 to 1976, under the regime of Mao Tse-tung, China's population grew quickly, with an average fertility rate of six children per mother. Since the beginning of 1979, the Chinese Government has pursued a **one-child policy** in order to reduce China's birth rate due to fears of overcrowding: China has very little habitable land, as over 75 per cent is covered in mountains and deserts.

- This policy is **especially strict in the urban regions of China**. In these areas couples are allowed only one child. In rural areas parents are allowed to have two children if the first child is a girl, because boys are more valued in Chinese society. People who have more children can face considerable fines.

- This one-child policy has led to an **imbalance of the sexes** in China. Official census figures show that the ratio of boys to girls in the country is 106.7 boys to 100 girls. It is suggested that these figures do not tell the true story. The ratio could be as high as 117:100. The reasons behind this are traditionally based:

- Boys are needed for agricultural labour, much of which is manual.
- Boys are more highly regarded in Chinese society than girls.
- If a family has only a female heir, this is regarded as a great dishonour.

1.7 A Chinese family in Shanghai with their only child

- Chinese couples, especially in rural regions, are so concerned about having a son that ultrasounds are performed to see if the foetus is female. This has led to an increase in **illegal abortions** of female foetuses. Female abortion has continued in the country even though the Government introduced a law banning abortion on the grounds of gender. This is supported by figures showing that in 95.7 per cent of all abortions the foetus is female. In Chinese orphanages 90 per cent of the children are abandoned girls.

- As a result of the one-child policy, over a very short period of time China has moved from stage 2 (early expanding stage) to stage 4 (low stationary stage) of the demographic transition model (see pages 12–14). The population of China is still growing by 9 million a year, because traditionally Chinese people marry young. This increasing population is an issue that the Chinese Government needs to address.

- In 2013 the policy was relaxed. Chinese couples living in urban areas could now have two children but only if one parent was an only child. This was implemented in 29 of the 31 provinces with very little effect.

- In 2015 an end to the one-child policy was finally declared as the Chinese Government stated that it would like to 'improve the balance of population'. It is believed that the Government is concerned about issues such as the male/female ratio and the growing ageing dependent population in the country.

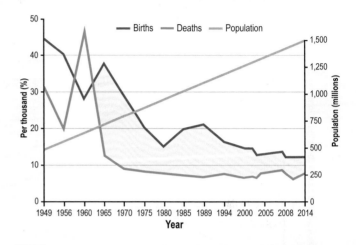

1.8 China's population growth, births and deaths from 1949 to 2014

Life expectancy and mortality rates

As the development of a country improves, its **infant mortality rate** declines. Approximately 10 million children under five years of age die every year. Half of these are killed by five diseases: malaria, measles, pneumonia, diarrhoea and acquired immune deficiency syndrome (AIDS). This equates to 1 child in 8 in the developing world and 1 child in 143 in the developed world.

In the developing world people often live in poor conditions, in shanty towns for example, where clean water and sanitation are not available. Children are often malnourished because they lack a balanced diet. **Malnourished children** are more likely to get sick. Improvements are needed in healthcare, water cleanliness, food supply, education and political stability (to prevent wars) to reduce mortality rates in the developing world.

Life expectancy is linked to the economic development of a country, healthcare, clean water, urban sewage systems and mass vaccinations. In the developed world, life expectancy averages in the high 70s. However, it can be as low as 40 years in some developing world countries. Some countries in the developing world have defied all odds and have life expectancies like those of developed countries. This is because their governments have prioritised the provision of healthcare services and clean water. One example is Cuba, where the life expectancy is 77 years. Other governments have neglected their health services. An example of this is Russia, where life expectancy has fallen from 69 to 65 years.

AIDS has become one of the newest and biggest threats to life expectancy worldwide. It is most devastating in the countries of sub-Saharan Africa. AIDS was

GEOTERMS ⓐⓑⓒ

- The **infant mortality rate** is the number of children per 1,000 live births who die before their first birthday.

- **Shanty towns** are slum areas of poorly built huts, with few services. They are normally located on the outskirts of large cities in the developing world.

first recognised in the 1980s but in 2007 there were almost 39 million sufferers worldwide. In the developed world antiretroviral drugs are helping to prolong the lives of people diagnosed as positive for **HIV**, the virus that causes AIDS. However, these drugs are too expensive for the majority of people in the developing world. Some countries in sub-Saharan Africa have failed to tackle the problem, but thankfully that is not the case everywhere. In Uganda the Government has launched a major campaign to raise public awareness about the disease. This has led to a reduction in the number of new cases being diagnosed in that country.

--- HIV infections (global, in millions)

--- AIDS-related deaths (global in millions)

1.9 The global number of deaths due to AIDS between 1990 and 2013

1.10 A man paints an AIDS poster in Uganda

Demographic transition model

The demographic transition model is used by geographers today to **explain population growth patterns** in countries. This model indicates that countries go through predictable changes in population as their economy improves. Countries in the developed world have gradually passed through this cycle, but in the developing world they are passing through it at a much faster pace. Economic development of a country greatly influences population growth rates.

This model can also be called the **population transition model**. Countries move from one stage of the model to the next as their economy becomes more developed. Most countries in the developed world are in stages 4 or 5 of the model. Most countries in the developing world are in stages 2 or 3 of the model. Today, **90 per cent of all population growth is in the developing world**.

Stage 1: High stationary stage

During the high stationary stage, both the birth rate and the death rate of a country are high and fluctuating (constantly changing). This is the case as famines, wars and natural disasters are commonplace. The infant mortality rate is high and life expectancy is short. **Population growth is slow.** These regions are underdeveloped and dependent on agriculture. European countries experienced this stage of the cycle in the 1700s. **Rwanda, during its civil war in the 1990s,** experienced this stage of the population cycle due to people's poor living conditions.

Stage 2: Early expanding stage

In the early expanding stage of the cycle, birth rates remain high as family planning has not been introduced and the status of women is still quite low. With the introduction of cleaner water supplies, basic healthcare and the wiping out of common diseases such as smallpox, the death rate of the country falls dramatically. This leads to a **massive increase in population growth**, with the birth rate far higher than the death rate. This occurred in Europe in the late eighteenth century during the Industrial and Agricultural Revolutions. Today countries such as **Nigeria** are typical of this stage of the cycle.

Stage 3: Late expanding stage

During the late expanding stage, the death rate of the country continues to fall but at a slower rate than before because people are living in a healthier environment. The birth rate is also decreasing as family size is getting smaller. This is due to a decrease in the infant mortality rate and large families being viewed as an economic liability. During this stage of the cycle, there is **still an increase in the population but at a more gradual pace**. This occurred in Europe during the end of the nineteenth century and the early twentieth century, as general living standards improved and countries became more economically developed and urbanised. Some of the countries representing this stage today are **Bangladesh**, **Mexico** and **Brazil**.

Stage 4: Low stationary stage

In the low stationary stage of the cycle, the birth rate is only slightly higher than the death rate and **population growth is very low**. This occurred in Europe from the 1950s onwards as society became richer and industrialised. Women improved their social standing through education and state equality laws. A large proportion of women are in full-time employment. This has had an impact on reducing family size. **Ireland** is in this stage of the demographic transition model. Some developing countries, such as Costa Rica, are also in this stage of the cycle.

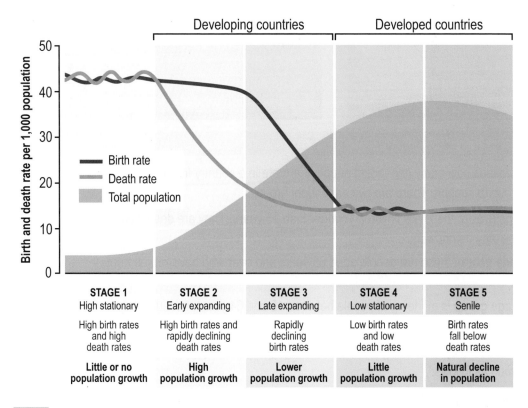

1.11 The demographic transition model

Stage 5: Senile stage

During the senile stage of the cycle, the death rate is higher than the birth rate for the first time because more people in the country die than are born each year. Life expectancy is greater during this stage than any other. The **population growth** of the country is said to be **in decline** or **negative**. Only some European countries, such as **Germany and Italy**, have reached this stage today. Inward migration is the only way to prevent these countries' populations from continuing to fall. It is expected that Ireland will reach this stage of the cycle in the next 20 years as the country's population continues to 'grey'.

NOTE

Ireland's population experienced stage 2 of the demographic transition model until the early twentieth century. After that, emigration kept the population in check. Ireland moved in to stage 4 of the model during the late 1990s as the economy developed, and over the next 20 years it is expected that the population will age and naturally decrease as Ireland moves into stage 5 of the demographic transition model.

GEOTERMS

A **'greying' of the population** is when a larger percentage of the population is older due to a decreased birth rate and long life expectancy.

Population structure

The population structure of a country refers generally to its **age and gender profile**. Specifically it examines the proportion of people in each of the different age groups and the proportion of males to females. It also examines the proportion of dependent population to economically active population, which is known as the **dependency ratio**. This information is displayed on a graph called a **population pyramid**.

QUICK QUESTIONS

1. Explain the 'one-child' policy in China and why the Chinese Government introduced such a radical scheme.
2. How is life expectancy linked to the economic development of a country?
3. Give another name for the demographic transition model.
4. Describe two stages of the demographic transition model. (Timed activity: 6 min; 6 SRPs)
5. In which stage of the demographic transition model is Ireland today?

EXAM HINTS

This topic has appeared a number of times as short questions on the exam papers at both Higher and Ordinary levels.

Dependency ratio

The dependency ratio determines how many dependent people there are in a country for the economically active age group to support. There are two dependent groups:

- **Young dependent age group:** these are children younger than 15 years. They are described as dependent because they do not work.
- **Elderly dependent age group:** these are people aged 65 years and over who have retired from the workforce.

The **economically active age group** is made up of people between 15 and 64 years, because they are of working age.

The dependency ratio is determined by expressing the dependent age groups as a percentage of the economically active age group as follows:

$$\frac{\text{Dependent age groups}}{\text{Economically active age groups}} \times \frac{100}{1}$$

The dependency ratio is **highest in developing countries**, where it can be up to 100 dependents for every 100 workers. It is the **lowest in developed countries**, where the ratio is between 45 and 70 per 100 workers.

Population pyramids

There are three main types of population pyramids: progressive, regressive and stationary. As a country develops it naturally moves from progressive through stationary to regressive.

- **Progressive population pyramids** have a wide base and a narrow top. This indicates a high birth rate and a high death rate. Countries with a progressive population pyramid would be in stages 1–3 of the demographic transition model. Mexico is an example of this.

- **Stationary population pyramids** are fairly uniform in shape, with all age groups well represented. Birth rates are moderate and life expectancy is relatively high. The country is in stage 4 of the demographic transition model. Ireland is an example of this.

- **Regressive population pyramids** have a wide top and a wide middle but a narrow base. This indicates a country that has a large number of older people and few births. The country has entered the senile stage (stage 5) of the demographic transition model. Germany is an example of this.

Population pyramids can be used to illustrate future changes or trends. Governments use these graphs for a wide variety of social needs. For younger people, the pyramids are taken into account when the government is deciding on budgets for funding of education, provision of new schools and teachers and allocation of children's allowances.

For the economically active age group in society, the population pyramids can affect their tax rates, development of new hospitals and services. They can also affect social welfare payments, care of the elderly and pensions.

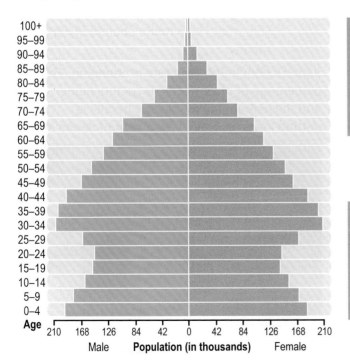

1.12 Ireland's population pyramid for 2014

EXAM HINTS

Population pyramids have appeared every year on the Ordinary Level exam paper as part of a long question. It is an area worth studying.

EXAM HINTS

If the birth rate of a country is low and the base of the pyramid is narrow, the population of the country is said to be **regressive**, or to have a **negative growth rate**.

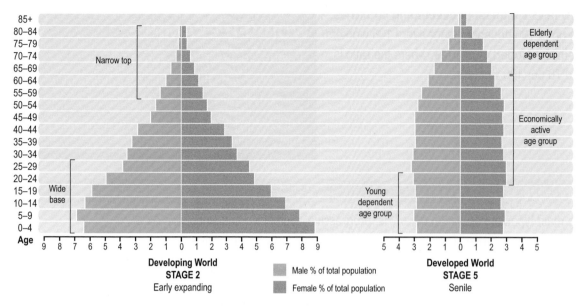

Developing World
STAGE 2
Early expanding

Developed World
STAGE 5
Senile

■ Male % of total population

■ Female % of total population

1.13 Population pyramids of a developing and a developed world country

CASE STUDY 1.3
Japan

Japan is an example of a country that has moved through the population cycle, or **demographic transition model**.

- In the 1920s Japan was moving through stages 2 and 3, the early and late expanding stages of the cycle, because it had a high birth rate and a declining death rate. The high birth rate was caused by a baby boom after the two world wars. During this time and up until the 1950s, the base of Japan's population pyramid was wide.

- From the 1950s, as Japan became more developed, the population began to decline. This was because of an increase in education, the status of women, family planning and prosperity. By 1985, the base of Japan's population pyramid had reduced significantly as the birth rate declined.

- Japan has now reached the final stage of the cycle. Its fertility rate is 1.3, well below the replacement level of 2.1 children per mother. This will cause an increasing narrowing of the country's population pyramid unless government initiatives, such as higher children's allowances for couples with larger families, are introduced to encourage increases in family size.

- The population of Japan is said to be 'greying' because many of its citizens survive beyond their seventies. It means that there will be

a large proportion of elderly dependents in the country in years to come. This will bring challenges to Japan. The following measures could help to lessen the problems of an increasingly dependent society:

- Postponing retirement to reduce pension costs.

- Encouraging inward migration from regions such as the Philippines for employment in Japan's industrial sector. This would be a major change in Japanese society.

Japan's population structure is changing. The percentage of older people is getting higher and the percentage of younger people is getting lower. In 1990, 12 per cent of Japan's

1.14 Japan is in the senile stage of the demographic transition model

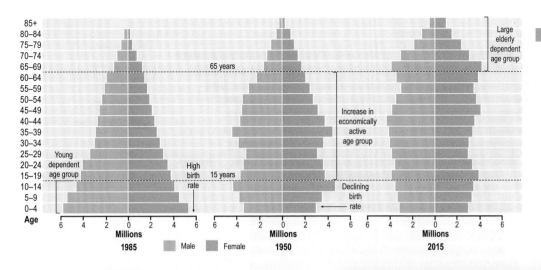

1.15 Changes in Japan's population structure from 1950 to 2015

population was aged 65 years or over. This is predicted to rise to 26 per cent by 2025. Japan is one of the most populous countries in the world, with over 830 people per km². If agricultural land alone was taken into account, this number would increase to 3,070 people per km². This is called the **physiologic population density** (population per unit of arable land).

GEOTERMS

Inward migration occurs when people from another place move to and settle in an area.

QUICK QUESTIONS

1. What is the dependency ratio? Give Ireland's ratio.
2. Name three ways in which governments can use population pyramids. (Timed activity: 3 min; 3 SRPs)
3. What are the three main types of population pyramid?
4. Why has Japan's population moved so quickly through the demographic transition model?
5. Why will the 'greying' of Japan's population be a challenge for the country in the future?

CASE STUDY 1.4
Ireland: A census study

Population distribution and density

The distribution and density of the population of twentieth-century Ireland is uneven. It is affected by **physical, political** and **economic factors**.

- **The lowest population densities are in areas where the physical environment is not suitable for cultivation.** The harsh climate, poor soils and mountainous terrain of the Western region can discourage settlement. The Central Plain of Ireland is also inhospitable to settlers because of the marshy landscape and poor-quality peaty soils. The islands off the coast of Ireland have also seen a decline in inhabitants. Their population figures have almost halved in the last 200 years. Fertile rural areas can also

have low population densities because the land is rich and needed for agriculture, so settlement is restricted.

- **The highest population densities in Ireland are in urban areas, on coastal lowlands and in river valleys.** Settlers are attracted to the well-drained valleys of the main rivers of the country, such as the Barrow, Liffey and Blackwater. For many centuries towns and cities have developed in these areas. At the mouths of these rivers many seaports have developed, and these have assisted industrial growth in the country. Agricultural villages have also been set up in the river valleys. Until the 1960s a higher proportion of the population lived in rural areas, dependent on agriculture.

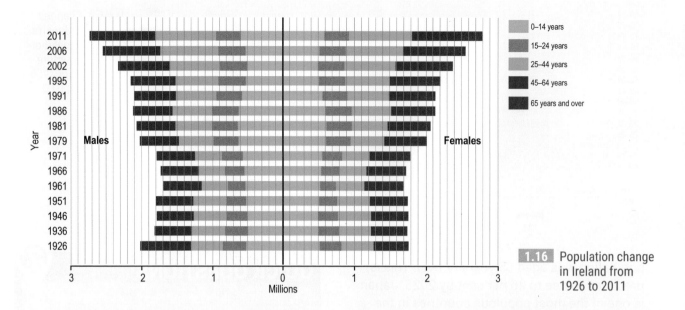

1.16 Population change in Ireland from 1926 to 2011

Change over time

- In the 1960s the Irish population reached its lowest level, 2.6 million, due to **increased unemployment** and **emigration**. The population of the 1960s began to slowly increase as more jobs were created in Ireland due to the new economic policies of Taoiseach Seán Lemass. Tax incentives and grants were put in place to encourage multinational corporations (MNCs) to locate here. Ireland experienced what could be described as an industrial revolution.

- Ireland's entry into the **European Economic Community** (EEC) in 1973 also helped to increase the country's economic growth as it opened up European markets to Irish products. People no longer had to leave Ireland in search of work. The country experienced its first population increase in over 120 years. For the first time, immigrants outnumbered emigrants. A natural population increase of 361,268 occurred between 1971 and 1981.

- Over the next couple of decades Ireland entered a cycle of **recessions** and **booms** that had drastic effects on the country's population.

During the 1980s, emigration returned as the country underwent a **severe economic depression**. Young people left Ireland again as economic migrants in search of work. More than 200,000 Irish people departed between 1981 and 1991.

During the 1990s and the early years of the twenty-first century the country entered an

economic boom period called the 'Celtic Tiger'. Employment figures for the country increased dramatically. Inward migration was needed to fill all the jobs available. This led to a marked growth in the Irish population. There was large-scale west-to-east, rural-to-urban and inward migration. The majority of the population growth during the Celtic Tiger era was absorbed by urban areas, where most of the industrial and service jobs were concentrated.

- During the **Celtic Tiger era, 1997 to 2007,** over 66 per cent of the Irish population has lived in urban areas. The largest increase was in Leinster, especially in Dublin and its commuter belt of Louth, Meath, Kildare and Wicklow, which had a 40 per cent rise in population. These counties grew at a rate that was faster than the national average of 8.1 per cent. The smallest proportion of this increase was felt in Connacht, and the counties of Cavan, Donegal and Monaghan.

- During the **2008–13 recession** migration began once more, with over 200,000 people emigrating from the country again. Since the 1960s, the population of the country has been slowly increasing, reaching a high of 4.59 million people in 2014.

Regional authority	2006	2011			Change in population 2006–2011	
	Persons	Persons	Males	Females	Actual	Percentage
Border	468,375	514,152	256,887	257,265	45,777	9.8
Dublin	1,187,176	1,270,603	618,541	652,062	83,427	7.0
Mid-East	475,360	530,437	263,764	266,673	55,077	11.6
Midland	251,664	282,195	141,267	140,928	30,531	12.1
Mid-West	361,028	378,410	188,929	189,481	17,382	4.8
South-East	460,838	497,305	247,802	249,503	36,467	7.9
South-West	621,130	663,176	329,326	333,850	42,046	6.8
West	414,277	444,991	222,182	222,809	30,714	7.4
State	4,239,848	4,581,269	2,268,698	2,312,571	341,421	8.1

Table 1.1 Population change in Ireland from 2006 to 2011

Changing fertility rates and population structure

As we have seen, the population of Ireland is said to be **'greying' rapidly**. There has been a notable increase in the percentage of the population over 65 years of age, which now stands at just over 17.4 per cent. This figure is set to rise over the next few years. It could be as high as 29 per cent in 2050. This is a major change in the structure of the Irish population.

At the other end of the scale the population of Ireland younger than 15 years of age has been declining in recent years. It reached its peak in the 1970s at just over 31 per cent and has slowly decreased to approximately 21 per cent today. From the 1940s to the 1980s, the average number of births per mother in Ireland was 4. This has more than halved to 1.98 today. It is unlikely to change over the next few years as the **trend towards later marriage and smaller family size continues**.

The **economically active age group** of Ireland, ranging in age from 15 to 64 years, has increased from 58 per cent to 68 per cent over the last 45 years. This amounts to an increase of 1.18 million people in this section of society. These figures represent an annual growth rate of 1.5 per cent.

The **dependency ratio in Ireland** reached its highest in 1966, at 74 per cent. This has been falling over the last few decades and reached just over 49 per cent in 2014. Over the next few years it is predicted that the dependency ratio in Ireland will rise as the population continues to age. It is

1.17 Ireland now has an ageing population demographic

predicted that the ratio will be as high as 65 per cent in 2040. This is nearly back to the 1960s level, but the main difference this time is that over two-thirds of the dependent population will be over 65 years. In the 1960s only one-quarter of the dependent population was in this age bracket and the rest were younger than 15 years.

An **ageing population** can lead to many socio-economic problems for future governments, as pensions, nursing home facilities and so on have to be accounted for. A **greater tax burden** will have to be placed on the economically active age group to pay for these facilities.

Ireland's TFR was at its lowest in 1994 at 1.85 but it has now increased to 1.98 children per mother. For a country to replace its population, it needs to be at 2.1. The population of Ireland can only grow in the future if migration into the country continues.

Life expectancy

The life expectancy in Ireland has increased for men, from 57.4 years in 1926 to 78.7 years in 2014, and for women, from 57.9 years to 83.2 years. This is in line with **some of the highest life expectancies in Europe**. Major improvements in life expectancy in Ireland were seen immediately after the Second World War (1946 to 1961). This was aided by advances in healthcare, especially maternity services, immunisation and the elimination of tuberculosis (TB), which claimed the lives of thousands of people each year. In 1948, Dr Noel Browne, Minister for Health, launched a campaign to eradicate TB, and by 1957 it had been reduced to one-fifth of earlier levels.

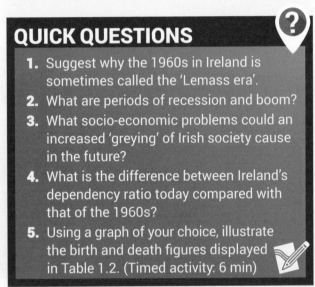

QUICK QUESTIONS

1. Suggest why the 1960s in Ireland is sometimes called the 'Lemass era'.
2. What are periods of recession and boom?
3. What socio-economic problems could an increased 'greying' of Irish society cause in the future?
4. What is the difference between Ireland's dependency ratio today compared with that of the 1960s?
5. Using a graph of your choice, illustrate the birth and death figures displayed in Table 1.2. (Timed activity: 6 min)

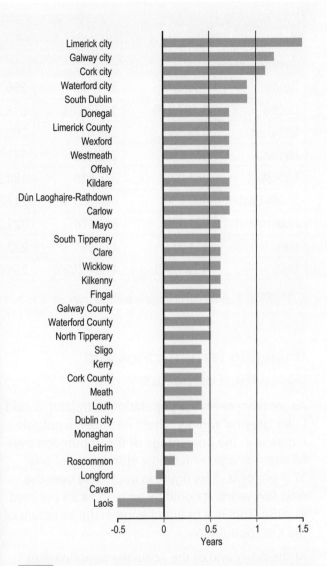

1.18 Change in elderly population by county since 2006

Period	Births	Deaths	Natural increase	Change in population	Estimated net migration
1926–1936	58	42	16	0	−17
1936–1946	60	43	17	−1	−19
1946–1951	66	40	23	1	−24
1951–1956	63	36	27	−12	−39
1956–1961	61	34	26	−16	−42
1961–1966	63	33	29	13	−16
1966–1971	63	33	30	19	−11
1971–1979	69	33	35	49	14
1979–1981	73	33	40	38	−3
1981–1986	67	33	34	19	−14
1986–1991	56	32	24	−3	−27
1991–1996	50	31	18	20	2
1996–2002	54	31	23	49	26
2002–2006	61	28	33	81	48
2006–2011	73	28	45	68	24

Table 1.2 The annual births, deaths and natural increase in Ireland from the first national census in 1926 to 2011 (figures are per 1,000)

Ordinary Level – Long Questions
Irish population

Irish population by age group in 2014	
Age group (years)	%
0–14	21
15–64	66
65–84	11
85+	2

Amended from US Census Bureau

1. Examine the table above showing Ireland's population by age group in 2014.

   (i) Using graph paper, draw a suitable graph to illustrate this data.

   (ii) State two ways that population statistics are used.

   2015, Section 2, Q10A, 30 marks

The marking scheme for a question like this on an Ordinary Level paper is as follows:

Graph paper	**2 marks**
Vertical axis labelled	**3 marks**
Horizontal axis labelled	**3 marks**
4 aspects identified @ 4 m each	**16 marks**
2 ways population statistics used @ 3 m each	**6 marks**
Total	**30 marks**

Population growth

Currently, the size of the Earth's population is 7.2 billion people. It is predicted that the Earth's population could be as high as 12.3 billion people by 2100. Infectious diseases like Ebola spread faster in densely populated areas. Scientists warn that the rising population could worsen world problems such as climate change, infectious disease and poverty. Most of the growth is expected to take place in Africa, where the population is expected to increase from around one billion today to four billion by the end of the century. In sub-Saharan Africa, fertility levels remain high and large families – typically with more than four children – are still common. Reductions in the death toll from HIV/Aids are said to be another contributing factor to the African trend.

Amended from Irish Examiner, September 18th 2014

2. Read the article at the bottom of the left-hand column and answer each of the following questions.

   (i) According to the article, what is the current size of the Earth's population and what is the predicted population by 2100?

   (ii) Calculate the predicted increase in the Earth's population by 2100.

   (iii) Name one problem mentioned in the article that could be made worse by this predicted increase in population.

   (iv) Where is most of the population growth expected to take place?

   (v) Explain briefly why this area is predicted to have the most growth in population.

   (vi) Explain briefly one advantage of predicting population figures.

   2015 Section 2, Q12A, 30 marks

Ireland's population

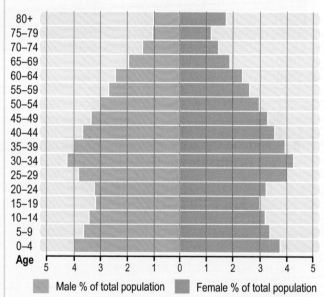

Male % of total population   Female % of total population

3. Examine the population pyramid for Ireland in 2011 and answer the following questions.

   (i) What percentage of the population was male and in the 0–4 year age group?

   (ii) What percentage of the total population was in the 35–39 year age group?

   (iii) Were there more males or females over 75 years of age?

   (iv) Explain briefly one way the shape of this population pyramid differs from the shape of a population pyramid for a developing country.

(v) Name two ways population pyramids are used.

2013, Section 2, Q11A, 30 marks

> The marking scheme for a question like this on an Ordinary Level paper is as follows:
>
> Each section @ 6 marks each = **Total 30 marks**

Population

4. 'One of the greatest challenges facing European governments in the future will be coping with ageing populations.'

   Describe the difficulties that an ageing population can cause.

   2012, Section 2, Q12C, 30 marks

Irish emigration

Component of annual population change – Emigration	
Year	Total
2005	29,000
2007	42,000
2009	65,000
2011	76,000

Amended from CSO figures

5. Examine the data above on Irish emigration.

   (i) Using graph paper, draw a suitable graph to illustrate this data.

   (ii) Explain one reason for the increase in emigration.

   2012, Section 2, Q10A, 30 marks

Higher Level – Long Questions
Population dynamics

Irish birth and death rates per 1,000 of population		
Year	Birth rate	Death rate
1950	21.5	13.0
1990	15	9.0
2013	15	6.5

Amended from CSO figures

6. Examine the data above showing Irish birth and death rates in 1950, 1990 and 2013.

   (i) Using graph paper, draw a suitable graph to illustrate this data.

   (ii) Explain briefly one reason for the decline in Irish birth rates between 1950 and 2013.

   2015, Section 2, Q11A, 20 marks

Population

7. Examine the population pyramids below and answer each of the following questions.

   (i) What percentage of males in Pyramid A are in the 40–44 year age group and what percentage of females in Pyramid B are in the 25–29 year age group?

   (ii) Are more people living longer in the area represented by Pyramid A or Pyramid B? With reference to the structure of the pyramid, give one piece of evidence to support your answer.

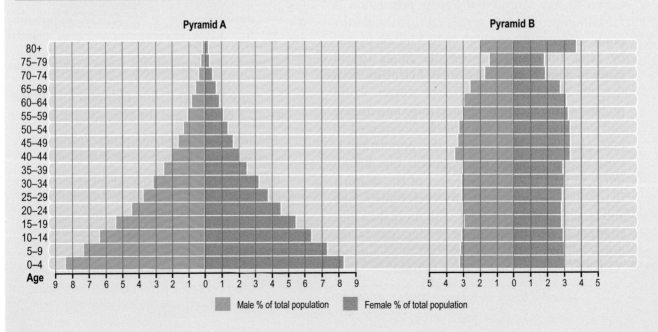

(iii) Which of the pyramids, A or B, represents a developing economy? Name an example of a developing economy.

(iv) Explain briefly two challenges facing an economy with a population pyramid similar to Pyramid B.

2015, Section 2, Q12A, 20 marks

Population dynamics

8. Examine the diagram below showing the Demographic Transition Model and answer each of the following questions.

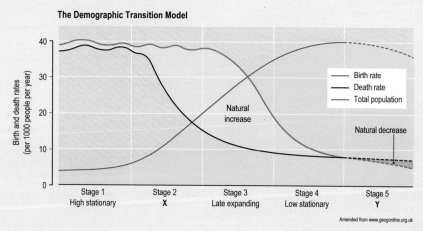

The Demographic Transition Model

Amended from www.geogonline.org.uk

(i) In which stage of the Demographic Transition Model is the total population at its lowest?

(ii) Name X, Stage 2 of the Demographic Transition Model and name an example of a country in this stage.

(iii) Name Y, Stage 5 of the Demographic Transition Model and name an example of a country in this stage.

(iv) Explain briefly one problem facing countries in Stage 5 of the Demographic Transition Model.

(v) Explain briefly what is meant by natural increase.

2014, Section 2, Q11A, 20 marks

Dependency ratio for a number of Irish regions, 2011	
Region	Dependency ratio
Galway city	35
Galway county	54
Cork city	42
Cork county	52
Waterford city	49
Waterford county	55

Amended from CSO figures

9. Examine the data above showing dependency ratios in a number of Irish regions in 2011.

(i) Using graph paper, draw a suitable graph to illustrate this data.

(ii) Explain briefly one reason why dependency ratios are usually higher in rural areas.

2014, Section 2, Q12A, 20 marks

Population

Percentage (%) of population aged 65 years and over, 2001 and 2011		
Country	2001	2011
Switzerland	15	17
Ireland	11	12
Germany	17	21

Amended from Eurostat

10. Examine the data in the table above showing the percentage of the population aged 65 years and over for a number of European countries in 2001 and 2011.

(i) Using graph paper, draw a suitable graph to illustrate this data.

(ii) Explain briefly the term dependency ratio.

2013, Section 2, Q12A, 20 marks

Population change

11. With reference to the graph below, describe and explain three changes in Ireland's population between 1956 and 2011.

2012, Section 2, Q10C, 30 marks

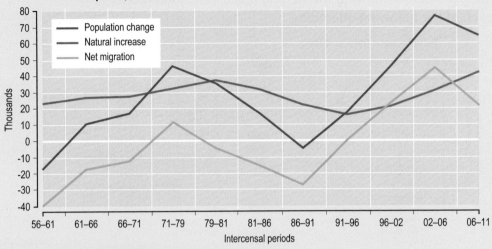

Components of Irish population change (average annual figures) for each intercensal period, 1956–2011

Demographic change

Female life expectancy at birth (years)		
Country	1990	2001
Bulgaria	75	77
Ireland	78	83
Germany	80	83

Amended from Eurostat

12. Examine the data in the table above showing female life expectancy at birth in a number of European countries.

  (i)   Using graph paper, draw a suitable graph to illustrate this data.

  (ii) State two reasons why life expectancy in general is increasing in Europe.

2012, Section 2, Q12A, 20 marks

13. Examine how improvements in technology impact on population growth, with reference to examples that you have studied.

2012, Section 2, Q11C, 30 marks

HOT TOPICS IN THE EXAMS

1. Reading population pyramids
2. Reading the demographic transition model

Chapter 2 Overpopulation
Chapter 3 Migration

Mind map

Population distribution and density

- **Distribution:**
  - Spread of people across the world
  - Factors affecting it: altitude, latitude, water, resources, history, urbanisation, government
- **Density:**
  - Number of people per km²
  - Densely: more than 100 per km²
  - Sparsely: less than 10 per km²
  - Bangladesh highest

Population structure

- **Dependency ratio:**
  - How many young and elderly dependent people are in the country for the economically active age group to support
- **Population pyramids:**
  - Show age and gender profile of a country
  - Progressive, stationary, regressive
  - Governments use them to budget for education, provision of new schools and hospitals, tax rate, old age pension and children's allowance

China

- 1949–76 fertility rate: 6 per mother
- 1979 one-child policy
- Urban areas 1 child, rural areas 2
- Imbalance of sexes: 106.7 boys to 100 girls
- Increased illegal abortions based on sex
- 95.7% of abortions female
- 90% of children in orphanages girls
- Moved from stage 2 to 4 in a short period of time
- Population still increasing 9 million a year as people marry young
- 2015 one-child policy abolished

The dynamics of population

Life expectancy and mortality rates

- Development of country improves, mortality rate declines
- 10 million children under 5 die per year
- 1 in 8 in the developing world, 1 in 143 in the developed world
- Life expectancy 70s developed world, 40s developing world
- AIDS biggest killer in sub-Saharan Africa, 39 million sufferers 2007

Demographic transition model

Countries go through predictable changes as the economy improves

- **Stage 1: High stationary stage**
  Birth and death rates high, infant mortality high, life expectancy short, Rwanda
- **Stage 2: Early expanding stage**
  Birth rate high, death rate drops dramatically, improved healthcare, Nigeria
- **Stage 3: Late expanding stage**
  Birth rate and death rate fall, population increase at a more gradual pace, Mexico
- **Stage 4: Low stationary stage**
  Birth rate only slightly higher than death rate, population growth low, Ireland
- **Stage 5: Senile stage**
  Death rate for the first time is higher than birth rate, population decrease, Germany

Mind map

The dynamics of population

Growth patterns

- Malthus: need natural disasters to keep population in check
- Agricultural Revolution: more food
- Industrial Revolution: more jobs
- Medical Revolution: better healthcare
- 1960–2015 population growth
- Average birth rate for a stable world population: 2.1 children per mother
- World fertility rate: 2.5
- Developing world fertility rate: from 2.5 to 3.3
- Developed world fertility rate: 1.56
- Life expectancy in developing world to rise from 50 to 66 by 2050
- Life expectancy developed world to rise from 75 to 82 years by 2050

Japan

- 1920s: stage 2/3, high birth rates
- 1950s: more developed, birth rate declined
- Today: stage 5, fertility rate 1.3, below replacement level
- Population 'greying'
- Increasingly dependent society
- Need inward migration or to postpone retirement
- 830 people per km²

France

- Unevenly distributed
- 77% urban based, 11 million Paris
- Primate city, 20% of population
- Vast number of jobs, home of government, education, fashion
- 'Empty diagonal', low population density, underdeveloped rural region, outward migration
- Population: rapid growth from 19 million to over 66 million
- Highest TFR in Europe

Changing fertility rates

- **Fertility rates low in the developed world:**
  - Working mothers
  - Education
  - Governmental encouragement
  - Increased cost of living
  - Cost of raising a child
  - Decline in influence of Catholic Church
  - Urbanisation
- **Fertility rates high in the developing world:**
  - Early marriages
  - Traditional roles
  - Lack of education
  - Children viewed as an asset
  - Governmental encouragement

Ireland

- Distribution and density uneven
- Highest in urban areas
- 1960s: 2.6 million, lowest population
- 1960s: boom, Lemass era, MNC, jobs, inward migration, EEC
- 1980s: recession, emigration
- 1990s: boom, 'Celtic Tiger', inward migration, urbanisation
- 2000s: recession, outward migration, unemployment
- Rapid 'greying' 17.4% over 65 years
- Under 15 years down 10% since 1970s
- Economically active age group increased from 58% to 68% in 45 years
- Dependency ratio highest 74% in 1966, now 49% increasing
- TFR now 1.98
- Life expectancy from 1926 to today:
  - Men 57.4–78.7 years
  - Women 57.9–83.2 years
- Advances in healthcare, Dr Noel Browne eradicated TB

Overpopulation

2

 SYLLABUS LINK

Population characteristics have an impact on levels of human development.

NOTE !

This section should be allowed at least 11 class periods (40 minutes).

By the end of this chapter, students will have studied:

○ The main terms associated with human development

○ How poor development of resources can lead to overpopulation

○ How a region's cultural differences, economic level, population growth, technological advancement and developments can all have a major impact on its population, either positively or negatively

Introduction

The growth or decline of a country's population is dependent on many factors, such as economic level, role of culture and society and resources. These can have a major impact on population levels, causing them to be **optimum**, **overpopulated** or **underpopulated**.

All these situations have a major impact on the people living in the region, and they affect every aspect of their daily lives. The population density of a region alone is not an accurate indicator of the region's level of population.

- Japan's population density is 830 people per km² but the region is not considered to be overpopulated because it has a high level of resources.

- In Mali the population density is only 9 people per km², yet it is considered to be overpopulated because it has huge economic and social problems and does not have the resources to provide an adequate standard of living.

Concepts of levels of population in a region are always changing as levels of technology, availability of resources and trade do not remain the same. They can improve or decline with time.

NOTE

Overpopulation is not the same as overcrowding. A country can be overpopulated but have very few people living there as there are not enough resources in the country to support the population.

Population levels

Overpopulation

Overpopulation occurs when there are too many people in a region for the natural resources to support. Therefore the **carrying capacity of the region's environment is exceeded**. This is happening in many parts of the world today and is slowing development. For example, Bangladesh and the Sahel in Africa lack adequate food

GEOTERMS

○ **Optimum** means the best or most favourable amount.

○ **Carrying capacity** is the maximum number of people that can be supported in a given area.

supplies, resources and energy supplies. Ireland experienced this during the famine years of the 1840s, when the main food source, the potato, failed. The country was highly overpopulated and many people died or emigrated. Migration acted as a release valve for the population that remained, as they had a better chance of surviving with the resources available.

Optimum population

Optimum population is **the number of people in a region who will experience a high standard of living given the region's level of development and natural resources** at any given time. It is difficult for a country to reach its optimum population because population is dynamic. It is hugely influenced by changes in the world market, employment opportunities and migration.

Underpopulation

Underpopulation occurs when **the number of people living in a region cannot use or exploit the natural resources of the region fully**. In an underpopulated region, an increase in population due to inward migration can lead to an increase in the standard of living for all people in the region. During the Celtic Tiger era, Ireland experienced underpopulation. Labour shortages were filled by incoming migrants, and this led to advances in the Irish economy.

EXAM HINTS

- Factors that can increase the carrying capacity of a region include new farming methods, irrigation and outward migration.
- Factors that can decrease the carrying capacity of a region include climate change, population growth/inward migration and natural disasters such as flooding.

CASE STUDY 2.1

Overpopulation and the development of resources: The Sahel

When natural resources such as wood, fuel, water and the soils of a region are exploited in a controlled manner, populations can thrive. Unfortunately, in some regions of the world this is not happening and people suffer. This has led to overpopulation in many parts of the world due mainly to the **depletion of the regions' natural resources**. We will now examine the Sahel region of Africa, where overpopulation is putting a major strain on the region's natural resources.

Impact of the development of resources

The Sahel is an **area of savannah** that lies just south of the Sahara Desert. It consists of grassland with some acacia trees. This region has a limited amount of resources and rainfall, which it receives during the wet season from June to September. The rains come in heavy downpours, which can be quickly evaporated. The grasslands can support only **nomadic herders**, as cattle need

to be moved frequently to make the best use of the limited resources available in the region.

The area is also under threat from the ever-growing Sahara Desert to the north, which is expanding at a rate of 5–10 km per year.

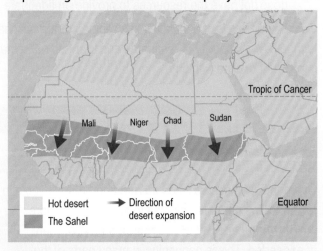

2.1 The Sahel region of Africa is located just below the Sahara Desert; Mali, Niger, Chad and Sudan are some of the countries in the region

The Sahel is under threat from desertification

Desertification is a growing problem in this arid (dry) and semi-arid region. The region has a very low carrying capacity of 30 people per km², as it has limited natural resources of soil, water and woodlands.

Causes of overpopulation in the Sahel

Climate change

Rainfall in the Sahel is unpredictable and the rainy season has shortened by almost 30 per cent over the last 30 years due to the effects of climate change. Between 2002 and 2006, Ethiopia did not receive enough rain for farmers in the region to grow crops.

When the rains do come, it is in very heavy downpours that can erode the region's precious soil resources. The soil becomes hard and baked in the hot sun, making it impossible for the rains to soak into it. The most fertile top layers of the soil can be washed away by **gullying** and **raindrop erosion**.

During the dry season the region's soils, which are made up of sand and **laterites** and so do not hold water well, are easily open to wind erosion (also known as **aeolian erosion**).

Higher temperatures in the region due to global warming are also causing **increased evaporation levels**. The resulting drop in the local **water table** causes the drying up of wells and subsequent droughts in the Sahel. Two main periods of drought occurred in the Sahel between 1968 and 1973 and 1983 and 1985. During these periods

Lake Chad reduced rapidly in size and rivers dried up, leading to disastrous famines in the region.

Unsustainable farming methods

Cattle numbers in the Sahel are often beyond the carrying capacity of the land, as cattle are viewed as a sign of a person's wealth and importance in society. Between 1950 and 1970 cattle numbers in the Sahel increased by 50 per cent. This has led to **overgrazing** of the region.

New wells have been drilled throughout the Sahel. These encourage once nomadic farmers to stay in one place for longer. Their animals are now stripping these areas of their grass cover. When the vegetation is removed, the roots can no longer bind the soil, and it erodes away.

Deforestation is also a problem in the region, as wood resources become less plentiful. People need wood for cooking and as a building material.

As the people are becoming more desperate, even small trees and shrubs are being cut down for fuel. Deforestation is especially disastrous at the desert edges, where the trees and shrubs would have acted as a barrier to prevent the spreading of the desert.

Population growth

The Sahel region is in **stage 2** (early expanding stage) of the **demographic transition model**. Sudan has a birth rate of 39 per 1,000 per year and a death rate of 10 per 1,000 per year. Owing to improvements in healthcare and the low status of

GEOTERMS

- **Desertification** is the spreading of the deserts.
- **Laterites** are soil types rich in iron and aluminium, formed in hot and wet tropical areas.
- **Gully erosion** occurs when fast-moving water concentrates on a small area and carves out channels in the land.
- **Raindrop erosion** occurs when raindrops dislodge pieces of soil, which makes it easier for water to wash away the soil.
- The **water table** is the area underground, beneath which soil and rock are saturated with water.

women, the population of the region has grown in recent decades.

This **population growth** has also been pushed up by the increase in **refugees** coming into the Sahel region from surrounding countries suffering from civil war and famine. For example, over one million people have fled from Ethiopia to the Sudan. This has put additional stress on the land to support the growing numbers of people.

The government of the region has put pressure on farmers to change from grazing animals to the growing of food and **cash crops** such as cotton and groundnuts on the region's most valuable land to help to increase the revenue of the country, by providing raw materials for export. This has had a disastrous effect on the **region's natural resource**, soil, as the crops have quickly **leached** the soil of its nutrients. This has happened because most farmers do not practise **crop rotation** and now use cattle dung as a fuel source rather than as a fertiliser.

Soils have become exhausted and larger areas are now needed to produce the same amount of crops. This has led to the **clearing and cultivation of lands** at the edge of the Sahel, which are the most vulnerable to desertification.

Effects of overpopulation in the Sahel

Socio-economic

Human activity is one of the main reasons for the exhaustion of soil resources in the Sahel region. Desertification, climate change and droughts have

2.4 A refugee camp in the Sahel

all made farming in the Sahel almost impossible. However, the frequency of **famine** in the Sahel in the last 20 years is directly linked to people's **overuse of the region's soil resources**.

The **increasing population** and **growing numbers of refugees** have put major pressures on these already stressed resources. The reactions of the region's governments and peoples have also not helped, as violence erupts between the refugees and the original inhabitants.

The introduction of **cash crops** has taken over valuable land that could be used for the growing of crops for the local people.

Farmers no longer move around, as water is more easily available from newly built **wells**. This means that cattle now strip areas of their grass cover.

EXAM HINTS

This is linked to the case study on the Sahel in Chapter 8: Soil characteristics and *Horizons* Book 1 Chapter 8: Mass movement.

GEOTERMS

- A **refugee** is a person who flees their own country for safety reasons and moves to another country.
- **Cash crops** are crops grown for selling.
- **Leaching** washes nutrients down through the soil.
- **Crop rotation** is the practice of changing the crop grown in an area regularly to prevent certain soil nutrients getting used up by the main crop.

2.3 Overgrazing of cattle in the Sahel region

Sahel people live in great **poverty**, with a gross domestic product (GDP) of $163 per person, less than one per cent of an Irish citizen's.

There is an economic need to have more children as they are the only form of assistance for elderly parents.

Refugees due to famines in the Sahel, as recently as 2010, have become dependent on food aid and other assistance. They tend to migrate to urban areas: for example, Dakar has more than doubled in size in the last 60 years, from 1 million to 2.5 million inhabitants.

Environmental

Due to a **change in rainfall patterns** in the Sahel region, Lake Chad has reduced to one-twentieth of its size in the last 40 years. A thriving fishing industry was once located on the shores of Lake Chad. Today stranded fishing boats lie in the area, many kilometres from where the shores of the lake are now located.

The fish stocks of the lake have also rapidly reduced because **overfishing** has taken place as people become more desperate for food.

Conflict has occurred between Nigerian and Cameroon fishermen and farmers. These people are fighting for valuable fishing areas and newly emerging farming lands. The borders of these countries are not as clearly defined as they were when Lake Chad was its original size.

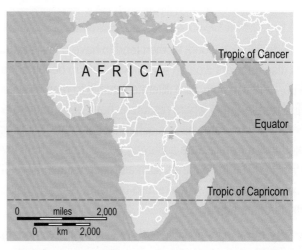

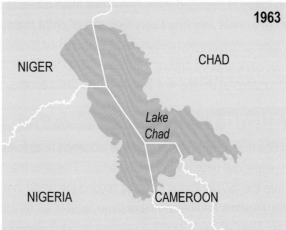

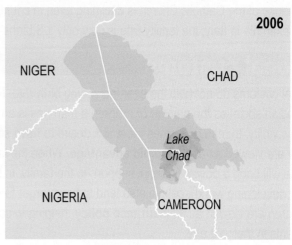

> **NOTE**
>
> There are two possible solutions to overpopulation:
>
> o **Development aid** could be introduced to the area so that teachers and nurses, for example, could teach the local people skills that would help them to live healthier lives.
>
> o It is well known that if money is put into **educating women** in an area, primary healthcare, family planning and basic education improve quickly.

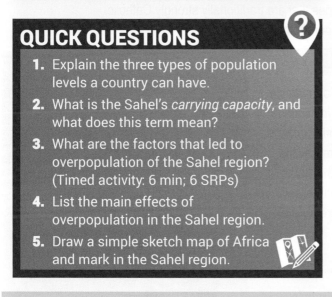

> **QUICK QUESTIONS**
>
> 1. Explain the three types of population levels a country can have.
> 2. What is the Sahel's *carrying capacity*, and what does this term mean?
> 3. What are the factors that led to overpopulation of the Sahel region? (Timed activity: 6 min; 6 SRPs)
> 4. List the main effects of overpopulation in the Sahel region.
> 5. Draw a simple sketch map of Africa and mark in the Sahel region.

2.5 The decreasing waters of Lake Chad in the Sahel region of Africa

Influence of society and culture on population

A high birth rate is not the only indicator that a region is overpopulated. If the **resources of the country are unable to cope with the needs of a growing population**, then the region is described as overpopulated. Many regions of the developing world are overpopulated. Birth rates are high in these regions for some of the following reasons: the status of women, religion, local customs and provision of healthcare.

Status of women

In the developing world, women tend to have a **low status** and therefore **lower levels of education**. This disempowers women and allows them to become the property of their husbands. In India, 65 per cent of women are illiterate (unable to read or write). However, in the Kerala State, where resources have been put into educating women, literacy rates have reached 92 per cent. This is directly linked to the Kerala Sate achieving below replacement levels of fertility in 2011. In countries such as Niger, women have little or no access to education. They remain unaware of opportunities for them outside of the home.

Fertility rates in these societies are very high. Women marry very young, often in arranged marriages. Their main role is to produce male heirs. India also has a very high rate of **child malnutrition**. The cycle continues as uneducated malnourished mothers give birth to malnourished children. India accounts for 20 per cent of the world's maternal deaths and 25 per cent of child deaths.

GEOTERMS

- In an **arranged marriage**, someone other than the couple getting married chooses the people to be wed.
- **Malnutrition** occurs when a person does not receive enough of the right nutrients to stay healthy.
- **Maternal death** is the death of a woman during or shortly after a pregnancy.

Religion

Societies that have a strong religious influence tend to experience **high birth rates** as most religions oppose artificial birth control and abortion. This was the case in Ireland, a strongly **Catholic** society, well into the 1970s. Today it occurs around the world in many **Muslim** countries, such as Saudi Arabia. Muslims traditionally have large families as devout followers believe that birth control is anti-Islamic. The Catholic Church dominates in South America, where birth rates are also very high. The influence of the Catholic Church is declining even in countries that are traditionally strongly Catholic. For example in Italy, the fertility rate is now only 1.3 births per mother per year.

Local customs

Local customs do not help the ever-increasing birth rate. For example in Indian societies the number of children a man has is an indication of his virility. In many countries there is a desire to have sons because they are viewed as an **economic advantage**. When they marry, the bride will bring a dowry, financial support, to the family. In the South (the developing world), people also tend to have larger families as children are viewed as an **insurance policy**, helping to care for their parents in their old age.

2.6 Many women in the developing world have large families

Provision of healthcare

Higher levels of **healthcare** and **access to clean water** are associated with countries that are well developed. In these areas of the world, **infant mortality rates** are lower. People have smaller families as they are sure of their children surviving. The opposite is the case in the developing world. This keeps the birth rate high in these areas. For example in Somalia, the infant mortality rate is 118.5 per 1,000 per year compared with Norway, where it is 3.7 per 1,000 per year.

CASE STUDY 2.2
Overpopulation and the influence of society and culture: Bangladesh

Bangladesh is one of the poorest countries in the world. It is located on the **floodplain** of the Ganges and the Brahmaputra Rivers and is constantly under threat from flooding. The people are mainly involved in **primary economic activities** such as agriculture, and they live in the countryside. In 2013 only 29 per cent of the population lived in urban areas. The population of the region in 2014 was over 158.5 million, with approximately 1,100 people per km².

Causes of overpopulation in Bangladesh

Risk of flooding

Bangladesh is located on the **low-lying delta lands** of the Rivers Ganges and Brahmaputra. Regularly during the annual **monsoon** season, this area is flooded by sea water as **typhoons** from the Bay of Bengal sweep up over the region. Even an increase in 1 m can flood 20 per cent of the land area of Bangladesh, making millions of people homeless.

The land resources of the region are constantly under threat because salt water can make agricultural land **sterile**. This makes it impossible to farm without the aid of expensive fertilisers.

Floodwaters also **contaminate drinking water** as wells and reservoirs are affected. This causes many people to contract **infections** that can be life-threatening, especially to malnourished people, from waterborne diseases such as typhoid and cholera.

Social factors

Bangladesh is in **stage 3** (late expanding stage) of the **demographic transition model**. The country's birth rate is starting to decline as family planning

> **GEOTERMS**
> - A **floodplain** is the area on either side of a river that floods when the river level rises.
> - A **delta** is alluvium above the water level that is deposited at the mouth of a river.
> - A **monsoon** is a seasonal wind created in South-East Asia. Heavy rain follows it.
> - A **typhoon** is a violent tropical storm that occurs in the western Pacific and Indian oceans.

has been introduced to the region. This has been difficult as it is a Muslim society, in which women have a very traditional role. However, the **fertility rate** has declined from four births per mother in 1990 to two in 2013. Women marry young in arranged marriages and there is a great desire for sons in the region.

The **adult literacy rate** is still very low, at 47.9 per cent.

Effects of overpopulation in Bangladesh

Migration

Land is very scarce in Bangladesh and people are forced to live in more vulnerable areas, such as the fertile islands in the Bay of Bengal. Here there is a greater **risk of flooding** from typhoons and subsequently a greater chance of loss of life.

Rural-to-urban migration is also occurring in the region as people move to the larger cities such as Dhaka in search of work. These people are agricultural labourers and lack skills. They often

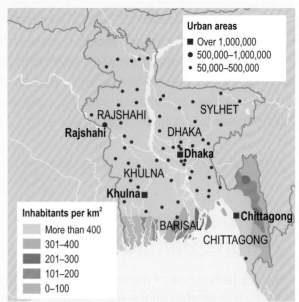

2.7 Bangladesh and its population densities

live in **shanty towns** on the outskirts of the larger cities where conditions are very poor. An example is Gulshan shanty town, Dhaka.

Overcrowding

Overpopulation occurs in both the rural and the urban areas of Bangladesh. In the shanty towns around the large cities of Bangladesh, **access to clean water** is limited, as are jobs. The majority of people are **unemployed** and extremely **poor**. **Mortality rates** in these areas are very high.

Women are forced to leave their homes because of overcrowding. They find jobs abroad, often in the Persian Gulf, as domestic servants. They send home **remittance**, which is often a lifeline for their families to pay for basic necessities such as food, healthcare and education.

GEOTERMS abc

Remittance is the sending home of money.

QUICK QUESTIONS ?

1. What impact can improving the status of women have on a region's population growth?
2. Briefly describe the impact of either the Catholic or Muslim religion on a country's population growth. (Timed activity: 3 min; 3 SRPs)
3. Why does flooding occur in Bangladesh?
4. What are shanty towns?
5. From your understanding, what is remittance, and why is it important to families in Bangladesh?

Impact of income levels on population

Trends suggest that the regions of the world that have the highest birth rates and population growth also have the **highest levels of poverty**. This is occurring in parts of India, South-East Asia and sub-Saharan Africa. According to the UN Development Programme, over 500 million people are malnourished in the world today.

Poor people tend to have larger families because they are seen as an economic asset. For example, in Nicaragua children work as labourers to support their families. Birth rates in these regions will fall only through **education**, such as the introduction of family planning. This helps parents to understand that larger families can be a drain on their limited resources.

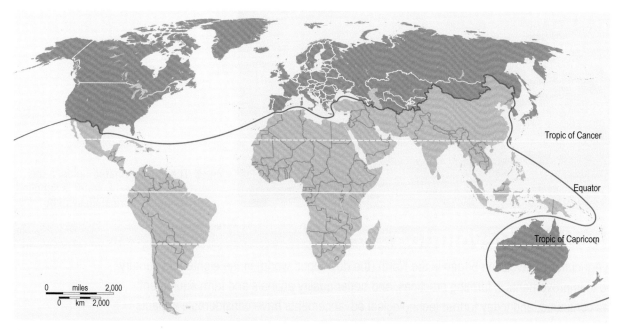

2.8 The world divided into the North (developed world) and the South (developing world)

High population density is not the sole indicator of poverty and overpopulation.

- In **South Korea** in 2014, there was a population of 50 million and a population density of 518 people per km². At first sight the region would be considered overpopulated, but South Korea has a large and profitable export-led economy. The region is therefore able to import foodstuffs and other basic necessities, allowing the country to offer its people a **good standard of living**.

- **Kenya**, with a fairly similar population of 45.5 million in 2014, has a population density of only 80 people per km². It is said to be **overpopulated** because its resources are not able to sustain the people living there. This is due to a combination of factors such as a mainly rural, isolated society, little foreign investment, poor infrastructure, low incomes, low status of women, a high incidence of AIDS, and political corruption in the region.

In regions with high-income levels, children are viewed as an **economic liability** because of the high costs of childcare and education. Figures in Ireland suggest it costs around €50,000 to rear a child from birth to 18 years. This has contributed to a drop in the country's fertility rate and therefore led to smaller families and a low birth rate.

Regions with low-income levels can suffer from increased **outward migration** as people search for a better standard of living elsewhere. Higher income alone does not bring about a decline in the region's birth rate. Central to this concept is the education of women.

Therefore we can see that many factors need to be examined when trying to determine whether a region is overpopulated.

Impact of technology on population growth

The world population has doubled in the last 40 years, putting massive pressures on the world's natural resources, such as arable land and water. **Technological advancements have helped to improve the carrying capacity of certain regions.** This has made food supply more secure so that an increasing population can be supported. Commentators have suggested that cereal production alone needs to increase by 35 per cent over the next 20 years to cope with the world's growing and urbanising population.

GEOTERMS

Arable farming involves growing crops.

The round irrigated fields in the
Sahara Desert – water is supplied
through a sprinkling system

Agricultural Revolution

- The Agricultural Revolution began in the North (the developed world) in the eighteenth century. It led to improvements in farming practices, and better quality animals and farm equipment. It has continued, and today further technological advancements have considerable impacts on farming.

- For example, **combine harvesters** allow larger areas of land to be cultivated more quickly and efficiently, increasing food output in the region. This has coincided with **improvements in transport**, allowing people easy access to nearby markets to sell fresh produce.

- In more recent years other advances have been introduced in the South. They include artificial **fertilisers**, **pesticides**, **herbicides** and **fungicides** to reduce crop losses. **Selective animal breeding** to increase meat and milk yields, and **irrigation schemes** improving soil conditions in drought-ridden areas, have also been implemented.

- Unfortunately, some of the agricultural improvements introduced from the North did not work in the South. **Greenhouses**, in which water, heat, humidity and pests can be controlled so that food can be grown all year round, proved **too expensive** for farmers in the South.

- Overall these improvements in agriculture have led to an **increase in food supply** to keep pace with the world's growing population, which is mainly occurring in the South.

- People in the South are malnourished not because food supplies are unavailable, but because the **price** of these products puts them beyond their reach. In the EU food mountains of surplus supplies have been allowed to form by governments to prevent excess products flooding the EU market and causing prices to drop. This excess food is sometimes sold to the South, but for a high price.

GM foods and the Green Revolution

- The Green Revolution was the name given to an **increase in food production**, **technology** and **research** developed by scientists in the 1960s.

- Today genetically modified (**GM**) foods have the potential to reduce food shortages in overpopulated parts of the world.

- These foods have been modified in laboratories to contain desired traits such as **disease resistance**, **increased nutritional value**, **increased yields** of two to five times greater than traditional varieties and **salt tolerance**.

- High-yielding crop varieties, for example **rice** and **maize**, have been introduced into areas such as India, China and Mexico. This has had a marked improvement on the region's capacity to support its growing population. In India the population increased over three-fold from 361 million in 1950 to 1.26 billion in 2014. They could not have been fed without the help of the Green Revolution.

- Supporters of GM foods and crops claim they are the way forward as land resources become more limited and globally people become more urbanised.
- There are also many **disadvantages** to the Green Revolution:
  - Many of the products and the equipment are very **expensive**. Therefore their services are often unavailable to the small farmers who need them most.
  - A lot of the fertilisers are made from **oil**, which is a finite resource that is becoming more expensive and limited as time goes on.
  - Many farmers are now abandoning traditional varieties of crops in favour of new higher-yielding GM crops. Therefore **genetic diversity is being reduced** as many people around the world are depending on a limited number of crops.

2.10 A scientist working on GM foods

GEOTERMS

GM foods are genetically modified in laboratories to yield higher quality food crops.

INTERESTING FACTS

The Teagasc Research Centre located in Oak Park, Carlow, is involved in the research and development of different food crops to make them higher yielding and less susceptible to disease.

QUICK QUESTIONS

1. Name some of the improvements that the Agricultural Revolution introduced in the South.
2. What effect have the EU food mountains had on the South?
3. What does *GM* stand for?
4. What are the positive arguments in support of GM foods? (Timed activity: 3 min; 3 SRPs)
5. What are the negative arguments against GM foods?

Medical improvements

Medical research has developed new **medications** and **vaccinations** to fight diseases such as measles and malaria. In the developing world, **preventative health services** have finally become widespread. This helps to greatly reduce infant deaths, as vaccinations are cheap and can be administered even in the most basic conditions.

The controversial developments in **gene and geneline therapy** (the insertion, alteration or removal of genes within cells or tissues to treat disease) in recent years have promised to finally eliminate fatal human genetic diseases. They also have the potential to substantially reduce world death rates. However, many commentators argue that these therapies are too premature and might cause more harm than good if implemented too early.

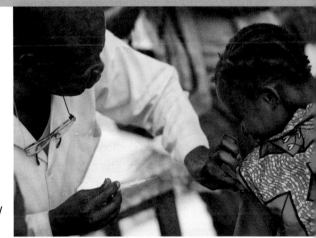

2.11 Vaccinations are hugely important in the elimination of deadly diseases

HIV

HIV/AIDS is causing rising death rates in Africa and India. Medical improvements, such as the use of **expensive antiretroviral drugs**, are not reaching the people who need them most. This is due to inaction by the region's governments and the power of multinational corporations (**MNCs**), which will not allow cheaper versions of the drugs to be made. In South Africa, where over 5.7 million people are HIV-positive, the South African Government changed its policies after legal action and allowed treatments to prevent pregnant mothers from passing HIV to their unborn child. The Government also delayed the introduction of the national HIV/AIDS treatment programme aimed at educating people about this disease.

Ecological footprint

An ecological footprint is the amount of forest land, agricultural land, recreational space and so on that is needed by a person to live. In the developed world this equates to huge tracts of land of several hectares per person, which is clearly unsustainable. By contrast, in the developing world it is less than 1 hectare per person. In 2014 in Sweden a person's ecological footprint was 5.8 hectares but in China it was only 2.1 hectares.

The health of the planet is at risk if this continues, as whole **habitats are being destroyed** to keep pace with the demands of wealthy societies. The planet will not be able to cope if the developing world copies the lifestyle of the developed world. People in the North need to lead simpler lives. They will have to make wiser **lifestyle choices**, such as buying food locally and reducing travel, especially by airplane.

Impact of population growth/decline

Developed world

It is generally accepted that as the economy of a country improves, the average family size reduces. This is seen in **stage 5** (the senile stage) of the **demographic transition model**. Women tend to start families later and therefore have fewer children. Medical advances such as immunisation have also helped to decrease population growth in the developed world. Today in the North most countries are in stage 4 (stationary stage) or stage 5 of the model. Therefore most of their populations are **stationary** or **declining**. Some countries are experiencing **underpopulation**, **labour shortages** and an **ageing population**. Inward migration from the South is needed to sustain the standards of living in these countries.

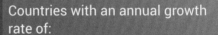

INTERESTING FACTS

Countries with an annual growth rate of:

- One per cent can double their population in 66 years
- Two per cent can double their population in 33 years
- Three per cent can double their population in 22 years

Developing world

Most countries in the developing world are in **stage 2** (early expanding stage) or **stage 3** (late expanding stage) of the demographic transition model, with more than 30 per cent of their populations below the age of 14 years. The major challenges for these countries are providing basic healthcare and education.

- Some of these countries are also experiencing **civil wars**, **corrupt leadership** and **poor management**, which are having a dramatic influence on their development.
- There is **very little, if any, inward investment by MNCs** in the South. Huge numbers of young people are unemployed so they have to move to nearby urban centres in search of work. They often end up living in the region's rapidly expanding shanty towns.
- The **populations of cities in the South can double in fewer than 15 years**. Mexico city grew from one million to 18.25 million in 50 years.
- **Overcrowding** of cities can lead to unrest and violence, as is seen in São Paulo, Brazil.

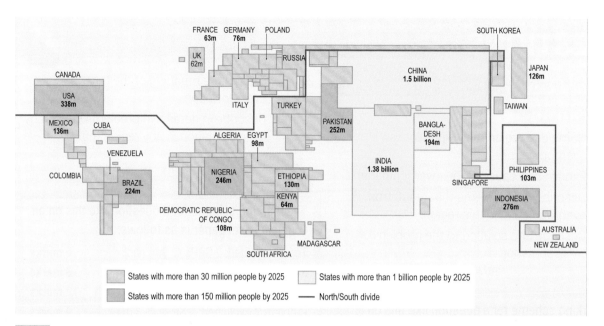

States with more than 30 million people by 2025	States with more than 1 billion people by 2025
States with more than 150 million people by 2025	—— North/South divide

2.12 The countries of the world with projected population figures for 2025 (they are drawn in relation to the size of their populations)

- **Overpopulation** of a region puts pressure on its food resources. People become malnourished and are more prone to diseases. They become less productive and the economy of the region suffers, as has happened in Sudan. The agricultural lands of an overpopulated region can become overworked and sterile, reducing the region's food supplies, for example in the Sahel.

- Studies have shown that **planning the number and timing of childbirths** can have a huge affect on the quality of life.

- Regions in the developing world are also at a major disadvantage as they did not experience rapid economic development or industrialisation as the developed world did. This is due mainly to an **unfair trading system** that benefits the wealthy nations of the world.

- Therefore there are fewer jobs in industry in the developing world, which has led to a **brain drain** in recent years. The small proportion of well-educated people who have failed to find work emigrate to the developed world, where well-paid jobs are available. In the South **outward migration** is viewed as a safety valve for these rapidly growing populations as it frees up more resources for those left behind.

GEOTERMS abc

A **brain drain** happens when the economically active age group moves away from a region in search of greater economic opportunities and a higher standard of living.

The quickly developing world

The newly industrialised economies (**NICs**) of the world are mainly located in Asia, and include China and Taiwan. Population growth here has helped their development. **Labour-intensive industries** have located in these regions to make use of their large populations and low wages. Some of these countries have almost reached the economic level of a developed country in one generation alone. Hopefully these NICs will lead the way for other countries in the developing world to overcome their problems. They can use their resources to attract foreign investment and bring about major improvements for future generations.

QUICK QUESTIONS ?

1. Explain how HIV/AIDS was dealt with by the South African Government.
2. What is an ecological footprint?
3. Why are people's ecological footprints in the developed world bigger than those of people in the developing world? (Timed activity: 3 min; 3 SRPs)
4. Why are populations in the developed world stationary or declining?
5. What is an NIC?

QUESTIONS

Ordinary Level – Long Questions

Overpopulation

1. (i)   Name one region that experiences overpopulation.
    (ii) Explain one cause of this overpopulation.
    (iii) Describe the problems that result from overpopulation in this region.
    (iv) Describe one solution to the problem of overpopulation.

    2015, Section 2, Q10C, 40 marks

The marking scheme for a question like this on an Ordinary Level paper is as follows:

Region named	**4 marks**
Explanation: 4 SRPs @ 3 m each	**12 marks**
Description: 4 SRPs @ 3 m each	**12 marks**
Description: 4 SRPs @ 3 m each	**12 marks**
Total	**40 marks**

Higher Level – Long Questions

Overpopulation

3. Describe and explain the causes and effects of overpopulation, with reference to examples that you have studied.

    2015, Section 2, Q10C, 30 marks

The marking scheme for a question like this on a Higher Level paper is as follows:

Cause identified	**2 marks**
Effect identified	**2 marks**
Examples @ 2 m each	**4 marks**
Explanation: 11 SRPs @ 2 m each	**22 marks**
Total	**30 marks**

2. (i)   Explain the meaning of the term *overpopulation*.
    (ii) Describe in detail two problems caused by overpopulation in any region that you have studied.

    2012, Section 2, Q10C, 30 marks

The marking scheme for a question like this on an Ordinary Level paper is as follows:

Term explained: 2 SRPs @ 3 m each	**6 marks**
Reference to country or region	**3 marks**
Problem 1 explained: 4 SRPs @ 3 m each	**12 marks**
Problem 2 explained: 3 SRPs @ 3 m each	**9 marks**
Total	**30 marks**

EXAM HINTS

The 2007 Chief Examiner reported that on this question some students confused the idea of overpopulation with overcrowding and lost marks accordingly.

HOT TOPICS IN THE EXAMS

1. Case study of the Sahel
2. Causes of overpopulation

Chapter 1 Population dynamics
Chapter 3 Migration
Chapter 8 Soil characteristics

Mind map

Overpopulation

Overpopulation and the impacts of society and culture

Bangladesh
- Poor country
- Primary economic activity: agriculture
- Population: 158.5 million
- 29% in urban areas
- 1,100 people per km²

Causes of overpopulation in Bangladesh
- Risk of flooding
  - Low-lying delta land
  - Annual monsoon season, typhoons
  - 1 m of water floods 20% of Bangladesh's land
  - Sterilises agricultural land, contaminates drinking water
  - Infections: typhoid and cholera
- Social factors
  - Stage 3 (late expanding stage)
  - Birth rates declining with family planning
  - 4 births per mother in 1990; 2 in 2014
  - Muslim: marry young, desire for sons
  - Adult literacy rate only 47.9%

Effects of overpopulation in Bangladesh
- Migration
  - Land very scarce
  - Rural to urban migration, lack skills, live in shanty towns
- Overcrowding
  - Both the rural and the urban areas
  - Shanty towns = high mortality rates
  - Domestic servants – remittance

South Korea
- Population: 50 million; population density 518 per km²
- Large and profitable export-orientated economy
- Good standard of living

Kenya
- Population: 45.5 million; population density 80 per km²
- Overpopulated – resources cannot sustain the people

Impact of income levels on population
- UN Development Programme: 500 million+ malnourished
- Poor people = larger families, economic asset
- High population density not sole indicator of poverty and overpopulation
- High income families – children an economic liability
- Education of women central to decline in birth rate

Underpopulation
- No. of people living in a region cannot use/exploit the natural resources fully
- Inward migration: increases living standards for all
- Ireland, Celtic Tiger (1997–2007), labour shortages

Impact of population growth/decline

Developed world
- As economy improves, family size reduces
- North (stage 4/5)
- Inward migration from South to sustain living standards

Developing world
- South (stages 2/3)
- 30% under 14 years
- Challenges: basic healthcare and education
- Civil wars, corrupt leadership, no MNC investment
- Migration to shanty towns
- Cities' populations can double in under 15 years
- Overpopulation
  - Agricultural lands – overworked and sterile
  - Overcrowding of cities – unrest and violence
  - Unfair trading system – benefits wealthy North
  - Brain drain
  - Outward migration – safety valve
- NICs, e.g. Taiwan
  - Labour-intensive industries
  - Large populations; low wages
  - Near levels of developed countries

Mind map

Overpopulation

- No. of people in a region too many for natural resources to support
- Carrying capacity exceeded
- Sahel, Africa; Bangladesh; Ireland 1840s
- Migration – release valve

Optimum population

- No. people in a region with high standard of living given region's level of development and natural resources at any given time

Overpopulation and development of resources: The Sahel

- Birth rates are high
  - Limited resources
  - Low carrying capacity

Causes

- Climate change
  - Rainfall: 30% less in 30 years
  - Heavy downpours = erosion
  - Sun-baked soil = hard
- Population growth
  - Sahel: stage 2
  - Sudan: 39 births per 1,000 per year
  - Healthcare improvements
  - Increase in refugees
  - Food and cash crops
  - Soil leached of nutrients, no crop rotation
- Unsustainable farming methods
  - Cattle exceed carrying capacity, up 50% 1950–70
  - Indicate wealth and importance
  - New wells, overgrazing
  - Deforestation: wood for cooking/building
  - Trees/shrubs cut: barrier to desertification
  - Gullying, raindrop, aeolian/wind erosion
  - Global warming: increased temperatures and evaporation
  - Drying up of wells and droughts 1968–73, 1983–5

Effects

- Socio-economic
  - Soil degradation
  - Cash crops on valuable land
  - Increasing population
  - Farmers more sedentary
  - Refugees not self-reliant
  - Reduction in cattle dung use
  - Cultivation of marginal lands
- Environmental
  - Change in rainfall patterns
  - Lake Chad one-twentieth of size in 40 years
  - Conflict: Nigerian and Cameroon fishermen and farmers

Influence of society and culture on population

- Status of women
  - Developing world: low status
  - Less education: India, 65% illiterate
  - Marry young, role = produce sons
  - High rate of child malnutrition
  - India: 20% world's maternal deaths, 25% child deaths
- Religion
  - High birth rates
  - Oppose artificial birth control and abortion
  - Ireland 1970s, Catholic; Muslim countries, Saudi Arabia; South America
  - Catholic influence declining – Italy, 1.3 births per mother per year
- Local customs
  - India: no. of children indicates virility
  - Desire for sons
  - Larger families – economic advantage, insurance
- Provision of healthcare
  - Developing world: infant mortality rates lower
  - Developed world: smaller families, survival

Overpopulation

Impact of technology on population growth

- Improved carrying capacity
- World population doubled in 40 years

Agricultural Revolution

- 18th century, North
- Better farming practices, animals and equipment
- Problems: greenhouses expensive, EU food mountain

GM foods and the Green Revolution

- Increase in food production, technology and research, 1960s
- Modified for desired traits, e.g. salt tolerance
- Disadvantages
  - Expensive products and equipment
  - Oil-derived fertilisers – non-renewable resource
  - Genetic diversity reduced

Medical improvements

- New medications and vaccinations
- Developing world: preventative health services widespread
- Gene and geneline therapy
- HIV/AIDS: rising death rates in Africa and India
- Expensive drugs, government inaction, MNCs' power

Ecological footprint

- Developed world: several hectares per person
- Developing world: less than 1 hectare per person
- Ecological footprints: Sweden 5.8; China 2.1

Migration

3

SYLLABUS LINK

Population movements have an impact on the donor and receiver regions.

By the end of this chapter, students will have studied:

- The changing migration patterns in Ireland since the 1950s
- The migration policies implemented by Ireland and the European Union
- The ethnic, racial and religious issues that can arise from migration
- The impact and issues that can arise from migration for donor and receiver countries
- The impacts of rural to urban migration in the developed and the developing world

NOTE

This section should be allowed at least eight class periods (40 minutes).

Introduction

Migration occurs as people move from one area to another for a variety of reasons. Migrants tend to be young people moving from their home for more than a year. Migration can be permanent, temporary, voluntary or forced. Migrations can be within a country (**intra-national**) or between countries (**international**).

Migrants are pushed (**push factor**) from their donor countries for reasons such as:

- Poverty
- Unemployment
- Natural disasters
- Violence or civil unrest
- Overpopulation

The donor country suffers the loss of their talents and subsequent economic, educational and personal contributions.

These migrants are pulled (**pull factor**) to host or receiver countries because of:

- A better quality of life
- Employment opportunities
- Personal reasons such as family ties
- Personal freedom

The host or receiver country benefits from this influx of migrants if the region is **underpopulated**. If the host country is **overpopulated**, as is the case in countries surrounding Somalia today as people flee the region because of famine, these new migrants can cause extra pressures on a country's already exhausted economy.

3.1 Migrations from Syria in 2015

Barriers to migration such as the cost, a country's migration polices and fear can all prevent migration of people across the world. Migration has played an important role in the distribution of people over time across the world.

GEOTERMS

- An **emigrant** is a person who leaves a country to settle in another.
- An **immigrant** is a person who comes to live in a country.

Changing migration patterns in Ireland

Emigration, 1950s

During this period in Irish history, there was a **deep economic recession**. The population declined by 4.8 per cent. In 1961, it fell to 2.82 million people from a high of 6.5 million (for the 26 counties) in 1841 before the Famine. During the 1950s, over 400,000 people **emigrated** from Ireland, with a record 58,000 people emigrating in 1958. The majority of people emigrating were young adults who had been employed in domestic service, construction or as agricultural labourers. They lacked skills and education. The countryside of Ireland suffered **rapid depopulation** and **social isolation**. Many areas were left with a **high dependency ratio** (large numbers of children and elderly people).

Economic prosperity, late 1960s and 1970s

During part of this period Seán Lemass was Taoiseach of Ireland and launched the programmes for **economic expansion**. Under his government, foreign investment and free trade were promoted by offering attractive grants, newly built industrial estates and financial incentives such as tax-free industrial exports. This helped to create jobs in manufacturing in large multinational corporations (MNCs) such as Braun. Therefore **outward migration from Ireland declined** as work at home could now be found. These industries tended to be flexible and located throughout the country. This resulted in large employment gains for the West, where the effects of emigration had been felt the most. By 1966, over 300 foreign companies were located throughout Ireland.

EXAM HINTS

This exam question has appeared a lot on the exam paper and is an area worth studying. It would also be beneficial to take some time looking at the CSO website to find more census facts and figures to back up your answers.

Further economic growth was achieved when Ireland joined the European Economic Community (EEC) in 1973. This enabled migrants to return home as more jobs became available due to EEC funds and its strong focus on manufacturing expansion. **Living standards rose** by 50 per cent in the country during this golden era. People began to take their first package holidays and car ownership increased significantly.

During this period, Ireland enjoyed an **industrial revolution** as thousands of jobs continued to be created in manufacturing and services. For the first time in 120 years **immigration outweighed emigration** as the migration balance shifted. Between 1971 and 1981 there was a population increase in Ireland of 15.6 per cent. Emigration was at its lowest level to date with only 5,000 people emigrating from Ireland in 1971. Later in the 1970s the country saw net inward migration for the first time and the trend continued until 1979.

3.2   Seán Lemass, Taoiseach from 1959 to 1966

GEOTERMS

- **Migration balance** is the difference between the number of emigrants moving out of a country and the number of immigrants moving into that country.
- A **package holiday** is a tour arranged by a travel agent with all-inclusive costs for travel, accommodation and food.

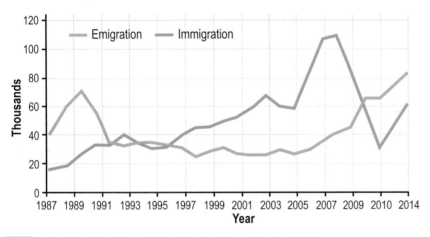

3.3   Ireland: emigration and immigration from 1987 to 2014

Recession, 1980s

A renewed period of emigration started in Ireland in the 1980s as another **economic recession** caused by the world oil crisis gripped the country. High unemployment rates resulted in over 200,000 young people leaving Ireland in search of work between 1981 and 1991. In 1988–9, 70,000 people became '**economic refugees**'. This was a new type of emigration as now highly educated young people were departing in search of work, causing a **brain drain** of talent. Government debt increased and many manufacturing companies, both MNCs and Irish, closed down.

Celtic Tiger era, 1997–2007

During the Celtic Tiger years Ireland became a country of **net inward migration**, reaching its highest ever level in 2006. Immigrants included skilled and unskilled workers and asylum seekers from outside the European Union (EU) and EU citizens. The latter group have the right to live and work anywhere within the EU. Irish society was becoming **multiracial** as people of many different nationalities came in search of work. This was especially noted after the expansion of the EU in 2004, when a large number of Eastern and central Europeans arrived. Numbers peaked at over 100,000 between 2006 and 2007, as Ireland was one of only three EU countries that allowed these new migrants immediate access.

During this period, there was also a **wave of investment** in Ireland by new high tech MNCs such as Dell and international service industries such as Google. They were attracted by the well-educated workforce and high quality transport and communications. Ireland contained 1 per cent of the EU population but achieved 20 per cent of new inward investment in Europe. At this time Ireland was underpopulated, and there weren't enough workers to fill the demand in areas such as construction, retail and the services industry. Ireland announced that it would allow unrestricted immigration from the newer members of the EU, which caused immigrants and their families to arrive in their thousands.

Applications for asylum in Ireland peaked in 2002 with 11,634 applicants, up from 362 in 1994. The highest proportion of these applications came from Nigeria, which made up nearly 35 per cent of all applications. Ireland's

3.4 An influx of new MNCs brings much-needed manufacturing jobs to Ireland

population grew rapidly during this time because of the influx of asylum seekers and migrant workers as the native Irish population levels were just below replacement levels.

Recession 2008–2013

Ireland experienced a **downturn in its economy**, and emigration became one of the main social issues. Many MNCs such as Wyeth and established Irish industries such as Jacob's Biscuits closed down or were taken over, causing extensive job losses. **Emigration** started again as young well-educated people left Ireland once more in search of work. These job losses coincided with a **large governmental debt**. This rose from €38.5 billion in 2005 to €84 billion in 2010, leading to a bailout from 'the Troika', which included the International Monetary Fund (IMF), the EU and the European Central Bank. This so called 'Euro Crisis' meant that the Irish Government was now answerable to 'the Troika' in regards to Irish governmental spending until they can once again prove that they are on a firm footing financially.

3.5 Economic recession in Ireland

This also caused a **rise in living costs and taxes** for Irish citizens. The **collapse in the housing market** led to a huge loss of building jobs and apprenticeships for young people in a once booming trade. In 2007 alone over 140,000 jobs were lost. The **unemployment rate** in Ireland rose from a low of 4.2 per cent in 2005 to a high of 15.1 per cent in 2012. Due to the major job losses in the building and construction industry, the majority of the unemployed (80 per cent) were men.

 Economics

Outward migration from Ireland has dramatically increased in this period owing to these major job losses. In 2009 over 65,100 people left, a 40 per cent increase on the previous year – 18,400 of these were Irish nationals.

The number of immigrants also decreased due to lack of available work in the country and the tightened regulations on the entry of unskilled people into the country. Immigration figures dropped from 83,800 to 57,300 people. Ireland experienced a **net outward migration** for the first time since 1995. Ireland exited this period of economic decline in December 2013, as the economy recorded a **growth** of 0.4 per cent in **gross domestic product** (GDP).

GEOTERMS

Gross domestic product (GDP) is one of the primary indicators used to determine the health of a country's economy.

Migration policy in Ireland

The Irish Government's main aim for its immigration policy is to treat migrants with justice and fairness. In 2014 the Government introduced the 'Employment Permits Act': stricter laws governing people entering Ireland from outside the European Economic Area (**EEA**) for work. They focus on permitting people into the country who provide skills that are in short supply here. There are nine in total, but the four main categories under which permission to work in Ireland is granted are as follows:

- **General Employment Permit**

  This permit was formally referred to as the 'work permit' and is now available to people with an annual salary of €30,000 or more. People will only be considered in exceptional cases for jobs with a lower annual salary. A labour market means test is required to gain this permit, ensuring that an equally skilled Irish or EEA person does not fail to gain the job over a non-EEA national.

- **Critical Skills Employment Permit**

  This permit was formally referred to as the 'Green Card permit' and is available for most occupations with an annual salary of over €60,000. It is also available for occupations with an annual salary of at least €30,000 if it appears on the 'Highly Skilled Occupations List', which shows that it is a skill highly required in Ireland because of a shortage. An example of this is a registered midwife.

- **Dependant/Partner/Spouse Employment Permit**

  This permit applies to spouses and partners of the holders of Critical Skills Employment Permits or existing Green Card permits. This allows them to also apply for work in Ireland.

- **Reactivation Employment Permit**

  This permit allows 'foreign nationals who entered the State on a valid employment permit but who fell out of the system through no fault of their own, or have been badly treated or exploited in the workplace, to work again' (citizensinfomation.ie).

Asylum seekers

Asylum seekers are people who arrive in the country without a work permit. They are allowed to apply for **refugee status** in Ireland. Once they are here, they cannot work or leave the State. They are entitled to state accommodation, healthcare, education and welfare. If refugee status is granted, they have the same rights as any other Irish citizen. If it is not granted, they are deported.

In 2003, the Government changed the policy of granting citizenship to foreign-born parents of children born in Ireland. In 2004 a referendum removed the automatic right to citizenship for Irish-born children of non-national parents.

INTERESTING FACTS

At present, Ireland is one of just two EU member states with a blanket working ban on all asylum seekers.

3.6 The number of applications for asylum in Ireland between 1994 and 2014

Migration policy in the EU

Migrants are needed in Europe as most of its countries are moving into stages 4 (low stationary) and 5 (senile) of the demographic transition model. Their **birth rates are declining**, so migrants help to fill the **labour shortages**. With the recent expansions of the EU to the east after the collapse of the USSR in 1992, the flow of both skilled and unskilled migrants to the core EU countries has continued as people seek a better standard of living and the protection of democratic laws. Migrants are also entering from outside the EU from Africa and Asia.

EU migration laws

The Schengen Agreement of **1995** allowed people to **move freely** between most of the member states of the EU. Ireland is not included in this, as border controls were largely eliminated. Since this agreement was implemented, the EU has aimed to develop a common set of laws to regulate immigration and asylum into and within the region. The EU wants to implement these laws to:

- Decrease the burden and share the responsibility of migration on its member states. Some countries, for example Spain, receive more migrants than others.
- Eliminate illegal trafficking of migrants (worth over $8 billion annually) and make processing of immigrants quicker and easier.
- Prevent readmission of migrants already refused from another member state.
- Make it easier for migrants to obtain work permits and residency.

In **2003** the **Dublin System** was introduced to **regulate asylum applications** and prevent 'asylum shopping'. Asylum seekers are now fingerprinted and their details entered on a central database.

In **2011** the **EU Blue Card** was introduced giving work and residence to **non-EU workers**, but they must be earning a salary of 1.5 times higher than the EU average.

Some people are hesitant to agree to a complete common policy on migration as they fear:

- It will lead to a '**Fortress Europe**', whereby migrants cannot easily enter Europe.
- Countries might **lose more sovereignty** if more power is handed over to the EU to rule its member states.
- The peoples of Europe will become **xenophobic** as the EU tightens and strengthens its immigration laws, possibly creating a fear and hatred of foreigners living here. This idea has been further promoted, as many countries within the EU seem to be experiencing asylum fatigue. There is growing support for right-wing parties that wish to limit inward migration. Globalisation is a welcome idea to many countries as goods, money and services flow across international borders, but governments are nervous of the flow of migrants. Today only 3.2 per cent of the world's population are migrants but 59 per cent of them were concentrated in the developed economies of the North in 2014.

Many other people believe that a common immigration policy is needed in Europe. This has especially come to light during the **mass influx of migrants** into EU countries in 2015. The

> ### GEOTERMS
> - **Fortress Europe:** a view that Europe is very difficult to enter
> - **Sovereignty:** a state having power over its own affairs

EUROPE A FORTRESS? WHAT ARE YOU TALKING ABOUT?! CAN'T YOU SEE - THE DOOR IS OPEN WIDE!

3.7 A cartoon illustrating Fortress Europe

figures for late 2015 reached the highest ever recorded: 499,826 migrants, mainly from Syria (54%), Afghanistan (13%) and Eritrea (7%). The EU is struggling to cope with the influx, and Frontex (a border control agency set up in 2004) has recorded numbers of over 100,000 migrants for the first time since it started records in 2008.

This mass migration is leading to **tensions at southern EU borders**. Border countries, such as Hungary and Croatia, the first point of entry for migrants, felt deserted as they were inundated with people fleeing desperate situations. They felt abandoned by the EU and made reactionary decisions to build razor wire defences and use tear gas to keep the migrants out of their countries. The United Nations (UN) voiced concern over the force used by riot police trying to disperse refugees at the Greek border. They called for the country to continue an 'orderly management of its borders'. Yet a common immigration policy was not implemented.

Migrants from the Middle East, Africa, Asia and Syria displayed **frustration and anger at border closures**. Macedonia declared a 'state of emergency' on 23 August 2015, as it was unable to deal with 1,500 to 2,000 migrants daily. They tried to seal off their frontiers to migrants completely as trains, buses and other modes of transport in the area were dangerously overcrowded and unable to cope with the vast numbers. The crisis spilled out into other EU countries and riots erupted in Germany, which took over 40% of the migrants. There a torn Koran led to attacks taking place on refugee centres, injuring 17 people.

These events have highlighted the need to upgrade the EU immigration laws to help these border countries as EU agreements such as the Dublin system have failed. This new **common immigration policy** needs to deal with issues such as human rights, anti-discrimination laws, family reunification and citizenship if it is to improve the lives of migrants and EU citizens alike.

QUICK QUESTIONS

1. List three push factors and three pull factors that can influence migrants.
2. What is the difference between an immigrant and an emigrant?
3. For each of the following time periods of Irish history, state whether it was a period of economic boom or recession: 1950s, 1960s–1970s, 1980s, 1997–2007, 2008–2013.
4. Explain Ireland's migration policy. (Timed activity: 3 min; 3 SRPs)
5. Explain the following terms: *Frontex, Schengen Agreement, Fortress Europe, Dublin system.*

The impact and issues that can arise from migration

Impact of migration on donor and receiver countries

Migration can bring many advantages as well as disadvantages to both donor countries (which they have left) and receiver/host countries (which they are emigrating to).

Advantages of migration for donor countries

- **Safety valve for population:** emigration from a country as people move in search of work can act as a safety valve, reducing the pressure on the resources of the country for the people still living there. This was the case in Ireland during the 1980s and the trend appears to have continued during the economic recession from 2008 to 2013. Migrants also tend to be young adults, which helps to lower the country's future birth rate and reduce the need for later generations to migrate.

- **Remittance:** the money sent home from migrant workers is a major source of outside funding for developing world countries. It is the second largest source of income in some of these countries.

For example, in Mexico remittance was worth €19 billion in 2006. Remittance in the Philippines is worth approximately €4.7 billion annually, three times the amount of foreign aid received by the country. It is a practice that the government of the country encourages.

Disadvantages of migration for donor countries

- **Depopulation of rural towns and villages:** this is a socio-economic problem as a growing youthful population is needed for government investment and job creation in an area. As more and more young people leave rural areas in search of work, local services such as post offices close down, schools amalgamate and social amenities such as Gaelic football teams decline. This leads to a lack of choice in the region, as was seen in the West of Ireland during the twentieth century. Farming practices do not improve, since there are no young people to train and take over farms. This can have a knock-on effect on the quality of the land and livestock of the region.

- **Brain drain:** migration of highly skilled workers from a region can have a major impact on the donor country. This occurred in Ireland during the economic recession 2008–13 as highly educated young people left in search of work in other countries, often as far away as Australia. This slows down the economic development of the donor country. The investment in education is reduced, tax contributions are lost and spending power on goods and services decreases. In 2005, 17 per cent of all Polish migrants to Ireland were aged 25 years and over, many with third level qualifications. This had a major negative impact on the Polish economy as their skills and talents were lost from their homeland, in some cases permanently.

Advantages of migration for receiver/host countries

- **Skills enrichment and labour shortages:** an influx of highly skilled workers can have a positive effect on the region, as renewed inward investment from the manufacturing and services sectors is likely. In countries that are suffering from labour shortages, migrant workers fill the gaps. This was the case in Ireland during the Celtic Tiger era. In 2006, 50 per cent of production jobs in the food industry were filled by migrant workers. Migrant workers pay taxes for goods and services, so they contribute to the governmental budget of the country. As most migrant workers are young adults, they have disposable incomes and are among the largest spenders.

- **Multiracial society:** as more and more migrants arrive in a country, it can lead to a greater diversity, tolerance and understanding of the new cultures that have located there. It gives people a chance to have a better awareness of the different cultures and races. This can be seen in Ireland with the vast variety of ethnic food outlets, for example Thai, and medical professionals, for example Chinese practitioners, available today. This helps to enrich Irish society and introduce people to other foods, music, religions and cultures.

3.8 Ireland is a multiracial society

Disadvantages of migration for receiver/host countries

- **Lack of integration** can cause problems of **ghettoisation**, **racism** and **discrimination** as immigrants tend to locate in the same areas of towns and cities. This prevents them from integrating fully into their new society. In countries in the developing world this has led to the growth of shanty towns on the outskirts of major cities such as São Paulo in Brazil, where

GEOTERMS

- **Integration** occurs when different cultures in a society live together peacefully. In an integrated society, members of the minority groups have full access to the opportunities, rights and services available to the members of the majority groups.

- A **ghetto** area is an urban area that is occupied by a minority group. The people live together for social support. These areas can often lack facilities and can become quite run down, as the majority of people living there are low-income earners. Ghettos can also prevent immigrants from integrating quickly in their host country as they are surrounded by their own culture, language and religion.

3.9 A ghetto area of a city

migrant workers locate in the hope of finding work in the cities. It is a significant problem for governments of host countries.

- A **Minister for Integration** was appointed in Ireland in 2007 to help migrant workers and their families integrate into Irish schools, social activities and workplaces. This role has now been replaced by the **Office for the Promotion of Migrant Integration**. It was set up to develop, drive and co-ordinate policy in relation to the integration of legally resident immigrants across government departments so that immigrants are fully integrated into Irish society. Official leaflets and documents throughout all areas of Irish social and economic life are now available in a range of languages to help bring about this integration.

- **Language** can be a major problem for migrant workers, especially in lower paid jobs, as **discrimination** and **exploitation** can occur. In 2007, the Irish Congress of Trade Unions claimed that migrant workers who didn't speak English were earning 31 per cent less than Irish workers in the same jobs. For example, in 2015 it was revealed that some migrant workers on Irish trawlers were paid less than half that of Irish workers. This lack of the dominant language can also cause problems for migrants' children. They have to settle into new schools, understand rules and regulations, make friends and study in a language with which they are unfamiliar.

- Large-scale immigration can put **pressure on a country's resources**, especially **housing**, **educational** and **medical services**. These services are needed by newly arrived immigrants immediately but the country's government cannot implement changes in these sectors quickly. These services are stretched, as is seen daily in hospital waiting times. The government will have to invest heavily in these areas in the future but funds may have to be diverted from other areas, such as transport, to facilitate this. This can lead to **resentment** and **xenophobic attitudes** from some people of the host country. They feel that the migrant population is a burden on their country's finances.

GEOTERMS

Xenophobia is the fear or hatred of foreigners.

Ethnic, racial and religious issues that can arise from migration

As people of many different cultures mix together, prejudice – often based on inaccurate stereotypes – can develop, preventing acceptance of the new migrant population. **Tensions** can also arise between the host population, which is under stress to deal with the rapid changes that are occurring in their society, and the migrant population, which is under pressure to try to adjust to a new society and way of life. Tensions normally occur under the broad headings of ethnic, racial or religious issues.

Ethnic issues

The word *ethnic* refers to the identity of a minority group with a collective self-identity within a larger population, for example Polish people in Ireland. It can be defined according to **place of birth**, **language** or **religion**. Their native language is important to immigrants as it is part of their identity, culture, traditions and beliefs. However, it is hard to maintain it as the receiver language is that of business and employment. In Ireland, the Government has addressed this complex issue in some way, as the Leaving Certificate offers exams in the languages of the major migrant populations.

> **GEOTERMS** (abc)
>
> **Ethnic cleansing** is the forceful removal by slaughter, threat or terror of a minority group from an area.

Ethnic cleansing is the removal of ethnic groups from a region. This term was first widely used to describe the forced elimination of the Muslim population from Bosnia-Herzegovina during the civil wars after the break-up of Yugoslavia in the 1990s.

Racial issues

Race refers to the **biological inheritance** of a person. It is usually based on their physical characteristics such as skin colour. Migrants often tend to locate in the same part of a city or town, often in **ghettos**. This type of social segregation can lead to a climate of fear and suspicion that can breed racist attitudes. Apartheid, the racial separation of black people and white people imposed by the South African Government, is an extreme example of these racist attitudes. It was eventually ended in 1994.

There have been an increased number of racist attacks on foreign nationals. In 2006, 35 per cent of immigrants surveyed by the Economic and Social Research Institute (ESRI) had experienced harassment in public places in Ireland. A national policy was developed against racism between 2005 and 2008. Its five main aims for immigrants are:

- To help them participate fully in all areas of life
- To raise awareness of who they are and help them be accepted for this
- To provide for them
- To include them in all areas of economic and social life in Ireland
- To ensure they have the same legal protection as everyone else in Ireland

France experienced race riots in 2005. The rioting was carried out by mainly French youths of North African descent over the accidental deaths of two teenagers from the working class commune of Clichy-sous-Bois, a suburb of Paris. The teenagers died while fleeing from police. This caused the French media to debate the issues of integration and discrimination in France. Unemployment rates of foreign migrants in France tend to be 1.5 times higher than French nationals. Tensions also exist between this community and the French Government over housing and lack of opportunities. The rioting spread to other poor suburbs of the rest of France. A state of emergency was declared for two weeks as 274 towns were affected. The rioting caused €200 million worth of damage and the death of one person. The French Government admitted that the rioting was a result of their failure to provide opportunities to young people of North African origin. A €30 billion aid package was announced for the areas that had been affected by the riots to help provide employment.

Religious issues

In *Horizons* Book 1 we studied migrations of people in India based on their religion or their beliefs. Muslim Indians moved to live in the state of Pakistan to avoid persecution from the Hindu-dominated India to the south. In the sixteenth and seventeenth centuries in Ireland, the plantations of Protestant people loyal to the Crown caused major problems. This was most notable in Northern Ireland, where up until recently people of Catholic and Protestant faiths clashed violently. Today in Ireland people of different religions pose a new, but thankfully not violent, problem for the Government.

3.10 An Educate Together school

Much of the **Irish educational system**, especially at national level, is under the trusteeship of the Catholic Church. This can make it difficult to integrate children of immigrants into the educational system without affecting their religious beliefs. The **Equal Status Act of 2000** allowed schools to offer first preference places to children of religions that helped to preserve the ethos of the school. Children who did not receive places in these schools were mainly of ethnic and racial minorities. The Irish State is legally obliged to provide education for all children under 16 years of age, so changes had to be made to accommodate these children. This was helped by the establishment of 74 multi-denominational **Educate Together** (also includes Education Training Board (ETB)) schools and three secondary schools throughout the country that are open to children of all religions. Planning is still needed by the Irish Government to make sure that children of immigrants are educated together with Irish children independent of their religious beliefs.

Migration holds many challenges for both the migrants themselves and for the countries that they move to. Countries have developed two very different and broad ways of dealing with the challenges that migrants bring. Countries such as Ireland have an **integration**, or 'melting pot', approach. Migrants are encouraged to adapt to the host country's culture. Countries such as Britain have a **multicultural** or 'salad bowl' approach, where many cultural groups keep their own cultures and traditions.

Rural to urban migration: Developed world

Ever since the Industrial Revolution in the eighteenth century, people have moved in large numbers to cities in search of work. This began the tradition of rural to urban migration that continues in most countries of the world today. Cities are growing more rapidly in the developing world. In 1900, a mere 10 per cent of the world population lived in cities. This increased to 50 per cent in 2005 and is expected to rise to 75 per cent by 2050.

QUICK QUESTIONS

1. How can migration act as a safety valve for donor populations?
2. What is a *brain drain*, and how can it affect the donor country?
3. Write three SRPs each on one advantage and one disadvantage of migrants for a receiver country. (Timed activity: 6 min; 6 SRPs)
4. Describe the difference between the 'melting pot' and 'salad bowl' approach to migrants.
5. What are the most recent experiences of migrants in Europe?

In Ireland, migration to towns was helped by the reduction in the people working in agriculture. Only a quarter of people work in this sector now compared with the 1960s. This has led to a population decline in the Border Midlands West (BMW) region of Ireland as more people move to the larger towns and cities located in the Southern and Eastern regions of the country. This trend has also occurred as the number of towns with a population of over 5,000 in the Western region is one-sixth that of the Mid-Eastern region.

Impact on the rural area

1. Rural depopulation

- Rural areas tend to have a **small, ageing population** as the populations of parishes decline. As young people are more inclined to move to urban areas in search of work, this has led to a reduction in the birth and marriage rates in the rural areas and a **'greying'** of the population. Donegal, Leitrim and Mayo lost up to 40 per cent of their populations between 1996 and 2002 through outward migration.

- Often in these areas there is also an **imbalance in the ratio of males to females**. This is the result of cultural attitudes: boys are more likely to remain in the area to work farms and girls are more likely to migrate to the city in search of jobs. This has led to a life of loneliness for many single men left behind in the rural areas.

2. Reduction of services

- The provision of services such as healthcare is **limited** in areas of low population density. Socially these areas have gone into decline as amenities such as local football teams are lost. There is also a reduction in other services, since the people living in the area cannot maintain the numbers needed to keep all the local schools, clubs and other facilities open. Rural areas have seen the amalgamation of schools and the closure of services such as post offices.

- This has created a **lack of choice** for people still living in rural areas. Feelings of bitterness and resentment can build towards the Government, which does not seem to be

as interested in their needs as in those of the more populated cities. Nine western counties lost 30 per cent of their post offices from 1992 to 2010.

3.11 Rural depopulation can result in few local services

Impact on the urban area

1. Urban sprawl

- With many people moving to cities to live, the rate of urban sprawl has increased in recent years. Cities expand rapidly to accommodate the growing numbers. Dublin has experienced high rates of urban sprawl. It has grown outwards in a westerly direction, and become a highly dispersed city. People are attracted to live in cities as there are plenty of services. They also tend to be **core economic regions** with plenty of jobs in the **secondary** and **tertiary sectors**.

- **Industries** are attracted to these regions by the well-educated workforce and well-developed transport links and infrastructure. Dublin is unlike other European cities, which are characterised by high-rise, high-density housing in the city centre. It has taken on the **model of American cities**, where low-rise urban sprawl is the norm. The expanding city is eating into the farmland and wildlife habitats of its hinterland.

2. Traffic congestion

- The **increase in car use** has been a common trend in Dublin city as more and more people commute to work. It is not helped by poor public transport, infrastructure and higher housing costs nearer to the city centre. The Government invested a lot of money in **Transport 21** to try to improve transport infrastructure. In recent years with the economic recession in 2008–13, funds have been transferred elsewhere, for example to create employment. Transport 21 was replaced by the **Planned National Roads Network 2020**.

- There has been a growth of **dormitory towns** such as Celbridge on the urban fringe of cities. Cheaper houses are available in these regions and people are able to commute to work. However, services such as schools and GPs have not grown at the same pace.

- A **sense of community** is often **absent** in these areas as many people are out of their homes for most of the day. This can lead to a sense of loss and loneliness.

- In recent years, **new towns** such as Adamstown have been built on the edge of the city to try to control this urban sprawl. The Government has made huge investments so that infrastructure and services have kept pace with new housing builds in the area.

3.12 Urban sprawl in Dublin

GEOTERMS

- A **core region** is the dominant region. It has the majority of the region's trade, industry, governmental influence, communications and affluent population.

- In **secondary economic activities**, raw materials are processed or semi-processed materials are further developed.

- People working in the **tertiary sector** provide services. Regions that are mainly involved in tertiary economic activities tend to be richer.

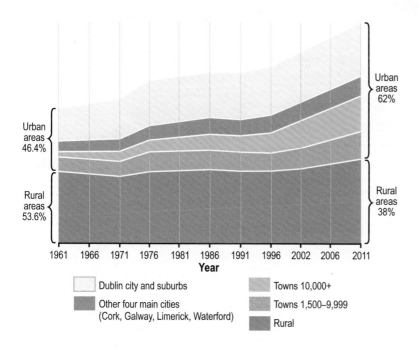

Legend:
- Dublin city and suburbs
- Other four main cities (Cork, Galway, Limerick, Waterford)
- Towns 10,000+
- Towns 1,500–9,999
- Rural

3.13 Ireland's rural and urban populations change over time

Rural to urban migration: Developing world

In the developing world, migrants have poured into cities out of desperation. The majority of these migrants have been young adults, which has led to an increased birth rate in these city areas. This natural increase accounts for about 60 per cent of the current urban population growth in developing countries. In many countries, this considerable increase in population has led to the development of **megacities**, those with populations of over 10 million people. In 1960 New York and Tokyo were the only examples. Today there are 35, such as Mexico city, mainly located in the developing world.

People in the developing world move to cities for different reasons to those in the developed world:

- The **countryside is overcrowded** with poor people, as is seen in Indonesia. In some ways rural to urban migration is seen as relieving the pressures of a growing population on the rural area.

- People migrate to the cities in the hope of creating a **better life** for themselves.

- **Services** such as drinking water are more easily available in cities.

- The hope of **finding work** can pull people in the developing world towards cities. However, in the developing world migrants to cities can find it very difficult to find accommodation.

Over-urbanisation occurs when a city's resources, such as employment and shelter, cannot cope with its growing population caused by rural to urban migration. As a result, **shanty towns** develop on the outskirts of these cities. These areas are unhealthy places to live since basic services are often not available. At least 600 million people live in these areas across the world. They are overcrowded and dirty, and diseases are widespread. Infant mortality is very high in these areas. Alcohol and drug abuse are common in shanty towns and children are sometimes sold into the sex trade. Developing world cities have inadequate street lighting due to power shortages, poor public transport and awful air pollution caused by traffic congestion and the burning of coal and wood.

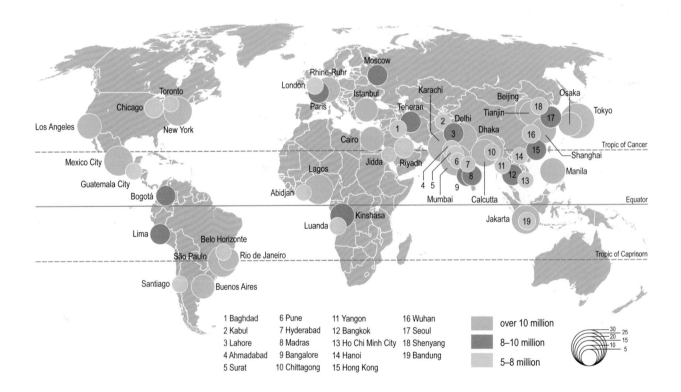

3.14 The location of the world's megacities, 2015

Today with a population of 22 million, Mumbai is the **most populous city in India** and the **sixth most populous city in the world**. Rural to urban migration is widespread, as people move to the already overcrowded cities in search of work. Those who move tend to be young people.

Impact on the urban area

1. Poor living conditions

- Mumbai is **highly congested**. Residential areas within cities are divided along religious and social lines. Lack of open space and clean water are some of the problems facing Mumbai's population of 22 million.

- **Overcrowding** is a major problem. In 2015, the population density was over 20,000 people per km² in the densely populated slum areas. This means there are not enough facilities and open spaces in the city.

- There has also been an increase in the number of **bustees**, which are made up of temporary dwellings made of plastic, tin or cardboard. The inhabitants are squatters (people without legal rights to their homes). Shanty towns are home to over 4 million people in Mumbai.

- There are **poor hygiene standards**, as there is no running water in some areas of the city. The risk of waterborne diseases such as typhoid and cholera spreading is high.

- **Pollution** is a huge problem, as rubbish is often not collected in parts of the city. Smog in Mumbai is also a problem as fossil fuels and cow dung are burned in people's homes.

2. Lack of employment opportunities

- Some 70 per cent of India's population live in rural areas. It is difficult to introduce improvements in rural areas because the people tend to be quite **traditional**. Rural areas are still experiencing outward migration of younger people as they are pulled to urban areas in search of employment opportunities.

- Most unskilled migrants find work in the informal sector or **hidden economy**. Here migrants are employed in areas such as the recycling industry, processing recyclable waste from other parts of the city.

- The Dharavi bustee has an estimated 15,000 single-room factories. These migrants are poorly paid and live a **subsistent lifestyle** and have no employment rights.

- Bustees are growing at a rapid rate around Mumbai as **landless labourers** come to the city in search of work. Dharavi, the largest bustee in Mumbai and in Asia, is home to nearly 1 million people.

- The government of the region has plans to demolish Dharavi. Through an €800 million development project, it plans to build business parks, a university and hotels in the area and to rehouse the inhabitants of the area in apartments elsewhere in the city.

EXAM HINTS

This is linked to the case study on Mumbai covered in *Horizons* Book 1 Chapter 17: Continental/subcontinental region: India.

GEOTERMS

- A **subsistence lifestyle** involves having just enough food, water and other necessities to survive.

- **Bustees** are shanty towns, slum areas of poorly built huts, with few services. They are normally located on the outskirts of large cities in the developing world.

- **Smog** is lowlying polluted air caused by smoke from factories, cars and homes.

QUICK QUESTIONS

1. What is a megacity? Name one example.
2. What is meant by the term *greying* of the population?
3. What is a bustee?
4. What is the hidden economy?
5. Write about rural to urban migration in Dublin city. (Time activity: 6 min; 6 SRPs)

Ordinary Level – Long Questions

Migration

1. Migration takes place due to push and pull factors.

    (i) Name one push factor and one pull factor associated with migration.

    (ii) Describe and explain the positive impacts of migration in Ireland.

    (iii) Describe and explain the negative impacts of migration in Ireland.

    2015, Section 2, Q10B, 40 marks

2. (i) State two reasons why people migrate from rural areas to urban areas.

    (ii) Describe and explain the effect of this migration on the urban areas that people migrate to.

    (iii) Describe and explain the effect of this migration on the rural areas they leave behind.

    2014, Section 2, Q12B, 40 marks

The marking scheme for a question like this on an Ordinary Level paper is as follows:

2 reasons stated	**4 marks**
Examination: 6 SRPs @ 3 m each	**18 marks**
Explanation: 6 SRPs @ 3 m each	**18 marks**
Total	**40 marks**

Migration – rural to urban

3. (i) Describe the push factors which contribute to migration from rural to urban areas.

    (ii) Describe the pull factors which contribute to migration from rural to urban areas.

    2013, Section 2, Q10B, 40 marks

Patterns in migration

4. (i) Explain two reasons why people immigrated (moved in) to Ireland in recent times.

    (ii) Explain two reasons why people are now emigrating (moving out) of Ireland in large numbers.

    2013, Section 2, Q12C, 40 marks

Higher Level – Long Questions

Migration

5. Examine the impact of migration on a city in the developing world that you have studied.

    2015, Section 2, Q11C, 30 marks

The marking scheme for a question like this on a Higher Level paper is as follows:

Named developing world city	**2 marks**
Impact identified	**2 marks***
Examination: 13 SRPs @ 2 m each	**26 marks**
Total	**30 marks**

* If named, a second impact would be awarded 2 marks or 1 SRP.

6. With reference to a developed region that you have studied, explain the impact of rural to urban migration on donor and receiver regions.

    2014, Section 2, Q10C, 30 marks

The marking scheme for a question like this on a Higher Level paper is as follows:

Named developed region	**2 marks**
Impact on donor region identified	**2 marks**
Impact on receiver region identified	**2 marks**
Examination: 12 SRPs @ 2 m each	**24 marks**
Total	**30 marks**

Patterns in migration

7. Describe and explain changes in the pattern of migration into and out of Ireland since the 1950s.

    2013, Section 2, Q10C, 30 marks

Migration

8. Examine how ethnic and religious issues can arise as a result of migration, with reference to example(s) that you have studied.

2013, Section 2, Q11C, 30 marks

The marking scheme for a question like this on a Higher Level paper is as follows:

Named example	**2 marks***
Religious issue identified	**2 marks**
Ethnic issue identified	**2 marks**
Examination: 12 SRPs @ 2 m each	**24 marks**
Total	**30 marks**

*A second named example will gain another 2 marks.

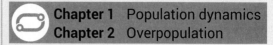

HOT TOPICS IN THE EXAMS

1. Developed world migration: rural to urban
2. Developing world migration case study

Chapter 1 Population dynamics
Chapter 2 Overpopulation

Mind map

Migration

Migration

- Intra-national/international
- Pushed from donor countries
- Pulled to host/receiver countries
- Barriers: cost, migration policies, fear
- Emigrant: a person who leaves a country
- Immigrant: a person who comes to live in a country

Religious issues

- Muslim Indians, Pakistan, plantations of Protestants, Northern Ireland
- Irish educational system: trusteeship of Catholic Church
- Equal Status Act 2000
- 74 multi-denominational Educate Together schools
- Ireland: integration/'melting pot' approach
- Britain: multicultural/'salad bowl' approach

Migration policy in the EU

- Migrants needed – labour shortages
- 1995 Schengen Agreement – free movement
- 2003 Dublin system, 2011 The EU Blue card
- EU common laws: share immigration between member states
- 'Fortress Europe', xenophobia, asylum fatigue
- Today: 3.2% migrants worldwide, 59% in North
- Migrant crisis 2015: tensions, closure of borders, southern EU countries abandoned, common EU policy needed

Migration policy in Ireland

- 2014: stricter laws
  - Focus on skills in short supply:
    General Employment Permit, Critical Skills Employment Permit, Dependent/Partner/Spouse Employment Permit, Reactivation Employment Permits
- Migrant and Irish workers = same rights
- 5+ years permanent citizenship possible
- Asylum seekers can apply for refugee status
- Irish-born children of non-nationals and their parents not automatic citizens

Changing migration patterns in Ireland

Emigration, 1950s

- Deep economic recession
- 1961 population: 2.82 million
- 400,000 emigrated
- Lacked skills and education
- Rapid depopulation, social isolation
- High dependency ratio

Economic prosperity, late 1960s and 1970s

- Taoiseach Seán Lemass
- Programmes for economic expansion
- Foreign investment and free trade
- Manufacturing jobs
- Outward migration declined
- 1966: 300+ foreign companies
- 1973: Ireland joined the EEC
- Living standards rose by 50%
- Immigration outweighed emigration

Recession, 1980s

- High unemployment rates
- Economic refugees
- Brain drain – 200,000 highly educated, young
- Manufacturers closed down

Celtic Tiger era, 1997–2007

- Net inward migration, highest in 2006
- EU and non-EU skilled and unskilled workers
- New wave of investment: high-tech MNCs
- Ireland: 1% of EU population, 20% of new inward investment in Europe
- 2002: applications for asylum peaked – 11,634

Recession 2008–2013

- MNCs closed
- Young well-educated people emigrate
- Governmental debt: €38.5 b (2005), €84b (2010)
- Housing market collapse
- 140,000 jobs lost since 2007
- Unemployment: 4.2% (2005), 15.1% (2012)
- Immigration decreased: tightened regulations
- Net outward migration
- Exited December 2013

Mind map

Migration

Migration impact and issues

Advantages for donor countries

- Safety valve: reduces pressure on resources, Ireland (1980s)
- Remittance: developing world countries

Disadvantages for donor countries

- Brain drain: slows economic development, education investment reduced, loss of tax and spending
- Rural depopulation: services close, farming practices stagnate

Advantages of migration for receiver/host countries

- Skills enrichment and labour shortages
  - Renewed inward investment
  - Labour shortages filled
  - 2006: migrants in 50% food industry production jobs
  - Contribute to the governmental budget
- Multiracial society
  - Greater diversity, tolerance and understanding

Disadvantages for receiver/host countries

- Language barrier: discrimination and exploitation
- Lack of integration: ghettoisation, racism and discrimination, shanty towns
- Pressure on resources
  - Housing, education and medical services
  - Xenophobia, stereotypes

Ethnic issues

- Identity of a minority group, collective self-identity in larger population
- Place of birth, language/religion
- Ethnic cleansing, e.g. Muslims in Bosnia-Herzegovina

Racial issues

- Biological inheritance, physical characteristics
- Social segregation: ghettos
- Apartheid, South Africa
- France race riots 2005

Religious issues

- Equal Status Act 2000
- 74 Educate Together schools
- Same laws and protection as everyone else

Rural to urban migration: Developing world

- Development of megacities
  - 35, e.g. Mexico city
  - Countryside overcrowded
  - Services more easily available in cities
  - Over-urbanisation – shanty towns develop on cities' outskirts
  - 600 m urban inhabitants in these areas
  - Infant mortality high

Case study: Mumbai, India

- World's 6th largest city
- 22 m people
- Megacity
- Poor living conditions
  - Difficult to provide basic services
  - Mumbai: 4 m people live in shanty towns
- Pollution
  - Rubbish not collected
  - Fossil fuels and cow dung burned in homes
- Lack of employment opportunities
  - 70% of India's population in rural areas
  - Informal sector/hidden economy: most unskilled migrants
  - Subsistence lifestyle

Rural to urban migration: Developed world

- 1900: 10% of world population in cities; 2005: 50%; 2050: 75% projected

Case study: Ireland

Impacts on the rural area

- Rural depopulation
  - Reduction in birth and marriage rates
  - 'Greying' of population
  - Imbalance in male to female ratio
- Reduction of services
  - Amalgamation of schools, closure of services
  - Bitterness and resentment

Impacts on the urban area

- Urban sprawl
  - Cities expand rapidly: core economic regions
  - Dublin: urban sprawl, highly dispersed, US model
- Traffic congestion
  - Poor public transport, infrastructure and higher housing costs
  - Funds transferred to employment
  - Growth of dormitory towns, e.g. Celbridge
  - Few services
  - Sense of community absent
  - Loss and loneliness

4 Settlement

By the end of this chapter students will have studied:
- The site, situation and functions of settlements
- The origins of settlements throughout Ireland from historic times
- The map skills necessary to locate and evaluate rural settlement patterns
- Rural planning, strategies and theories
- The reasons why a town's functions can change over time

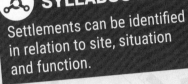

SYLLABUS LINK

Settlements can be identified in relation to site, situation and function.

NOTE

This section should be allowed at least 12 class periods (40 minutes).

Introduction

The development of towns and cities in Ireland began many centuries ago when settlers came to this island and made it their home. Many factors were taken into account when they chose their first locations. However, many of these factors have changed over time as the settlements expanded and the needs of the people changed.

We will now examine the various time periods in Ireland's past and see the many remains of the ancient civilisations that have lasted until today. We will also examine the reasons why these places were chosen by settlers to become the towns and cities of Ireland as we know them today.

Site, situation and function

The following are terms used to describe the location of settlements.

Site

'Site' refers to the area or the land that the settlement is built on, the **area's main physical characteristics**.

Here are examples of reasons why an area might have been chosen by earlier settlers:

- **Close to water supplies:** this could be used as a source of food and water, as a shallow bridging point to cross the river or a mode of transport for trading.
- **Altitude:** areas of low-lying land, below 200 m, are usually selected because of ease of construction of buildings and access to communications.
- **Aspect:** south-facing slopes have a gentler climate.
- **Avoidance of areas of flooding:** dry point sites on gently sloping, well-drained lands.

- **Good defensive sites:** on the meander bends of a river or higher land that could be easily surveyed in times of attack.
- **Nodal points:** meeting places where routes focused so trade could take place.
- **Resources:** settlements developed where natural resources such as minerals were found.
- **Coastal areas:** sheltered harbours and bays developed into ports where fishing, trade and shipping took place.

GEOTERMS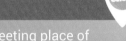

- A **nodal point** is the meeting place of roads.
- A **bridging point** is a shallow area along a river where bridges can be built.

EXAM HINTS

- The material in this chapter has appeared on the exam papers almost every year since 2006.
- For this chapter you will need to revise your map work and aerial photograph skills from *Horizons* Book 1 Chapters 19 and 20.

Situation

'Situation' refers to the **location of the settlement in relation to the surrounding area**, its features and landforms. This affects the modern growth and expansion of towns.

Here are some of the main examples of access:

- **Natural routeways:** these natural features, such as gaps and valleys, were created by rivers, glaciers or the sea. They attracted the first settlers to the area.
- **Developed routeways:** these are transport lines that have been developed over the years by people in the area as the settlement expanded.

Function

'Function' refers to the **main economic and social activities of the town**. It shows the services that the town provides for the people living there. These functions may change over time. Most towns today are **multi-functional** and provide many different functions at one time. Here are the most important functions of towns today:

R **Religious (ecclesiastical) and residential**

I **Industrial**

C **Commercial and communications (transport)**

E **Educational**

P **Port**

O **Open spaces (recreational)**

T **Tourism**

S **Services**

The following functions can be located on aerial photographs:

Religious	Church, cathedral, graveyard
Residential	Housing estate
Industrial	Industrial estate, port facilities
Commercial	Coloured shop front, market square
Communications/ transport	Road network, railway station, canal, ferry terminal, airport
Education	School, college, university
Ports	Harbour, quay, pier, marina, warehouse, large ship
Open spaces	Car park, picnic area, walking trail, nature reserve, national park
Recreational	Swimming pool, tennis court, golf course, race course, marina, football pitches
Tourism	Tourist information office, hostel, caravan/camping site, view point, antiquities
Services	Hospital, garda station, fire station, post office

Later we will see that these functions can change over time when we examine the case study on Galway.

CASE STUDY 4.1

The site and situation of Carrick-on-Suir

Site

From the OS map of Carrick-on-Suir on page 78 we can see that the town developed on gently sloping low-lying land, under 50 m. This is evident from the map's contour lines. It is also located close to the River Suir. This site was chosen by ancient settlers because the **fertile alluvial soils** created by the annual floods of the river were easily worked.

The river could be used as a mode of **transport and trade** with the surrounding areas. It was also used by ancient settlers as a source of **food and water**.

The gentle nature of the land allowed for the ease of **construction of houses and communication lines** at a later date. The low-lying aspect of the area also allowed for the **expansion of the town** on both sides of the river over the centuries, as is evident at S 40 22 and S 39 21.

Situation

The situation of the town of Carrick-on-Suir is a major crossing point on the River Suir, with roads developing in all directions from its central location. It has now developed as a major route

focus, or **nodal point**. The area appears to have developed on the shallower part of the river because deposition is occurring in S 408 217 in the form of alluvial islands. The river appears to be braiding due to a decrease in velocity and a wider channel.

Carrick-on-Suir is ideally situated to develop as a market town for the surrounding hinterland because it is fed by a **variety of modes of communication**. The town has a railway station at S 407 220 and a national primary road marked on the OS map from east to west. It is also linked by numerous regional and third class roads that can be used by local farmers and traders to buy and sell their produce in the town.

GEOTERMS

- **Braiding** of a river occurs where the river channel is broken up into a number of distributaries/channels due to deposition.
- The **hinterland** is the area surrounding a town or city.

EXAM HINTS

Things to ask yourself when answering this type of question:

1. On what type of land is the settlement built?
2. What is the altitude and aspect of the settlement?
3. If it is near a river, what are the reasons for this?
4. What are the prominent physical features of the region and have they affected the settlement's location?
5. What types of communications are found in this area and what does that tell you about the settlement?
6. Is there evidence the town has expanded and if so, why?

Back up your answers where relevant with map evidence and skills such as calculating area and measuring distance.

Distribution and density of settlement

From studying the various factors that affect the site and situation of settlements, we can also determine the reasons behind the variations in **population distribution and density** across the country. Many social and economic factors affect where people choose to live. However, they are also restricted by the physical factors of the region. Fertile lowlands that are well serviced are very attractive areas for people to live and farm, often creating high population densities in these areas. Harsh, steep, isolated upland areas with poor soils tend to discourage settlers, creating low population densities in these areas.

GEOTERMS

- **Population density** refers to the number of people per km².
- **Population distribution** refers to the spread of people across an area.

CASE STUDY 4.2

The distribution and density of settlement in Killarney

An area of low population density

The density of population on the map tends to be lower in certain areas, depending on the physical characteristics of the region.

- **Low population density** is evident in the north-west corner of the map on page 79 close to the River Laune, at V 88 92. This decrease in the density of the population is probably due to the annual flooding of the river, as settlement is absent on the floodplain on either side of the river.
- The **poor condition of the soil** is further evident by the presence of an area of mixed woodland at V 884 924. Coniferous trees are often planted in areas of low land that are not suitable for farming.

An area of high population density

The density of population in this region tends to be highest in the north-east section of the map, where the town of Killarney is located, at V 96 91. This is due to the **low-lying** nature of the area below 100 m, which allows for the **ease of construction** of buildings and communication lines.

The town seems to have developed over the years into a large market centre as it is the **focus of many routeways**, such as N72, N22, a railway station at V 970 907 and many regional and third class roads. It has a higher population density per km² than any other area of the map.

An area of absence of population

An absence of population appears in the south-west corner of the map, at V 89 87. This is due to the **upland** nature, of the region with altitudes as high as 568 m. Most settlements occur in areas below 200 m.

This high land area would be characterised by a **harsh climate** because it is exposed to winds and has colder north-facing slopes. The area also discourages agriculture as it has **poor thin soils** due to a lack of vegetation cover.

Part of the region is inside **Muckross National Park**, which would restrict the building of settlements.

EXAM HINTS

Things to ask yourself when answering this type of question:

1. Does the area have a high population density, a low population density or an absence of population?
2. What are the physical factors, for example drainage, altitude, aspect and soil fertility, that could have contributed to this?
3. What are the historical factors, for example availability of resources, nearby markets and centres, that could have contributed to this?
4. What are the social factors, such as communication lines, tradition of agriculture and tourism, that could have contributed to this?

Back up your answers where relevant with map evidence and skills, such as calculating area and measuring distance.

QUICK QUESTIONS

1. Define the terms *site* and *situation* of a settlement.
2. Give four examples of the functions of a town.
3. Define the terms *population density* and *population distribution*.
4. Pick out an area of low population density from the map of Carrick-on-Suir on page 78 and give reasons, supported by map evidence, for your answer. (Timed activity: 3 min; 3 SRPs)
5. Pick out an area of high population density from the map of Carrick-on-Suir on page 78 and give reasons, supported by map evidence, for your answer. (Timed activity: 3 min; 3 SRPs)

Pre-historic and historic settlement

The New Stone Age (Neolithic)

Time period: From 3500 BC until 2000 BC

Overview

The New Stone Age settlers were the first people to leave remnants of their civilisation behind because they were the **first farmers**. They settled in areas for longer periods of time. They grew crops and herded animals but their homes have not survived because they were made from wattle and daub. These settlers chose areas that were low lying and close to a river because the soil was fertile and easily worked. The river could be used as a source of food and water and for transport.

The first farmers built many and varied **megalithic tombs**, often in upland areas, for their dead. Many of these structures have survived. Some of these tombs have beautiful stone carvings or are aligned with the sun, for example Newgrange. The weight of the large stones used for these tombs leads us to believe that these people had great skills in engineering.

Map evidence

Midden (rubbish heap), megalithic tombs (large stone tombs), dolmens, court cairns, cist graves, barrows (burial mounds), passage graves, stone circles, standing stones

Named examples

The Boyne Valley especially Newgrange, Co. Meath; the Burren, Co. Clare

4.1 The Brownshill Dolmen, Carlow, created during the Neolithic period by the first farmers. The capstone is the largest in Europe, weighing over 100 tonnes.

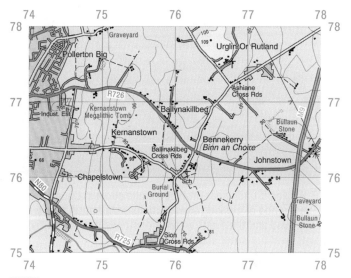

4.2 Carlow OS map showing Neolithic antiquities

Celtic settlement

Time period: From 500 BC until AD 400

Overview

Many Celts spoke an Indo-European dialect. They came to Ireland from central Europe. They brought with them iron weapons and were a powerful people. They lived in a structured society that was divided into kingdoms called tuaths. The Celts were **warriors** and built **defensive structures** to protect themselves from attack. These were often located on elevated sites or cliff edges that could be easily protected or in the centre of a lake built on a man-made island with hidden steps for access. These structures were constructed of earth or stone, and were often built in isolated areas. They are scattered across the country. In the West of Ireland, the ring forts are mainly made from stone because there is less soil cover.

Map evidence

Fulacht fiadh/fia (cooking place), ring forts, hill forts, promontory forts, crannógs, Ogham stones (Celtic writing), stone circles, souterrains (underground passages for escape)

Named examples

Placenames with Rath, Lios, Dun or Caiseal. Cahir and Cashel, Co. Tipperary.

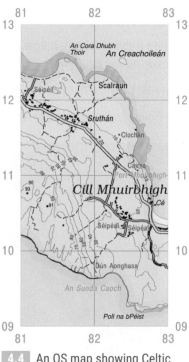

4.3 A fulacht fiadh near Drombeg stone circle in County Cork. This was a method of cooking used in the Bronze Age. A hole was dug in the ground and filled with water. Hot stones from a nearby fire were added to heat the water and thus cook meat.

4.4 An OS map showing Celtic antiquities on Aranmore

Christian period

Time period: From AD 432 (fifth century)

Overview

St Patrick was the first person to bring Christianity to Ireland. He helped to convert the pagan Celts over the following century. Pagan ritual sites such as holy wells were converted to Christian places of worship. The majority of people in Ireland at that time were illiterate. Therefore stone crosses with pictures carved into them were used by Christians to help teach people about Christianity.

4.5 St Kevin's monastery, Glendalough, Co. Wicklow

Most of the Christian people during this period were monastic and dedicated themselves to lives of prayer. They often lived in isolated places. Women became nuns and set up **convents**. Men became monks and established **monasteries**. Round towers were built near to the monasteries for protection during times of attack. Some of these monasteries became the first towns in Ireland because people settled close to them for education, alms (charity) and protection.

Map evidence

Church, monastery, holy well, cillín (small church), stone crosses, high crosses, round towers

Named examples

Placenames with Kill/Cill/Ceall/Manister (Church). Clonmacnoise, Co. Meath; Sceilig Mhicil, Co. Kerry; Kells, Co. Meath; Cill Dara (Kildare).

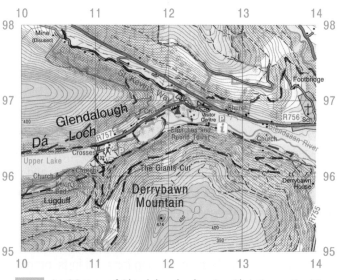

4.6 An OS map of Glendalough, showing Christian antiquities

Viking settlement

Time period: From AD 795 (eighth century)

Overview

The Vikings came to Ireland from Scandinavia on longboats. They created their first towns at **sheltered river mouths**, mainly located in the south and south-east of the country. Vikings raided many of the local monasteries in the region, especially those situated on navigable rivers.

Viking towns became **trading centres** between Ireland, Britain and central Europe. The ports were also located in sites that were easily defendable from the native Irish. Little of the original Viking settlements have remained because they were wooden structures. However, the radial layout of the original street patterns has survived in town centres such as Dublin (Dubh Linn/Black Pool) and Waterford.

Map evidence

Located at river mouths, have a radial street pattern

Named examples

Placenames with ford (fjord). Wexford, Waterford, also Wood Quay in Dublin, Limerick.

4.7 Wexford town, a Viking settlement in the south-east corner of Ireland

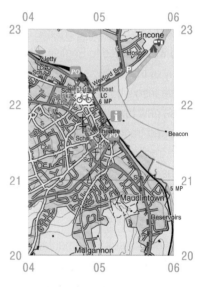

> **GEOTERMS** abc
>
> **Radial** means spreading out from a central point.

4.8 An OS map of Wexford town, showing Viking antiquities

Normans

Time period: From AD 1169 (twelfth century)

Overview

The Normans originally came from Scandinavia but settled in Normandy in France and travelled to Ireland from Britain. They were **castle builders** and sought out defensive sites, often on the bend of a river or elevated land. The majority of Norman towns developed around these castles for defensive and trading purposes. They tend to be located in the south and east of the country at **important route centres**. The Normans also valued **bridging points of rivers** because both sides of the river were accessible for trade. Many earlier Viking towns on the east coast were taken over by the Normans. Town walls and gates were built to protect the town further from attack and also to control trade and disease.

4.9 Cahir Castle, Co. Tipperary, an example of a Norman castle

The Normans were Christians and encouraged religious orders such as the Franciscans to establish religious institutions called **abbeys**. These provided education, alms and accommodation for the locals of the nearby town.

Map evidence

Castles, motte and bailey (wooden castle), moat, town walls, town gates, abbeys, priories

Named examples

Kilkenny; Trim, Co. Meath

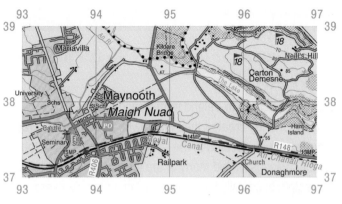

4.10 An OS map of Maynooth, showing Norman antiquities

Plantation town

Time period: From the 1500s (sixteenth and seventeenth centuries)

Overview

Plantation towns were created during the sixteenth and seventeenth centuries when land was granted to English planters who had been loyal to the English Crown. Many of these towns have **fortified buildings and defensive walls** because the native Irish who had lost their land often attacked the new inhabitants. Many of these new towns have a main street and a market square or diamond where weekly fairs and trading of goods took place. Plantation towns were **well planned**, with wide treelined streets and fine buildings three or four storeys high. Most of these towns were located near to a large estate or **demesne** owned by the local landlord. Roads and canal networks developed along with trade during this period.

4.11 The market square in Donegal town

Map evidence

Fortified houses, ornamental gardens, market square or diamond, demesnes, canals, wide streets with a grid pattern

Named examples

Towns in Laois-Offaly, Munster and Ulster; Maynooth, Co. Kildare; Birr, Co. Offaly; Abbeyleix, Co. Laois

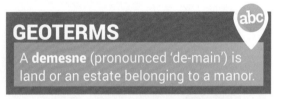

GEOTERMS

A **demesne** (pronounced 'de-main') is land or an estate belonging to a manor.

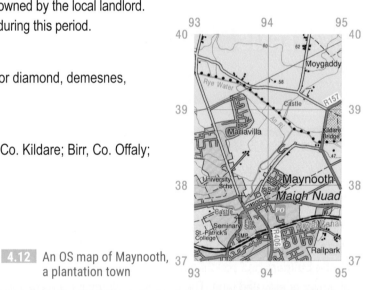

4.12 An OS map of Maynooth, a plantation town

New towns

Time period: 1960s (twentieth century)

Overview

New towns were created from the 1960s and laid out as a result of **urban planning issues**. Around Dublin city, towns such as Tallaght were created from smaller villages and developed by planners to counteract the effects of urban sprawl. These towns have now become part of the Greater Dublin area. Others, such as Shannon, were built to accommodate the growing numbers of people moving to the area to work at the nearby airport and industrial estates.

Map evidence

Planned streets, large housing estates and industrial estates

Named examples

Shannon, Co. Clare; Tallaght, Blanchardstown and Adamstown, Co. Dublin

4.13 Aerial view of planned town of Adamstown, Co. Dublin

GEOTERMS

Urban sprawl is the spread of a city out into the suburbs and into rural areas.

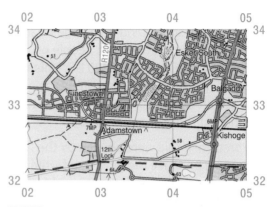

4.14 An OS map of Adamstown, a new town

EXAM HINTS

You must always back up map work questions with evidence from the map, such as grid references. Remember SEE: statement, evidence and explain!

QUICK QUESTIONS

1. What are the main characteristics of a Celtic settlement?
2. Why were ring forts made of stone in the West of Ireland?
3. What was a diamond used for in a plantation town?
4. Why were new towns built from the 1960s?
5. Transfer the table below into your copy and complete it using the following words and phrases (timed activity: 8 min).

   - Sixteenth and seventh century
   - Church
   - Norman
   - 3500 BC to 2000 BC
   - Wood Quay
   - Castle
   - Ring fort
   - Shannon
   - Christian
   - Eighth century

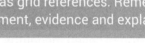

Type of settlement	Time period	Map evidence	Named example
Neolithic		Midden	Newgrange
Celtic	500 BC to AD 400		Rath
	From AD 432		Cill Dara
Viking		Radial streets	
	Twelfth century		Kilkenny
Plantation town		Fortified house	Abbeyleix
New town	1960s	Planned streets	

CASE STUDY 4.3
The development of a historic settlement at Dingle

The New Stone Age (Neolithic)

On the OS map extract of Dingle on page 80 the earliest settlers were the Neolithic people or the first farmers in 3500 BC to 2000 BC. This is represented by a Galtan (standing stone) at Q 478 008, which was used to **mark burial sites** or the position of the sun and the stars.

Low-lying areas like this were chosen by the Neolithic people because the land was **fertile** and the soils were easily worked and could be used for growing crops. It was also less than half a kilometre to the Garlinny River, which was probably used as a source of **water and food** and also for **transport**.

Located in upland areas of the region are **megalithic tombs** (tuama meigiliteach), for example at V 525 994, which is 205 m above sea level. These were often located on elevated sites and marked the graves of the dead. They were made with large stones called megaliths.

Celtic period

This time period is evident from the large number of **ring forts** at Q 445 032, **fulacht fias** at Q 470 001 and **Ogham stones** (clocha oghaim) at V 464 997 located in the region. Celts arrived in Ireland in 500 BC from central Europe. They were a warlike people who built ring forts to protect themselves from attack from the native Irish. These ring forts were often located on elevated sites for protection.

Many of the cooking places or fulacht fias of the Celts remain. This was a hole in the ground that was filled with water. Hot stones from a nearby fire were added to heat the water and cook meat.

Ogham was the writing of the Celts. It consisted of lines cut into the edge of an upright stone. These Ogham stones often marked the territorial boundaries of a Celtic tuatha, a tribe, laying claim to a particular area.

Christian period

Christian settlement dating from AD 432 is also evident on the OS map extract of Dingle. This period is when **St Patrick** arrived in Ireland and helped to **convert the pagan Celts**. It is evident from the two churches located in Dingle town at Q 446 013 and Q 448 013. These are situated on low-lying land below 50 m and close to Dingle harbour, which could have been used as a food source and later for trade. Religious sites often grew into towns as people settled near them for education and alms.

Rural settlement patterns

There are four types of settlement pattern to be found in the countryside:

- Nucleated (clustered)
- Linear (ribbon)
- Dispersed
- Absence

Nucleated (clustered)

Nucleated settlements consist of houses located **in groups**, often in housing estates or where roads meet (nodal points). These would have originally developed near demesnes (landlord estates) or a bridging point. They grew over time to become small towns with a market function and services such as schools, churches and post offices.

Linear (ribbon)

Linear settlements consist of houses **in a line**, usually built along a road due to ease of access to communications. This pattern is common in rural areas. Farmers often sell off land that faces a road because it can fetch a higher price. Linear settlements have developed since the 1960s. These sites have also been used by shops, petrol stations and B&Bs, which have benefited from their roadside locations. They can offer large parking areas at a fraction of the cost of town centre locations.

Today planning authorities do not favour this type of housing because it can contribute to urban sprawl and car dependency, which is not sustainable. There is also a fear of pollution of groundwater from an increase in septic tanks in the area.

Dispersed

In dispersed settlements, houses are **dotted around the countryside**, indicated by a small black square on the map. They are usually **farmhouses with their own farm** and are generally located near minor and third class roads. Before the eighteenth century, there was an open-field system of farming called 'common land' where all the farmers grazed their animals together. It was surrounded by a central settlement. After the eighteenth century land ownership changed. The common land was divided up and enclosed by individual farmers, working their own land for their own profits. An individual farmhouse was usually built on this land. Dispersed settlement also tends to show areas of fertile land. These farms can be very widely spaced in the east and south of the country where farms are large.

Absence

If there are no houses in the area, it usually means the **land is not suitable for settlement**, for example bogs, marsh, high land and areas prone to flooding. This can also be due to social factors, such as outward migration, and exhaustion of natural resources.

Rural planning

One-off housing in rural areas has become increasingly popular in recent years as people have moved out of towns in order to build bigger houses surrounded by larger gardens. They would tend to commute to the nearby town for work. This gave rise to an **explosion of linear housing** in Ireland along most towns' exit routes. Most Irish planning authorities felt that this was unsustainable. These areas have experienced rapid population growth and demands on services. During the Celtic Tiger era (1997–2007), there was a huge increase in the purchase of **second homes, holiday homes and B&Bs**, especially in scenic rural and coastal areas, which attract tourists. The building and sale of these units have now gone into decline. The recession and the Government's introduction of tax levies on second homes and holiday homes in Ireland has made these houses less affordable.

4.15 An area of rural 'one-off' housing

County development plans

Rural development plans have been introduced by local authorities as a response to the massive building boom during the Celtic Tiger era. They want to protect the distinctiveness of the rural areas and prevent them from becoming more suburbanised. **Strict planning laws** contained in a County Development Plan have been introduced in all counties in Ireland. These restrict the number of housing developments taking place each year. Restrictions include living a certain distance from the property, for example 10 km, being a native of the county, showing a need for housing, and limits on building heights and materials.

Planning authorities are also concerned about:

- The **provision of services** in rural areas
- **Traffic management and pollution** of local water supplies with an increase in septic tanks in the area
- **Reduction in scenic quality** of an area
- An **expanding commuter belt** because of a lack of jobs in rural areas

These issues are all examined and strategies to deal with them are contained in **county development plans**. These plans list organisations, groups and agencies concerned with the local socio-economic developments of the county. These plans are revised and updated every five years. They are of great importance for managing the developments in the county for current and future generations.

National Development Plan

On a national level, the National Development Plan 2007–2013 and the introduction of the Commission for the Economic Development of Rural Areas (CEDRA) 2012 both have developed planning strategies that will protect the rural environment of Ireland. This attempts to prevent **rural depopulation** and **counterurbanisation** by encouraging rural development. This means that social and economic development of rural areas must be balanced with the needs of the environment and the present and future generations. The NDP's areas of investment are:

- **Infrastructure** to link rural to urban areas
- **Village renewal**, to make villages more interesting places for people to live and increase their employment potential through tourism
- **Programmes** such as LEADER, and the IDA and Enterprise Ireland because they help in the development of much needed resource-based industries in Ireland
- **Social inclusion** with the provision of improved rural amenities and services, especially for older people
- **Preservation** of scenic areas, sensitive development and the maintenance of farmlands
- **Education and training schemes** in rural areas

GEOTERMS

Counterurbanisation occurs when urban workers move to the countryside. There are various reasons for this, such as a better quality of life, the acquisition of a family site or cheaper land. Counterurbanisation can lead to suburbanised villages, which can become dormitory villages as people commute to work.

QUICK QUESTIONS

1. Name the four rural settlement patterns.
2. How did linear settlements develop?
3. What is a County Development Plan?
4. What is counterurbanisation?
5. What promises have the NDP and CEDRA made for rural areas? (Time activity: 4 min; 4 SRPs)

Central Place Theory

Central Place Theory was developed by Walter Christaller in Germany in 1933. His theory tries to explain the size and spacing of towns across the countryside to prevent competition with each other. The term *central place* is used by Christaller to describe an **urban centre** that provides goods and services for an area larger than itself (hinterland). A central place can vary in size from a small village to a large city. The main ideas linked to the Central Place Theory are **range**, **threshold**, **hierarchy of goods**, **urban hierarchy** and **hinterland**.

Range

The range is the distance that people are prepared to travel for particular goods or services. These are divided into two categories:

- **Small range:** people need these goods or services frequently. They are not prepared to travel long distances for them. Examples are milk and petrol.

- **Large range:** these are one-off goods or services that people are prepared to travel longer distances for. Examples are cars and furniture.

Threshold

Threshold is the **minimum number of customers that a business needs to operate**. Local shops need only a small number of customers to stay in business. They provide a small range of goods that people buy frequently so therefore have a small threshold. A larger more specialised retailer such as a PC shop needs a greater number of customers to survive. People purchase these goods less frequently, so therefore the shop has a large threshold.

Hierarchy of goods

Goods and services can be further divided into three categories, depending on the importance of the product and the willingness of people to travel to obtain them:

- **Low order goods and services:** these are goods that are widely available to people. Therefore they have a low range and a low threshold. Examples are newspapers and petrol.

- **Middle order goods and services:** people do not use these as frequently and will travel further to find them. Examples are GP services and supermarkets.

- **High order goods and services:** these are used less frequently, and people will travel long distances for them. Examples are cars and universities.

Urban hierarchy

Urban hierarchy is the **ranking or grading of the importance of urban centres** in relation to each other. All the main urban centres in a country are arranged like a pyramid, with the largest primate city at the top extending down to small villages at the bottom. In Ireland, Dublin is at the top of the hierarchy pyramid because the city has the greatest number of high, middle and low order goods and services to offer its customers. Below Dublin are Ireland's other cities, such as Cork and Waterford. Normally below this is the county town, as it offers a mixture of middle and high order goods. And finally at the bottom of the pyramid are the smaller villages (hamlets) of Ireland because they offer only a limited number of low order goods.

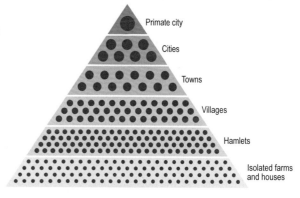

4.16 The urban hierarchy pyramid

Hinterland

The hinterland is the **area surrounding an urban centre** where the customers live. It can also be called its trade area or market area. For Christaller, this area had to be hexagonal in shape so that there was no overlapping or missed hinterlands of urban centres. The size of a hinterland is partly dependent on the size and functions of its central place and the population density of the area. Central places located in areas with a low population density tend to have a larger hinterland because people have to travel longer distances for lower order goods and services.

Christaller's Central Place Theory explains why towns of different sizes exist throughout the world today. It concludes that:

- **Small urban centres** with a small hinterland greatly outnumber larger urban centres with larger hinterlands.

- **Larger urban centres** provide a greater number of goods and services that people are prepared to travel longer distances for.

Christaller's theory has been criticised:

- **Physical landscape**, for example mountains, exploitation of natural resources and upgrading of transport networks, has allowed certain urban centres to advance at the cost of others. This is not necessarily based on their range of goods and services or their distribution across the countryside

- Christaller assumes that people have **equal purchasing power** and will always travel to the nearest central place.

Christaller's Central Place Theory is thought by geographers today to have **limited use** because the layout of most towns and cities does not follow the patterns outlined. However, the spread of educational facilities such as schools, colleges and universities and the spread of shopping centres in larger cities do seem to follow Christaller's ideas of distribution and spacing. At a simple level, Central Place Theory can be **helpful in regional planning and in market analysis of trade**.

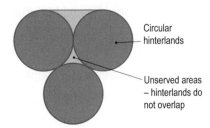

Circular hinterlands

Unserved areas – hinterlands do not overlap

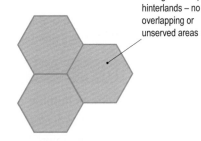

Hexagonal-shaped hinterlands – no overlapping or unserved areas

4.17 A hinterland that is hexagonal in shape gives the best coverage of an area

How functions and services of urban centres change over time

All cities, towns and villages are **dynamic** and are in a constant state of change that allows them to survive and prosper. Functions of an urban centre or town change over time according to the changing needs and activities of the people within the area. Most urban centres in Ireland developed as religious settlements, such as Cashel, Co. Tipperary, or defensive settlements, such as Trim, Co. Meath. Most towns have lost these functions today. They have developed more modern functions, for example retail and commercial. We will now examine the changes in the function of Galway city over time.

QUICK QUESTIONS

1. What is a central place?
2. Define the term *threshold*.
3. Give two examples of low, middle and high order goods.
4. Why have people criticised Christaller's Central Place Theory? (Timed activity: 2 min; 2 SRPs)
5. In which areas can Christaller's Central Place Theory be used today?

Galway is the fourth largest urban centre in Ireland and is the main urban centre for the Western region. It is located to the north of Galway Bay on the River Corrib. The city has sprawled to the east and the west of the river along the flat land close to the sea. On the OS map extract on page 81 it is approximately 21 km². It is a **nodal point**, with a train station at M 302 253, and is fed by many national primary (N84), secondary (N6), regional (R338) and third class roads.

Defensive function

Galway was a **medieval city**, as can be seen by the random pattern of roads in the left foreground of the OS map on page 81. These narrow streets were not developed with the car in mind. In the thirteenth century the Norman lord Richard de Burgh built a castle in the centre of the town. This established the town as a **trading centre** on the bridging point of the River Corrib. Galway also had access to the sea with a port for overseas trade, especially of wine, with France.

A town developed around the castle as people moved near to it for **protection in times of attack**. Trade in the city was later controlled by 14 merchant families or tribes. Hence the city gained its name 'City of the Tribes'. In the fifteenth century, Lynch's castle was built at M 300 253. It has been used as a bank in the city since 1927. Galway continued its defensive function into the seventeenth century when two star-shaped forts were built further out from the city, at M 305 265 and M 312 247. These were used as military bases to protect the city. More importantly, they kept watch over the port in case of attack. This function has declined in relative importance over the centuries.

Educational function

Galway has developed as the location of many **leading educational facilities**, from schools at M 293 253, colleges at M 329 258 to a university at M 294 259. In 1845, it was chosen as the location for one of the Queen's colleges in Ireland. These have been renamed as the National Universities of Ireland. NUIG is the National University of Ireland, Galway. Galway is also home to the main centre for the Galway-Mayo Institute of Technology (GMIT). The city supports the medical sector as it offers teaching and training of medical staff at the University College Hospital located at M 288 256.

All these educational facilities have established Galway as an **important centre of teaching and learning** in the Western region and throughout Ireland. It offers some of the leading courses in medicine and healthcare in the country.

Manufacturing function

Galway has established itself as the **leading manufacturing centre** in the western region. It is the base for most of the foreign-owned industries in the area. They are attracted to Galway because of its highly educated and English-speaking workforce, ease of access and advanced communications networks.

It is also a large urban centre that is able to offer a wide variety of services to **new industries** such as industrial estates, for example at M 325 275. Galway is the location of many **multinational companies**, especially in the fields of medical devices as well as pharmaceuticals and IT, for example Boston Scientific and Apple, respectively.

Galway's **functions** have therefore **grown and changed over time** from a defensive area to a thriving city leading the way in primary, secondary and third level education and international manufacturing.

4.18 Galway is the main urban centre for the western region

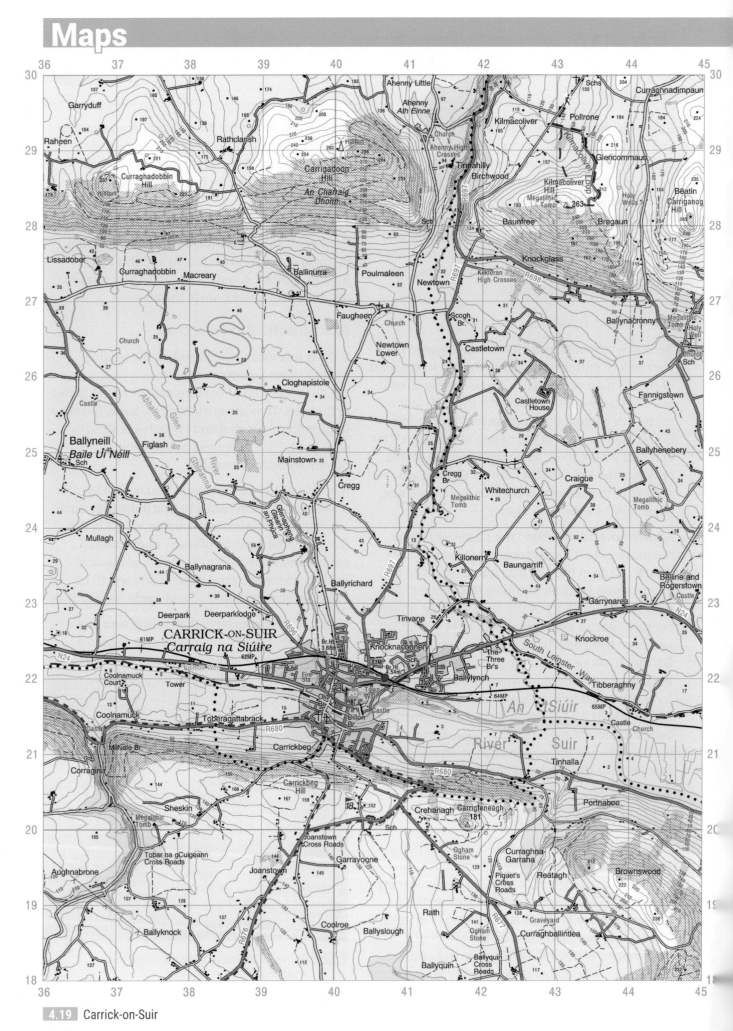

4.19 Carrick-on-Suir

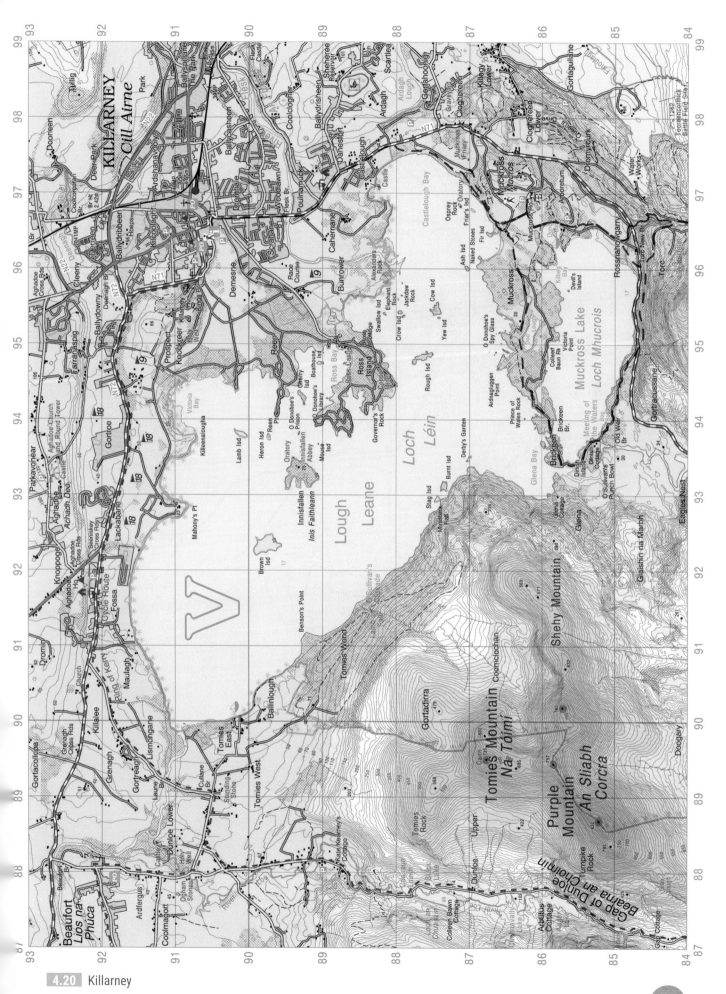

4.20 Killarney

4.21 Dingle, 2011

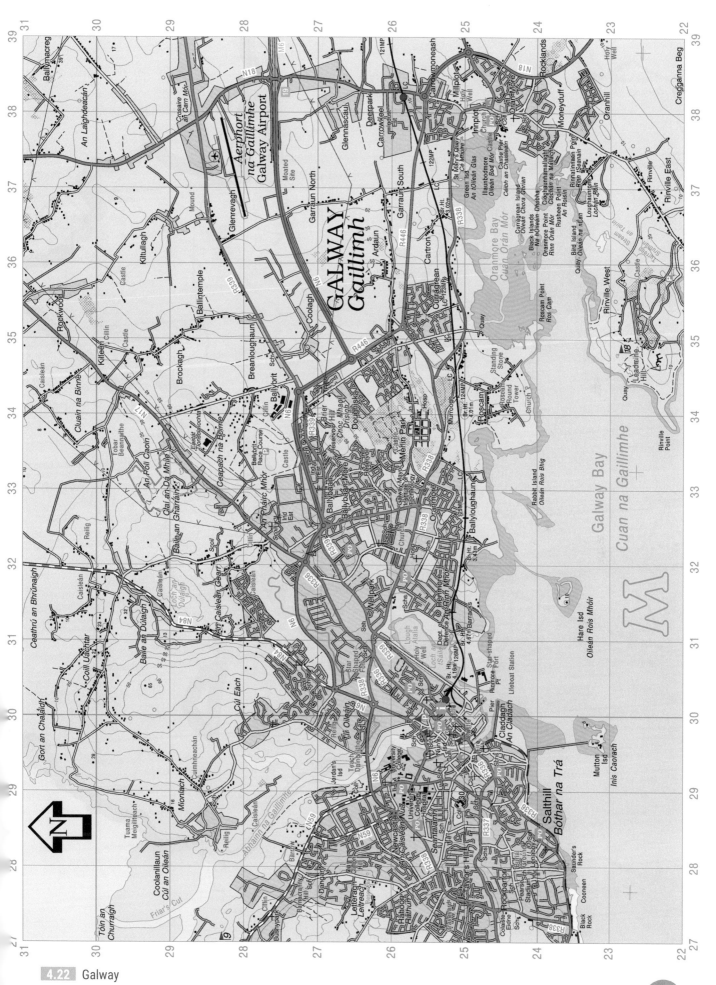

4.22 Galway

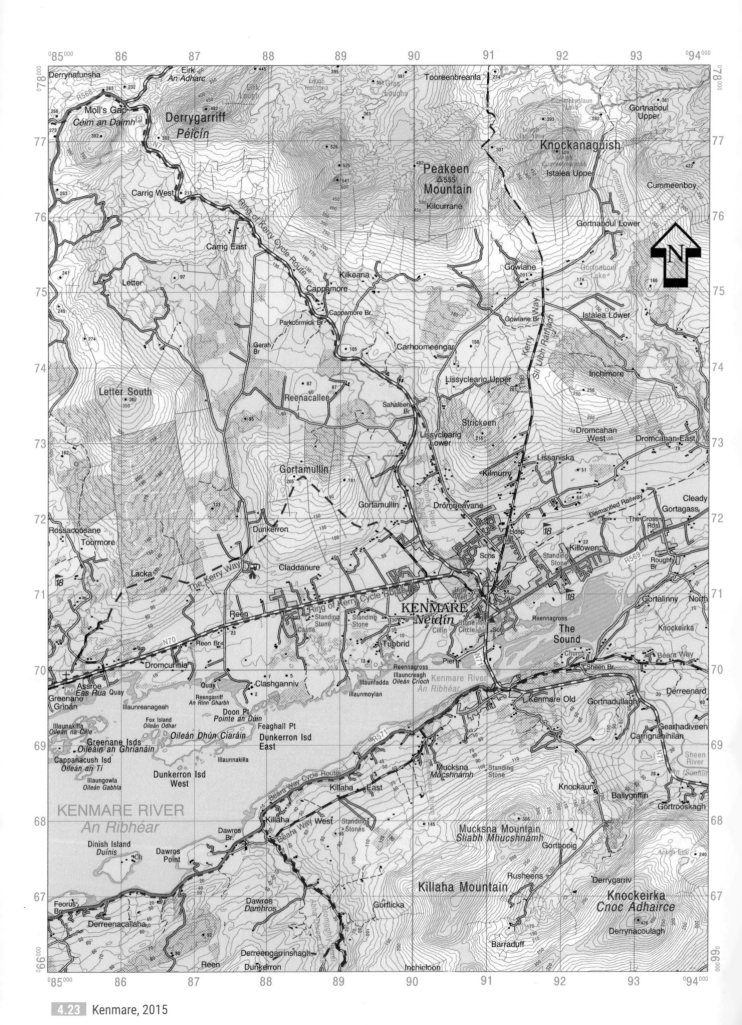

4.23 Kenmare, 2015

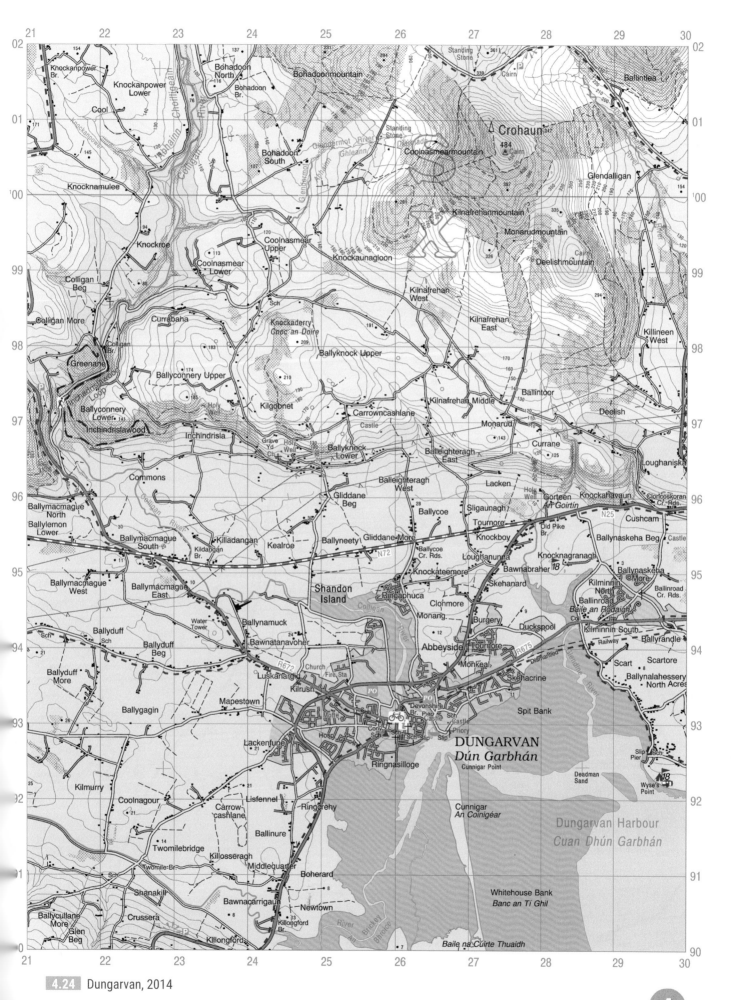

4.24 Dungarvan, 2014

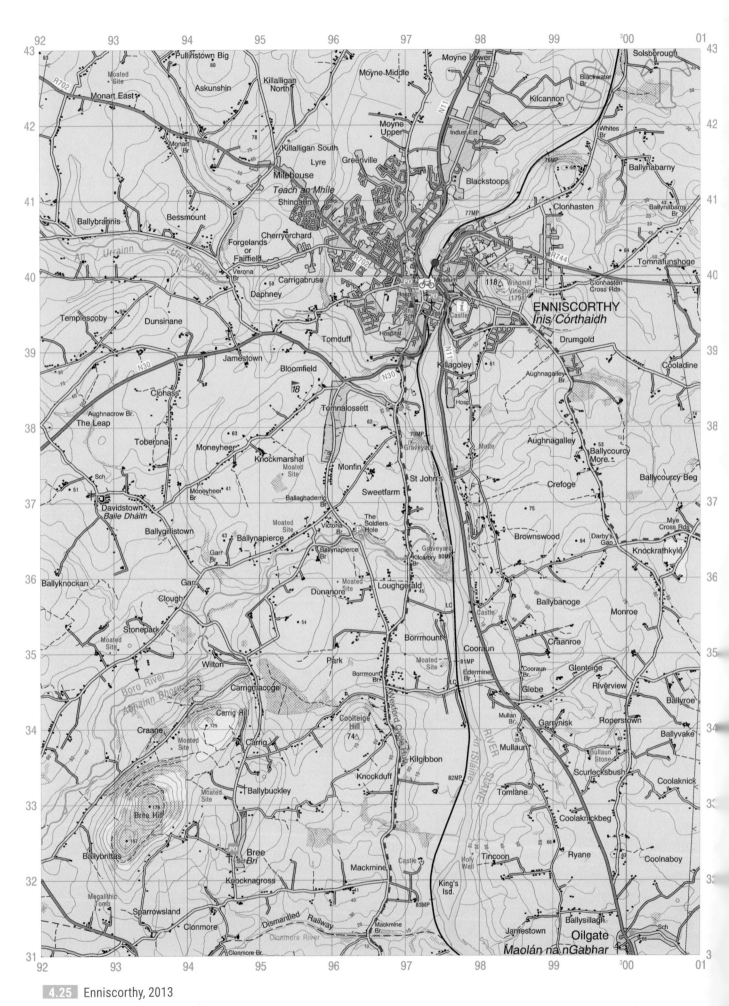

4.25 Enniscorthy, 2013

Legend Eochair

M 1 □1 Mótarbhealach
Motorway (Junction number)

N 11 Bóthar príomha náisiúnta
National Primary Road

N 71 Bóthar tánaisteach náisiúnta
National Secondary Road

Carrbhealach dúbailte
Dual Carriageway

Bóthar príomha /tánaisteach
náisiúnta beartaithe
Proposed Nat. Primary
/ Secondary Road

R 574 Bóthar Réigiúnach
Regional Road

4 metres min / 4 metres max Bóthar den
tríú grád
Third Class Road

Boithre de
chineál eile
Other Roads

Bealach
Track

Líne tarchurtha leictreachais
Electricity Transmission Line

SUMMIT INFORMATION

● Above 600m
◉ 599m - 400m
◉ Below 400m

NOTE Over 600m summits must have a prominence of 15m Between 400m and 599m a prominence of 30m and from 150 to 399m a prominence of 150m

The summit classification is courtesy the Mountain Views hillwalking community.
The lists used, updated to 2009, include:
The "Arderins" 500m list,
The "Vandeleur-Lynam" 600m list,
and other lists for smaller tops and county high points.

⊕ **Mountain Rescue Base**

Céim imlíne comhairde 10m
10m Contour Interval

Céim imlíne comhairde 50m
50m Contour Interval

△ Cuaille triantánachta
Triangulation Pillar

123 · Spota airde
Spot Height

+ Trasnú cliathráin
Graticule Intersection

IRISH NATIONAL GRID

	A	B	C	D	E
	F	G	H	J	K
	L	M	N	O	P
	Q	R	S	T	U
	V	W	X	Y	Z

○ Stáisiún cumhachta (uisce)
Power Station (Hydro)

◉ Stáisiún cumhachta
(breosla iontaiseach)
Power Station (Fossil)

Ⅹ Crann
Mast

▲ Brú de chuid An Óige
Youth Hostel (An Óige)

Ⓐ Brú saoire Neamhspleách
Independent Holiday Hostel

⇌ Láithreán carbhán (idirthurais)
Caravan site (transit)

♠ Láithreán campála
Camping site

⊓ Láithreán picnicí
Picnic site

☼ Ionad dearctha
Viewpoint

P Ionad pairceála
Parking

A T An Taisce
National Trust

Tearmann Dúlra
Nature Reserve

⊥ Feirm Ghaoithe
Wind Farm

Foirgnimh le hais a chéile
Built up Area

ℹ Ionad eolais turasóireachta
(ar oscailt ar feadh na bliana)
Tourist Information centre
(regular opening)

ℹ Ionad eolais turasóireachta
(ar oscailt le linn an tséasúir)
Tourist Information centre
(restricted opening)

★ Garda Síochána
Police

PO Oifig phoist
Post office

† Eaglais no séipéal
Church or Chapel

✟ Ardeaglais
Cathedral

✈ Aerfort
Airport

✦ Aerpháirc
Airfield

⑨ ⑱ ㉗ Galfchúrsa, machaire gailf
Golf Course or Links

🚲 Bealach rothar
Cycle route

Siúlbhealach le
comharthaí; Ceann Slí.
Waymarked Walks;
Trailheads.

This is a sample reference only

(Discovery Sheet 23)
Sample reference: G 103 079

Compiled and published by Ordnance Survey Ireland,
Phoenix Park, Dublin 8, Ireland.
Arna thiomsú agus arna fhoilsiú ag Shuirbhéireacht Ordanáis Éireann, Páirc an Fhionnuisce, Baile Átha Cliath 8, Éire.

Irish Transverse Mercator Not used on this extract.
(ITM) is a newly derived GPS compatible mapping projection that is associated with the European Terrestrial Reference System 1989 (ETRS89). For further information on ITM and for coordinate conversion visit our website.

CENTRE OF SHEET ITM CO-ORDINATES:
EXAMPLE: ⊕ 499973E 827008N

Loch
Lake

Canáil, canáil (thirim)
Canal, Canal (dry)

Abhainn nó sruthán
River or Stream

Líne bharr láin
High Water Mark

shingle,mud sand or loose rock Líne lag trá
Low Water Mark

Trá
Beach

Ferry V Bád fartha (feithiclí)
Ferry (Vehicle)

Ferry P Bád fartha (paisinéirí)
Ferry (Passenger)

🕯 🕯 Teach Solais in úsáid / as úsáid
Lighthouse in use / disuse

⛵ Bádóireacht
Boating activities

Iarnróid
Railways

Iarnród tionscalaíoch
Industrial Line

Tollán
Tunnel

LC Crosaire comhréidh
Level Crossing

Staisiún traenach
Railway Station

Teorainn idirnáisiúnta
International Boundary

Teorainn chontae
County Boundary

An Ghaeltacht
Irish speaking area

Páirc Náisiúnta
National Park

Páirc Foraoise
Forest Park

Seilbh de chuid an
Aire Chosanta
Dept. of Defence
Property

Foraois bhuaircíneach
Coniferous Plantation

Coillearnach Dhuillsilteach
Deciduous Woodland

Foraois mheasctha
Mixed Woodland

· Séadchomhartha
Ainmnithe
Named Antiquities

○ Clós, m.sh. Ráth nó Lios
Enclosure, e.g. Ringfort

⤬ Láthair Chatha (le dáta)
Battlefield (with date)

SCALE 1:50 000 SCÁLA 1:50 000

www.osi.ie

1 KILOMETRES 0 1 2 3 4 5 6 7 KILOMETRES 8
1 STATUTE MILES 0 1 2 3 4 STATUTE MILES 5

2 ceintiméadar sa chiliméadar (taobh chearnóg eangaí) 2 centimetres to 1 Kilometre (grid square side)

4.26 Legend

4.27 Dungarvan aerial photograph, 2014

QUESTIONS

Ordinary Level – Long Questions

Kenmare OS map: Development of urban settlements

1. Examine the 1:50,000 Ordnance Survey map and legend of Kenmare accompanying this paper.

    Explain three reasons why the town of Kenmare developed at this location, using evidence from the Ordnance Survey map to support each reason.

    2015, Section 2, Q10C, 30 marks

Kenmare OS map: Historic settlement

2. Examine the 1:50,000 Ordnance Survey map and legend of Kenmare accompanying this paper. Draw a sketch map of the area shown on the Ordnance Survey map. On it show and name the following:

    o The built up area of Kenmare

    o Four different examples of historic settlement evident on the map

    2015, Section 2, Q11A, 30 marks

Kenmare OS map: Population density and distribution

3. Examine the 1:50,000 Ordnance Survey map and legend of Kenmare accompanying this paper and answer each of the following questions.

    (i)   Give a four-figure grid reference for an area on the map where there is an absence of settlement.

    (ii) Explain in detail, using map evidence, why there is an absence of settlement at this location.

    (iii) Give a four-figure grid reference for an area on the map which has a relatively high population density.

    (iv) Explain in detail, using map evidence, why there is a relatively high population density at this location.

    2015, Section 2, Q12C, 40 marks

EXAM HINTS

Refer to the section on population density and distribution in Chapter 1 to help you when answering this question.

Dungarvan OS map: Historic settlement

4. Examine the 1:50,000 Ordnance Survey map and legend of Dungarvan accompanying this paper.

    (i) Name and locate, using six figure grid references, three different examples of historic settlement evident on the Ordnance Survey map.

    (ii) Describe and explain each of the examples of historic settlement named in part (i) above.

    2014, Section 2, Q11B, 30 marks

The marking scheme for a question like this on an Ordinary Level paper is as follows:

3 settlements named @ 2 m each	**6 marks**
3 settlements located @ 2 m each	**6 marks**
Settlement 1 explanation: 2 SRPs @ 3 m each	**6 marks**
Settlement 2 explanation: 2 SRPs @ 3 m each	**6 marks**
Settlement 3 explanation: 2 SRPs @ 3 m each	**6 marks**
Total	**30 marks**

Dungarvan aerial photograph: Development of towns

5. Examine the aerial photograph of Dungarvan accompanying this paper. Using evidence from the aerial photograph, explain three reasons why the town of Dungarvan developed at its present location.

    2014, Section 2, Q12C, 30 marks

Enniscorthy aerial photograph and OS map

6. Examine the 1:50,000 Ordnance Survey map and aerial photograph (see page 106) of Enniscorthy accompanying this paper, explain three reasons why the town of Enniscorthy developed at its present location.

    2013, Section 2, Q11B, 30 marks

Higher Level – Long Questions

Dingle OS map: Population density

7. Examine the 1:50,000 Ordnance Survey map and legend of Dingle accompanying this paper. Explain using evidence from the map, why the area to the east of easting 44 and north of northing 03 has such a low population density.

2011, Section 2, Q11C, 30 marks

Kenmare OS map: Phases of historical settlement

8. Examine the 1:50,000 Ordnance Survey map and legend of Kenmare accompanying this paper and answer each of the following questions.

   (i) Name three different phases of historical settlement evident on the Ordnance Survey map.

   (ii) Name and locate, using six-figure grid references, examples of each of the three phases of historical settlement named above.

   (iii) Explain briefly each of the three phases of historical settlement named above.

2015, Section 2, Q12C, 30 marks

Dungarvan OS map: Population distribution

9. Examine the 1:50,000 Ordnance Survey and legend of Dungarvan accompanying this paper. Explain three reasons why the area north of Northing 97 is less attractive to human settlement, using evidence from the Ordnance Survey map to support each reason.

2014, Section 2, Q11B, 30 marks

The marking scheme for a question like this on a Higher Level paper is as follows:

3 reasons @ 10 m each:	
Pattern identified @ 2 m each	**6 marks**
OS map evidence @ 2 m each	**6 marks**
Examination: 3 SRPs @ 2 m each	**18 marks**
Total	**30 marks**

Central Place Theory

10. Explain the importance of hierarchy and hinterland in Central Place Theory.

2014, Section 2, Q11C, 30 marks

Enniscorthy OS map: Rural settlement patterns

11. With reference to the 1:50,000 Ordnance Survey map of Enniscorthy accompanying this paper, describe and explain three rural settlement patterns evident on the map.

2013, Section 2, Q10B, 30 marks

The marking scheme for a question like this on a Higher Level paper is as follows:

3 patterns @ 10 m each:	
Reasons stated @ 2 m each	**6 marks**
Map evidence @ 2 m each	**6 marks**
Explanations: 3 SRPs @ 2 m each	**18 marks**
Total	**30 marks**

HOT TOPICS IN THE EXAMS

1. Historical settlement in an area
2. Reasons a town developed
3. Rural settlement patterns

Chapter 19 Map skills, Book 1
Chapter 20 Aerial photographs, Book 1

Mind map

Central Place Theory

- Walter Christaller, 1933
- Size and spacing of towns across the countryside to prevent competition with each other
- Central place: urban centre

Range

- Distance people prepared to travel for particular goods/services
- Small range: frequent
- Large range: one-off goods/services

Threshold

- Minimum no. of customers a business needs
- Local shops: small no. and threshold
- Larger specialised shop: larger no. and threshold

Hierarchy of goods

- Low order goods and services: low threshold
- Middle order goods and services: less frequent, longer distance
- High order goods and services: less frequent, long distance

Urban hierarchy

- Ranking/grading of the importance of urban centres in relation to each other
- Pyramid
  - Top: largest primate city – greatest no. of high, middle and low order goods and services
  - Bottom: smaller villages (hamlets) – limited no. of low order goods

Hinterland

- Area surrounding an urban centre where customers live
- Trade area/market area
- Hexagonal in shape
- Criticised as ideal
  - Exploitation of natural resources
  - Upgrading of transport networks
  - Assumes equal purchasing power
- Limited use: educational facilities, shopping centres
- Useful in regional planning and market analysis of trade

Rural settlement patterns

- Nucleated (clustered)
  - In groups at nodal point
  - Bridging point/demesne
  - Small towns, market function
- Linear (ribbon)
  - Line usually built along a road
  - Ease of access
  - 1960s 'Bungalow Blitz'
  - Planning authorities dislike
  - Urban sprawl, not sustainable
- Dispersed
  - Dotted around the countryside
  - Farmhouses near roads
  - After 18th century land enclosed
  - Shows areas of fertile land
  - Farms: widely spaced, in east and west, large
- Absence
  - No houses in the area
  - Land unsuitable for settlement

Settlement

Rural planning

- One-off housing
- Explosion of linear housing – exit routes
- Unsustainable
- Celtic Tiger era (1997–2007)
- 2nd/holiday homes, B&Bs
- Declined – tax levies

Site, situation and function

Site

- Area's main physical characteristics
- Close to water supplies
- Altitude: low-lying
- Aspect: south-facing slopes
- Dry point – good defensive sites
- Nodal points
- Resources: minerals
- Coastal areas

Situation

- Location of settlement in relation to surrounding area
- Natural routeways: gaps and valleys
- Developed routeways: transport lines

Function

- Town's main economic and social activities
- Towns today multi-functional
- R: Religious (ecclesiastical) and residential
- I: Industrial
- C: Commercial and communications (transport)
- E: Educational
- P: Port
- O: Open spaces (recreational)
- T: Tourism
- S: Services

Mind map

Settlement

Viking settlement
- From AD 795 (8th century)
- Longboats
- Plundered local monasteries
- Towns developed on dry sites
- Trading centres, sheltered river mouths
- Radial street patterns
- Map: ford (fjord) place names

Normans
- From AD 1169 (12th century)
- Castles: bend of a river/elevated site
- Defensive and trading purposes
- Bridging points of rivers
- Town walls and gates: trade and disease control
- Encouraged religious orders
- Map: castles, town walls, abbeys

Plantation towns
- From the 1500s (16th and 17th centuries)
- English planters
- Fortified buildings, defensive walls
- Main street, market square/diamond
- Weekly fairs
- Well planned
- Near large estate/demesne
- Map: fortified houses, market square/diamond

New towns
- 1960s (20th century)
- Urban planning
- Counteracted urban sprawl, e.g. Tallaght
- Shannon, accommodated airport workers
- Map: planned streets, large housing estates, industrial estates

County development plans
- Rural development plans
  - Protect the distinctiveness of the rural areas
  - Prevent suburbanisation
- Strict planning laws
- CEDRA 2012
- Rural service provision, traffic management, pollution, scenic quality, expanding commuter belt
- Updated every 5 years

National Development Plan
- NDP 2007–2013
- Preventing rural depopulation and counterurbanisation
  - Infrastructure – Transport 21
  - Broadband provision
  - Financial support to industry, agriculture and food industries
  - Social inclusion
  - Preservation of scenic areas

Distribution and density of settlement
- Variations in population distribution and density
- Social and economic factors
- Physical factors
  - Fertile lowlands: high population densities
  - Harsh steep isolated uplands: low population densities
- Population density: no. of people per km^2
- Population distribution: spread of people across an area

The New Stone Age (Neolithic)
- 3500 BC–2000 BC
- First farmers
- Low-lying areas close to a river
- Soil: fertile
- River: food, water and transport
- Megalithic tombs, stone carvings, aligned with sun
- Map: dolmens, passage graves, standing stones

Celtic settlement
- 500 BC–AD 400
- From central Europe
- Iron weapons
- Defensive structures: elevated sites, cliff edges, centre of a lake
- Scattered across the country
- Map: fulacht fiadh/fia, ring forts, Ogham stones

Christian period
- From AD 432 (5th century)
- St Patrick converted the Celts
- Illiterate: stone crosses, carved pictures
- Monastic: lives of prayer
- Round towers: protection
- Monasteries became the first towns
- Education, alms and protection
- Map: cillín, high crosses

Urban settlement and planning issues

SYLLABUS LINK

Urban settlements display an ever-changing land use pattern and pose planning problems.

By the end of this chapter students will have studied:

- The different land use zones within modern cities
- Theories of urban land use
- Changes in land use and planning issues
- Land use values in cities and how this can lead to social stratification
- The recent expansion of cities and the pressures that this causes on the surrounding rural landscape

NOTE

This section should be allowed at least 10 class periods (40 minutes).

Introduction

Cities today expand and change from day to day. As they change, the needs of cities also change. Planning issues can arise because of this. Land in cities is **zoned** by the local authorities. This means that land can be used for a specific purpose in accordance with the growth plan for the city.

Sometimes local authorities decide to **rezone** areas of the city, thus changing its original land use to help it grow. Europe ranks as one of the world's most highly urbanised areas. In northern Europe alone, 84 per cent of the population live in urban areas.

Land use zones within cities

Commercial

Commercial land use is prominent in many cities and towns. Commercial activities include **retail shops**, **offices**, **financial services** and **personal services** such as hairdressers. Commercial activities can be focused in a **commercial centre** where the services are grouped together, for example in a shopping centre. Alternatively, they can be stretched out along streets and roads, called **commercial ribbons**.

The busiest and most dominant commercial centre for any urban area is the **central business district** (CBD).

- The CBD is normally located in the **centre of the town** where the main roads into the area meet.
- It is normally made up of **multi-storey buildings**. This is because rents are expensive due to high demand and land space is limited in this area.
- Usually businesses with a high customer threshold locate here because the area is easily accessible. In multi-storey buildings, shops and banks are often located on the ground floor, with services such as solicitors and accountants on the floor above. The top floors are generally residential.

- **In the past, industries located in the CBD.** However, increased rents have caused large industries to move to the urban fringe.
- **Commercial shopping centres** have become very popular in recent years. These multiretail outlets are usually located on the outskirts of the urban area on cheap land with ample parking facilities.

5.1 Dublin's CBD

Transport

Land use related to transport within an urban area includes **roads**, **car parks**, **railway lines** and **railway stations**. Transport takes up a lot of valuable space but is needed by people entering and exiting the area.

Many European cities have developed from medieval cores and often have **narrow streets** that find it difficult to cope with the ever-increasing traffic in today's urban centres. By contrast, cities in the USA were developed with the car in mind. They have **wide streets** that are laid out in a grid-iron pattern to deal with their high volumes of traffic.

5.2 Aerial view of narrow network of streets in Dublin city

Residential

Residential is one of the largest uses of land in an urban area. There are **differences in the density of housing** throughout urban areas. The two main factors that explain this are the **cost of land** and the **age of the area**.

The cost of the land increases as you move towards the city centre. As a result, housing density also increases. There is more **high-density housing** close to the city centre, such as terraced housing and multi-storey apartment blocks. More spacious detached and semi-detached houses, known as **low-density housing**, are found on the urban fringe, where land costs are lower.

5.3 Low-density housing

5.4 High-density housing

The age of residential areas decreases as you move away from the city centre. From the 1950s onwards, car ownership became more commonplace and people could travel to jobs in the city centre. A **commuter zone** is often created on the edge of a city as people travel to and from work daily.

> **NOTE**
>
> A zone of transition can be found on the edge of the CBD. It is an older part of the town and often consists of multi-storey or terraced housing that may be in poor condition. These areas have been highlighted in many cities today for redevelopment.

Industrial

Traditionally industrial land was located in the city centre near the main transport lines, waterfront locations or close to large residential areas. In more recent years, **industrial areas have moved to the edge of cities**. In addition, traffic and land prices have increased. Industrial sites have therefore moved to the perimeter of the city to take advantage of a large workforce, more modern transport routes and cheaper land. This allows for expansion in the future.

Movement of industry has also been helped by the fact that most of today's industries are modern growth or light industries such as computer manufacturing. **Light industries** are not as tied to locational factors as the heavy industries of the past, such as steel making.

The edge of the city is now often a suburb of **industrial estates** and **business parks** due to large cheaper sites with traffic-free roads and ease of access to the main transport routes. The moving of large industries from their city centre locations has left behind large **brownfield sites**. These former industrial areas have been targeted by urban planners for **urban renewal**.

5.5 An industrial estate

Recreational

A proportion of all development plans for cities includes the provision of **large green areas that cannot be rezoned**. These **green belts** consist of open spaces within urban areas made up of parklands, woodlands and playgrounds. They are essential for the people living in the urban area to maintain their physical health and mental well-being. People partake in a wide variety of relaxing activities in these green areas.

5.6 The Phoenix Park in Dublin is an example of an urban green space

Central business district

Dublin's CBD is concentrated around **Grafton Street, O'Connell Street and Henry Street**. The majority of the city's retail outlets and services are located here.

The area is made up of **multi-storey buildings**. Because of the high rents in these areas, even the basements are used as extra shop space or storage. Banks, insurance companies and offices are also located here but often on the upper floors of the buildings, where rents are cheaper.

EXAM HINTS

The Dublin case study can be added to the previous information on urban functions to answer a question on this topic in the exams.

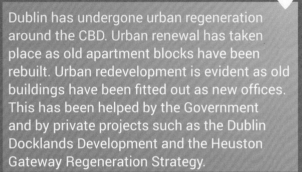

NOTE

Dublin has undergone urban regeneration around the CBD. Urban renewal has taken place as old apartment blocks have been rebuilt. Urban redevelopment is evident as old buildings have been fitted out as new offices. This has been helped by the Government and by private projects such as the Dublin Docklands Development and the Heuston Gateway Regeneration Strategy.

In more recent years this area has extended along the docks with the development of the **International Financial Services Centre (IFSC)**, restaurants and hotels by the Liffey.

5.7 Land use in Dublin

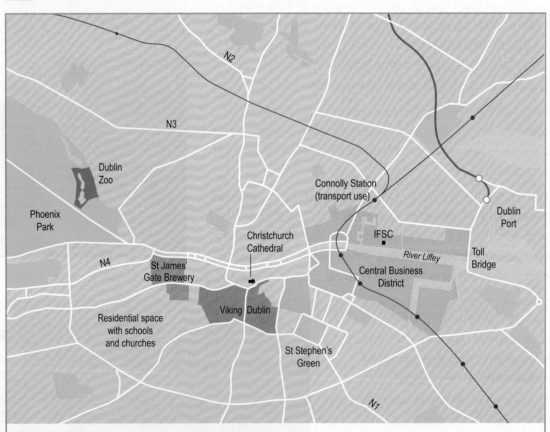

- Viking Dublin is visible in the narrow network of streets around Christchurch Cathedral.

- Commercial activities take place in the CBD.

- The port area is located around the toll bridge.

- There is open space for leisure activities in St Stephen's Green and Phoenix Park.

- Manufacturing takes place in the Guinness brewery.

Industrial zone

Some of Dublin's **old traditional industries** are still located in the **city centre**. An example is Guinness at St James' Gate, which has become identified with the area. However, the **majority of industries** have **moved to the urban fringe** because of traffic congestion and increasing costs. These new industrial estates on the edge of the city are easily accessible. They speed up import and export times and are near to new housing estates for workers. There, large sites are cheaper and there is room for expansion. An example is Intel, which is located in Leixlip.

Residential land use

Housing in Dublin has been **divided along social lines** for many decades. Many middle and high-income areas are located south of the city in suburbs such as Blackrock or further north of the city in places such as Swords. Low-income housing is located close to the city centre.

Due to high house prices in Dublin city centre in recent years, people have moved out of the city to live in more affordable areas. Some have moved out of the county altogether and commute from towns such as Navan in Meath. This has allowed a **commuter zone** to develop on the city's urban fringe. Shopping centres such as Liffey Valley have located in these areas to facilitate the large numbers of people living here.

Open spaces

Small open spaces are scattered across the city in the residential areas and are essential for people to escape the stresses of city life. **Larger**

5.8 Dublin city

open spaces are located nearer to the city centre – St Stephen's Green and the Phoenix Park, for example. These are referred to as green belt areas. They are maintained by the local councils. These areas help to reduce urban sprawl and are places where people can exercise, relax and unwind.

Inside the city centre there are some shared **walled gardens** formerly owned by the wealthy people that lived in the city during the eighteenth and nineteenth centuries. These are now open to the public and offer a relaxing atmosphere in a busy city. An example is Merrion Square Garden.

GEOTERMS

- **Urban fringe** is the edge of the city.
- **Commuter zone/commuter belt** is an area from which people travel for work.

QUICK QUESTIONS

1. Name and write two SRPs on each of the three different types of land use found in a city. (Timed activity: 6 min; 6 SRPs)
2. Define the terms *urban renewal*, *commuter zone* and *brownfield site*.
3. Define the term *bid rent*.
4. Give three examples in Dublin city of different types of land use.
5. In which zone would the Phoenix Park be?

Theories of urban land use

A number of theories have been put forward to explain how urban areas are laid out. These include:

- The concentric zone model proposed by Ernest Burgess in 1925
- The sector theory devised by Homer Hoyt in 1939
- The multiple nuclei theory developed by Chauncy Harris and Edward Ullman in 1945

The concentric zone theory – Burgess, 1925

Ernest Burgess, an American sociologist, put forward the concentric zone theory in 1925. His theory aimed to explain **how land is used** in different parts of urban areas. It also looks at the **distribution of social groups** in urban areas.

The theory observes that urban areas are made up of **five concentric circles** of different land use zones. The model in Figure 5.9 shows each of the five zones:

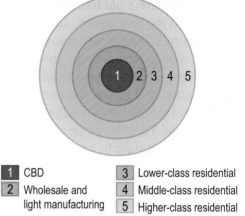

1 CBD		**3**	Lower-class residential
2 Wholesale and light manufacturing		**4**	Middle-class residential
		5	Higher-class residential

5.9 The zones of Burgess' concentric model

- **Zone 1** is the **CBD**. This is located in the city centre and is the commercial heart of the city, including hotels and offices. Buildings here are tall as land is expensive and there is competition for space.

- **Zone 2** is the **transition zone**. It has a mix of residential and commercial uses. There is some industry here. There is a high density of low-quality housing in this zone. These are often the areas occupied by large numbers of migrants today.

- **Zone 3** is a **lower-class residential zone**. Working-class people live in this zone, mostly in terraced housing. The residents here are better off than those in zone 2. Population densities are high and people from here often work in zone 2.

- **Zone 4** is a **middle-class residential zone**. Houses in this area are detached or semi-detached and have gardens. The residents in this zone are well-off.

- **Zone 5** is a **commuter zone**. This is a high-class residential area made up of towns and villages on the outskirts of the city. Many of the residents of this zone commute to the city centre to work.

Distribution of social groups

Burgess observed two main patterns in residential land use with his theory. First, as you move out from the CBD, **population decreases** and **housing becomes less dense**. Also, **social status increases** as you move out from the CBD. Poorer people live in the inner circles, with people getting richer as you move to the outer circles.

Problems with the theory

Burgess' theory is outdated and not relevant to many of today's cities. It is based on the cities of 1920s America, particularly Chicago. Many migrants had settled in the poorer inner-city areas of American cities. This led to **social stratification**, whereby people of similar incomes settled in the same areas. Areas were divided by class.

Today, advances in transport and an increase in car use mean that many people live outside the city. This way of living was not considered when Burgess developed his theory and has changed the pattern of land use in cities.

GEOTERMS

Social stratification describes the tendency of people of similar incomes and social backgrounds to live in the same part of an urban area.

The sector theory – Hoyt, 1939

Homer Hoyt devised the sector theory of urban land use in 1939. The sector theory was based on Burgess' idea of concentric zones but also considered the **impact of transport routes on land use**. Hoyt's theory shows that cities develop along major transport routes that extend out from the city, such as roads, railway lines and canals. Because of this, urban areas have grown in sectors radiating out from the CBD. Figure 5.10 shows the zones that can be identified using Hoyt's theory:

- **Zone 1** is the **CBD**. This is located in the city centre and is the commercial centre of the city.
- **Zone 2** grows outwards from the CBD. It grows in **wedges along transport routes**. This zone contains factories and light manufacturing. Housing in this zone is low quality.
- **Zone 3** is a **low-income residential** area. Many of the residents of zone 3 work in the factories and industries in zone 2. These areas have high levels of noise and air pollution from traffic and nearby industries.
- **Zone 4** is a **middle-income residential** area. The practice of social stratification results in zone 4 housing being found away from poorer areas.
- **Zone 5** is a **high-income residential** area. This is a desirable area in which to live since it is the furthest away from factories and manufacturing activity. People who live in this zone commute to work.

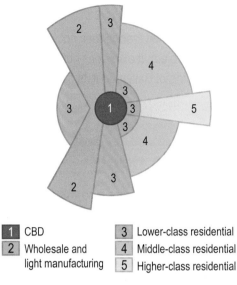

1	CBD	3	Lower-class residential
2	Wholesale and light manufacturing	4	Middle-class residential
		5	Higher-class residential

5.10 The zones of Hoyt's sector model

Limitations of Hoyt's model

Hoyt used a bigger sample for his study (142 cities) and also included a city's expansion along transport routes, but geographers today still feel that it is still too **generalised and unrealistic**. Hoyt is believed to be outdated on his views that residential areas would remain segregated due to their income levels. This is not the case today, as some of the most sought-after and expensive accommodation today is in the inner city, where new modern apartment blocks have been constructed near lower-class housing areas. The study was also only based on US cities – he needed to examine a wider range of world cities.

The multiple nuclei theory – Harris and Ullman, 1945

The multiple nuclei theory was developed by Chauncy Harris and Edward Ullman in 1945. This theory suggests that urban areas grow up around **multiple business districts** (multiple nuclei).

Harris and Ullman believed that it was possible to have more than one business district in an urban area. In this model, the CBD is located in the city centre, where access is good. As the city grows, other business districts grow to meet different functions and economic needs. For example, an industrial district may grow up around a busy port or a business district may grow near a residential area. These separate districts attract growth and further development.

- **Similar services and industries** establish close to each other and benefit from their proximity (closeness).
- **Social stratification** is evident, with separate lower-class, middle-class and higher-class areas. Lower-class residential areas build up around manufacturing areas. Higher-class residential areas are located away from heavy manufacturing, with business and commercial districts nearby.
- **Industrial suburbs** with light manufacturing activities can be found on the outskirts of the city, where land and property are cheaper.

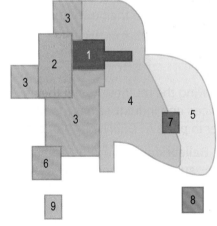

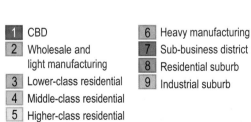

1	CBD	6	Heavy manufacturing
2	Wholesale and light manufacturing	7	Sub-business district
3	Lower-class residential	8	Residential suburb
4	Middle-class residential	9	Industrial suburb
5	Higher-class residential		

5.11 Harris and Ullman's multiple nuclei model

Problems with this theory

The multiple nuclei theory does not take into account areas of urban renewal such as the Dublin Docklands project. It also does not take into account responses to the housing crisis in Dublin, such as the building of Ballymun flats on the urban fringe.

CASE STUDY 5.2
Multiple nuclei theory – Dublin

The Dublin region fits into the multiple nuclei theory set down by Harris and Ullman in many ways.

Central business district

Dublin city centre is the CBD of the region. Access to the city centre is good, as all major transport routes meet there (it is a **nodal point**). Dublin city centre is the main commercial and financial centre of the region. There are low-class residential areas close to the CBD.

Multiple nuclei

The Dublin region has multiple nuclei. These developed as the city expanded into nearby villages and towns, each with their own **retail and business centres**. Areas such as **Blackrock** in the south of the city and **Swords** in the north have their own business districts and retail areas. These were once towns on the outskirts of the city, which were absorbed as the city expanded. Also, new towns such as **Blanchardstown** and **Adamstown** have their own business districts and services for people of the area.

Location of services

Following the multiple nuclei theory, similar services and industries have located close to each other in parts of Dublin city. For example:

- **Ballsbridge** has a large number of embassies – such as the American embassy – and commercial offices
- Many financial institutions are located in the **IFSC** area of the city
- **Fitzwilliam Square** is home to many medical consultants and is located near to hospitals

Industrial suburbs

There are a number of industrial suburbs around the edges of the city. **Sandyford Industrial Estate** on the south side of the city and **Ballymount Industrial Estate** on the north side are two

5.12 Over 430 international operations trade from the IFSC in Dublin

examples. These have grown up on the outskirts of the city, where they can take advantage of cheaper land and property prices.

Social stratification

In the multiple nuclei theory, social stratification results in **separate lower-class, middle-class and higher-class areas**. Social stratification occurs in Dublin, as is shown in the map in Figure 5.13. The map shows that residential areas in Dublin can be divided into two zones by a line running south-west from Howth to Rathcoole:

- Residents of **south-east** Dublin generally have a **high income**
- Residents in the **north-west** of the city generally have a **low to middle income**

A difference in the type of houses in different parts of a city can reflect social stratification. In Dublin:

- Houses in **higher-income areas** of the city are generally detached with large gardens
- In **middle-income areas**, houses are detached or semi-detached with smaller gardens
- In **lower-income areas**, people often live in terraced houses or apartment blocks

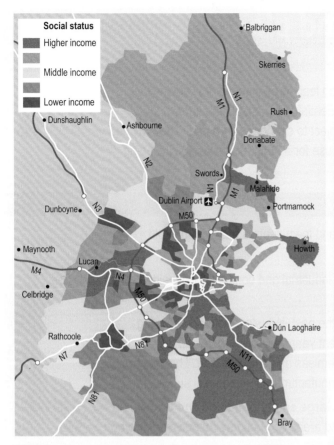

Social status
- Higher income
- Middle income
- Lower income

Balbriggan
Skerries
Rush
Donabate
Swords
Malahide
Portmarnock
Dublin Airport
Howth
Dún Laoghaire
Bray
Dunshaughlin
Ashbourne
Dunboyne
Maynooth
Lucan
Celbridge
Rathcoole
M1
N1
N2
N3
M50
M4
N4
M50
N7
N81
N81
N11
M50

5.13 Social stratification in Dublin based on income levels

Participation in third-level education is also used as an indicator of social stratification. In Dublin, people from middle-class and higher-class areas are more likely to go to college than those from lower-income areas.

5.14 Local authority apartment blocks can be found in inner-city Dublin

5.15 Large affluent homes can be found on the south side of Dublin

QUICK QUESTIONS

1. Name three theories of urban land use.
2. What theory did Burgess put forward in 1925?
3. What usually occupies zone 1 in urban land use theories?
4. What does the term *social stratification* mean?
5. Describe social stratification in Dublin city. (Timed activity: 4 min; 4 SRPs)

Social stratification in cities

As mentioned in the case study above, the division of people in cities depends on their income and status. It is noted in cities across the world that people of similar education levels and earning power live in similar areas of the city. This is reflected in the house prices of the areas and why certain addresses in a city are more sought after than others. In the past social stratification was referred to as 'social class' with the richer, or so-called 'higher class', people choosing the most desirable places to live. This is often reflected in the quality, size and design of the houses in these areas, where the housing density is usually low. Therefore the so-called 'lower class' housing was often smaller and of higher density. This social stratification is evident in developing countries today with the presence of townships and bustees.

Changes in land use and planning issues

As an urban area grows, its functions may change. This can lead to changes in how land in the area is used. For example, land use can change from residential to industrial. Changes in land use can lead to planning issues. People in an area may object to change of land use if they will be negatively affected by it. People object to changes in land use for a number of reasons, including **environmental**, **social** or **economic** reasons.

Changes in land use

An area can change from one land use to another. In city and town centres, for example, old residential streets often become office and retail space.

- **Greater demand for services** in an area can cause industrial and commercial development to spread into residential areas.

- **Manufacturing locations** can change over time. In the past, industry and manufacturing activities were located close to the city centre. In recent years, factories have relocated to the outskirts of urban areas where they can get larger premises and cheaper land. These areas of once rural or agricultural land change over time to manufacturing or residential suburbs.

- The movement of industry and manufacturing leaves **large empty buildings and brownfield sites** in the inner city. These once highly industrialised areas can become rundown and derelict.

- However, renewal of these derelict areas leads to many brownfield sites being **redeveloped**. The old buildings are replaced by modern commercial and residential buildings.

GEOTERMS

A **brownfield site** is a derelict (abandoned, rundown) industrial or manufacturing site.

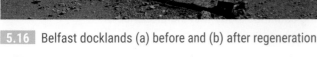

5.16 Belfast docklands (a) before and (b) after regeneration

In the 1800s, the docklands area of Dublin became an important commercial hub of the region. Canal and rail transport links meant that it became a **major distribution area** for goods imported through Dublin port. Many people lived and worked in the docklands area in **industries** such as milling, clothing workshops and iron foundries.

Urban decline

In the 1950s, transport and industrial advances caused the Dublin docklands to go into **decline**. Dublin port moved nearer to the mouth of the River Liffey to more modern facilities, and the old port became derelict. Coal imports decreased and new equipment replaced manual labour. Usage of vans and trucks increased and roll-on roll-off ferries were introduced. Many **jobs were lost** as a result of these changes.

The area further declined as unemployment increased. It became rundown and deprived. Large industrial buildings became **derelict** and social problems, such as **low education levels** (only 35 per cent of children reached Leaving Certificate level) and **crime**, increased. The area needed governmental intervention.

Urban renewal

This intervention first came in 1987 with the **development of the IFSC** where abandoned warehouses once stood: 450 companies set up business in the high-rise office blocks, engaging in banking and financial services.

Next in 1997 the **Dublin Docklands Development Authority (DDDA)** was set up to renew the docklands both economically and socially. The project covers 520 hectares of land in and around the docklands area. The DDDA is responsible for transforming the area by **regenerating brownfield sites and derelict factories**. It aims to provide a sustainable and well-developed inner-city area with access to education, services, employment, amenities and housing.

It is also hoped to **repopulate the area** with 45,000 people, with many new apartment blocks in the area. In the 2011 census North Dock B district had almost doubled its numbers since 2006 to approximately 7,000 people living there.

GEOTERMS

o **Roll-on roll-off ferries** are designed to carry wheeled cargo such as cars, trailers and lorries that are driven on and off the ship on their own wheels. For lift-on lift-off ferries, a crane is used to load and unload cargo.

o **Social integration** is the movement of minority groups or underprivileged sections of society into mainstream society.

o **Urban gentrification** is the improving and renovating of areas of the city that have undergone urban decay/decline with the arrival of young professional people.

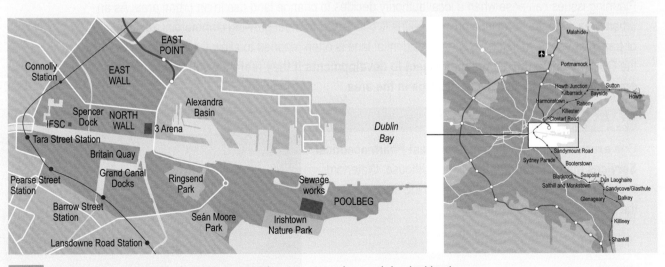

5.17 The DDDA is responsible for renewing 520 hectares in and around the docklands area

5.18 The renewed docklands area of Dublin

The project aims to create up to 40,000 new jobs and 11,000 new homes. **Social integration** will be achieved by providing 20 per cent of new homes as social and affordable housing. **Urban gentrification** is evident as young professional people move back into this area to work and live in what were once deteriorating neighbourhoods.

The **public transport network** in the area has been improved by the extension of the Luas line. The Port Tunnel has led to a decrease in traffic. These developments have helped to reduce traffic congestion and air pollution in the area, making it a more desirable place to live. As a result, there is a move towards young professional people living in the area.

New offices, hotels and retail outlets provide much-needed employment for the local community, both skilled and unskilled. **Leisure facilities** such as the Grand Canal Theatre,

amenities such as the 3 Arena, and **educational centres** such as the National College of Ireland in the IFSC have been established in the area.

A pleasant ambiance has been created in the area with the introduction of **new shopping areas**, **restaurants** and **street furniture**. These developments help to ensure that the local community has adequate facilities and a good quality of life.

Result

The Dublin docklands project has **successfully renewed and revitalised the area**. Employment has been created for the local community. Services and recreational amenities have been provided. Air pollution has been reduced and the landscape has been greatly improved.

QUICK QUESTIONS

1. Describe two ways that land use can change in urban areas.
2. What is a brownfield site?
3. Why did the docklands area of Dublin go into decline in the 1950s?
4. Describe two ways that the docklands area was renewed. (Timed activity: 6 min; 6 SRPs)
5. Why do local communities sometimes object to changes in land use in their area?

Planning issues

Planning issues can arise when a local authority decides to change land use in an urban area. As an urban area expands, rural land on its outskirts is often used to meet growing commercial, residential or transport needs. In inner-city areas, residential land is often rezoned to allow for the expansion of the CBD. **Local people sometimes object to developments if they feel they will impact on the environment, the landscape or heritage in the area.**

Waterford Ringfort

One example is the **development of West Pharmaceutical Services manufacturing plant** in Knockhouse, Waterford in July 2015. The move to create jobs in the area changed the land use from rural to industrial.

5.19 Waterford Ringfort

Local residents and historians objected to the development of the manufacturing plant, as it passed through part of an **archaeological site**. People felt that this would have a negative impact on the historical area. They created a Facebook page to raise awareness of the importance of the ringfort found at the site and continue to object to the proposed development. However, the local authority is fully behind the development and the company has been issued with a licence to demolish the ringfort when archaeological work has ceased at the site. Local historians are disappointed at the news and feel that Waterford city and County Council have let commercial interest outweight historical interests.

Land values in cities

Land values in cities vary. Land close to the CBD is the most expensive. **The value of land decreases as you move away from the CBD.** The diagram in Figure 5.20 shows how land value varies in different parts of a city.

Bid rent

The value of land in a city is based on how much someone is prepared to pay for it. The **price someone is willing to pay for land** is known as the bid rent. The most desirable land in an urban area is in the CBD. Property in the CBD is in short supply. As all transport routes merge there, the CBD is the most accessible part of the city. As a result, bid rents in the CBD are the highest.

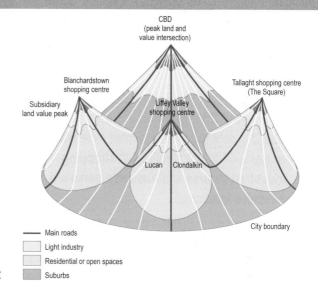

5.20 In most cities, land values are highest in the CDB and lowest in suburban areas but rise where major roads meet

Land use and land value

Shops

The **Peak Land Value Intersection (PLVI)** is the most valuable site within the CBD. Large shops and department stores are usually located in this part of the CBD. In Dublin, Arnotts and Brown Thomas are examples of large department stores located in valuable city-centre locations. These locations are highly accessible, so the stores experience a large volume of trade. The space has been maximised by building multi-storey department stores in these areas.

As you move further away from the CBD, the value of land decreases and bid rents are lower. Shops located outside the CBD are not as accessible, therefore they attract fewer customers. The bid rents that retailers are prepared to pay further from the CBD are lower.

5.21 Brown Thomas is located on Grafton Street, the most expensive part of Dublin city for retail space

Offices

Offices for **service industries**, such as law firms, financial institutions and accountants, tend to be located on the edge of the retail area. They do not rely on passing trade as much as retail outlets so are not prepared to pay high rents for ground floor or shop front sites.

They tend to be located further away from the city centre. They are usually located on the second floor, above retail outlets.

Industry

Industry and manufacturing are usually located on the **outskirts of the city**, where rents are cheaper and sites are bigger. They rely on good transport links, so are usually located near main routeways.

Some manufacturers will locate in **rezoned areas** that are being renewed, such as Dublin's docklands. Some will locate in suburban industrial estates and business parks near good transport links and residential areas, for example Sandyford Industrial Estate in south Dublin.

Suburbs

As suburbs grow, the value of land in these areas can also grow. Land in suburban areas is most expensive where main transport routes meet. Often **shopping centres**, **industrial centres** and **business parks** are developed in these locations.

The upgrading of many of Dublin's main routes has resulted in the development of **large shopping centres** in places such as Blanchardstown and Liffey Valley. It has also led to the development of industrial estates and business parks in places such as Santry and Sandyford.

5.22 Sandyford Industrial Estate has good transport links and a workforce close by

5.23 Developments such as Dundrum Shopping Centre push up the value of land in suburban areas

QUICK QUESTIONS

1. How does land value in a city vary?
2. What does the term *bid rent* mean? Draw a simple labelled diagram to support your answer. (Timed activity: 3 min)
3. In which part of a city are department stores usually located?
4. Why are manufacturing facilities usually located on the outskirts of a city?
5. Where is land most expensive in suburbs?

Expanding cities and the pressures on rural land use

As cities expand they can encroach on the surrounding countryside. At its worst this process is called **urban sprawl** and it can create huge pressures on the rural land use. For example, Dublin city now occupies an area four times that of the city in the beginning of the nineteenth century.

There are a range of factors that cause cities to expand such as:

- Population increases due to **rural to urban migration**
- New commercial and residential **developments on the urban fringe**
- Improvements in roadways and a **growing commuter belt**

This expansion has had a negative impact on the rural land use in the following ways:

- The city has expanded and **engulfed former rural villages** such as Dundrum, causing them to lose their unique character.
- There is **heavy traffic** on secondary and third class roads that were not designed to take these volumes of commuter traffic.
- Developers have been accused of interfering with **rural historical sites**.
- **Agricultural land** has been split into unworkable parts to build larger motorways.
- **Hedgerows** have been removed as agricultural land has been built upon, therefore destroying unique habitats for flora and fauna (the wren, for example).
- Cities have been built on natural river floodplains and the concrete landscape can contribute to **flooding** in the region by dramatically reducing the lag time.

> **GEOTERMS** abc
>
> - **Lag time** is the time it takes rainwater to soak into the ground, to eventually return to the water table beneath.
> - **Green belts** are areas in the city that have been set aside and where building is strictly controlled.

A limit or control that can be introduced by governments in the region is the introduction of **green belts**. These are areas around the city that have been set aside where building is strictly controlled.

- They help to **limit urban sprawl and protect rural land use and villages** by preventing the city from continuing to expand into rural areas.
- They **improve the environmental health** of the area due to the increased number of trees, which help to absorb pollutants and release oxygen through the process of photosynthesis for people to breathe.
- These areas allow urban dwellers to **interact with nature** – allotments and small farms are often located in this space to allow people to grow plants and rear animals.
- These areas also act as a soakage point for excess rainfall and create the lag time needed to **prevent flooding**, which concrete does not.

> **EXAM HINTS** ✓
>
> This information links to Chapter 6: Urban problems.

5.24 A cartoon showing urban sprawl

Aerial photographs

5.25 Enniscorthy, 2013

5.26 Carrick-on-Shannon, 2012

5.27 Dingle, 2011

QUESTIONS

Ordinary Level – Long Questions

Urban functions

1. Describe and explain how the functions and services of urban areas change over time, with reference to example(s) that you have studied.

2014, Section 2, Q10B, 30 marks

The marking scheme for a question like this on an Ordinary Level paper is as follows:

Example	**3 marks**
Description and explanation: 9 SRPs @ 3 m each	**27 marks**
Total	**30 marks**

Enniscorthy aerial photograph: Land use in Irish towns

2. Examine the aerial photograph of Enniscorthy accompanying this paper. Draw a sketch map of the area shown on the aerial photograph. On it, show and name the following:

   - The Central Business District (CBD)
   - An industrial area
   - A residential area
   - A religious building
   - A river

2013, Section 2, Q10A, 30 marks

Higher Level – Long Questions

Aerial photograph

4. Examine the impact of urban planning strategies with reference to example(s) that you have studied.

2015, Section 2, Q12B, 30 marks

The marking scheme for a question like this on a Higher Level paper is as follows:

Impact identified	**2 marks**
Example	**2 marks***
Explanation: 13 SRPs @ 2 m each	**26 marks**
Total	**30 marks**

The marking scheme for a question like this on an Ordinary Level paper is as follows:

Sketch map: limits/frame	**1 marks**
Sketch map: proportions (landscape)	**2 marks**
Overall impression	**2 marks**
Showing items: 5 @ 3 m each	**15 marks**
Naming items: 5 @ 2 m each	**10 marks**
Total	**30 marks**

Carrick-on-Shannon aerial photograph: Land use in Irish towns

3. Examine the aerial photograph of Carrick-on-Shannon accompanying this paper. Draw a sketch map of the area shown on the aerial photograph. On it, show and name the following:

   - An unfinished building
   - A row of modern apartments
   - A main shopping street
   - A church
   - A recreational (leisure) area

2012, Section 2, Q11A, 30 marks

Dungarvan OS map: Settlement patterns

5. Examine the 1:50,000 Ordnance Survey map and legend of Dungarvan that accompany this paper (see pages 83 and 85). Draw a sketch map of the area shown to half scale. On it correctly show and label each of the following:

   - The built up area of Dungarvan
   - An area of Linear/ribbon rural settlement
   - An area of dispersed rural settlement
   - An area of clustered rural settlement

2014, Section 2, Q10A, 20 marks

Changing urban functions

6. Examine how the functions of urban centres can change over time, with reference to Irish example(s).

   2014, Section 2, Q10B, 30 marks

The marking scheme for a question like this on a Higher Level paper is as follows:

Function identified	**2+2 marks**
Example Irish urban centre	**2 marks***
Land use zones explained:	
12 SRPs @ 2 m each	**24 marks**
Total	**30 marks**

*Second example would gain 2 marks.

Urban functions

7. Examine the aerial photograph of Dungarvan accompanying this paper (see page 86). Describe and explain three different functions of Dungarvan, using evidence from the aerial photograph to illustrate each function.

   2014, Section 2, Q12B, 30 marks

Changing land use patterns

8. Describe and explain the changing land use patterns in an urban area that you have studied.

   2012, Section 2, Q12C, 30 marks

Dingle aerial photograph

9. Examine the aerial photograph of Dingle accompanying this paper. Draw a sketch of the aerial photograph, half the length and half the breadth.

   On it show and name each of the following:

   - The Central Business District
   - Residential land use
   - Educational land use
   - An example of traffic management

   2011, Section 2, Q10A, 20 marks

HOT TOPICS IN THE EXAMS

1. Drawing a sketch map of an aerial photograph
2. Functions of a town and how they can change over time

  Chapter 6   Urban problems

Mind map

Theories of urban land use

The concentric zone theory – Burgess, 1925
- Land use and distribution of social groups
- Urban areas: 5 concentric circles, different land use zones
- Outdated, many commuters

The sector theory – Hoyt, 1939
- Impact of transport routes on land use
- Urban areas grown in sectors radiating from CBD
- Outdates views of residential areas remaining segregated

The multiple nuclei theory – Harris and Ullman, 1945
- Urban areas grow up around multiple business districts
- 1+ business districts possible
- Proximity of similar services and industries, social stratification, industrial suburbs

Urban settlement and planning issues

Expanding cities and pressures on rural land use
- Urban sprawl
- Migration, developments, roads
- Engulf villages, heavy traffic, historical sites, split agri land, destroy habitats
- Green belts

Case study: Dublin land use zones
- CBD: Grafton, O'Connell and Henry Streets, docklands and IFSC
- Multi-storey buildings: retail outlets, services, banks, offices
- Industrial zone: urban fringe, accessible and near housing
- Residential use: social divisions, commuter towns
- Open spaces: small (residential), larger (city), reduces urban sprawl

Land use zones within cities

Commercial
- Retail shops, offices, financial services, personal services
- Commercial centres/commercial ribbons
- CBD: central, limited land, high rents, multi-storeys, bid rents

Transport
- Roads, car parks, railway lines and railway stations
- Uses valuable space but necessary
- European cities: medieval, narrow streets
- US cities: developed for car, wide streets
- Urban fringe, commuter belt

Residential
- One of the largest uses of urban land
- Different density of housing in different areas – cost of land, age of area

Industrial
- Moved to perimeter from city centre
- Suburbs of industrial estates and business parks
- Brownfield sites – urban renewal

Recreational
- Large green areas – cannot be rezoned
- Open spaces: vital for health and well-being

Mind map

Urban settlement and planning issues

Case study: Multiple nuclei theory – Dublin

- CBD: city centre, major transport routes converge, main commercial and financial centre, low-class residential areas close
- Multiple nuclei, e.g. Swords
- Proximity of similar services and industries, e.g. IFSC
- Industrial suburbs, e.g. Sandyford
- Social stratification: 2 residential zones, high income, low income, social stratification affects participation in 3rd level education

Expansion of urban areas

- Cities expand and change – needs and functions change
- Planning issues – rezoning
- Europe: 84% live in urban areas

Land values in cities

- Land values decrease further from CBD
- Bid rent: price someone is willing to pay for land
- CBD: most desirable and expensive
- Shops: PLVI most valuable sites
- Offices: edge of CBD
- Industry: outskirts of city
- Suburbs: shopping centres, business parks, industrial estates

Planning issues

- Functions change as area grows – land use changes
- Planning issues, objections Waterford Ringfort vs West Pharmaceutical Services (historical vs commercial)

Changes in land use

- Industrial and commercial – spreads to residential areas
- Manufacturing: outskirts of city
- Renewal of brownfield site

Case study: Dublin Docklands

- 1800's commercial hub, distribution area, industries
- 1950's port moved, industrial decline, manual labour vs machinery, derelict, crime, low educational levels
- 1987 IFSC, urban renewal
- 1997 DDDA regeneration brownfield sites
- Results: 2011 census, population doubled by 7,000 people since 2006, urban gentrification, social integration, improved public transport network

Urban problems

6

SYLLABUS LINK

Problems can develop from the growth of urban centres.

By the end of this chapter, students will have studied:
- Urban problems of traffic movement and congestion
- Urban decay, urban sprawl and the absence of community
- Heritage in urban areas
- Environmental quality in urban areas
- Urban planning and renewal
- Expansion and problems in developing world cities
- Issues related to the cities of the future

NOTE

This section should take approximately 12 class periods (40 minutes).

GEOTERMS

Rush hour is the name given to the busiest times of the day, when people are travelling to and from work and traffic is at its heaviest.

EXAM HINTS

This is a very important chapter in the exams and is well worth studying. It often appears on both the Ordinary Level and Higher Level exam paper for more than one part of a long question.

Introduction

The growth of urban centres, such as towns and cities, can cause problems. These include **traffic congestion**, **urban sprawl**, **heritage issues** and **environmental damage**.

Urban problem 1: Traffic movement and congestion

A large number of vehicles use the roads around urban centres. As a result, these roads may become congested with traffic. Traffic can become heavy around the busiest times of the day, known as **rush hour**. This may also occur if the transport network in an area is poor. Traffic congestion results in slower speeds, long queues and increased journey times.

Causes of traffic congestion

In many cities and towns, a large number of people work in the **central business district (CBD)**. This means that many people commute to the CBD, which may have narrow streets that are easily congested. Inadequate, inaccessible or expensive public transport systems can cause people to drive to work rather than take a bus or train. This means there are more cars on the road.

6.1 In Ireland, commuters can spend up to four hours a day in their car

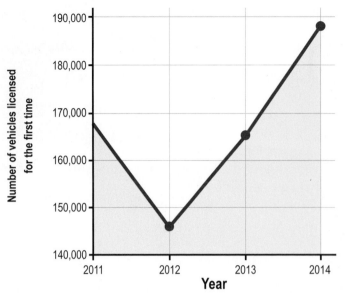

6.2 The total number of vehicles registered in Ireland, 2011 to 2014

Urban planners need to ensure that adequate public transport systems are in place to encourage commuters to leave their car at home. Today, more people own and use cars than ever before.

Effects of traffic congestion

Traffic congestion can have a **social impact**. As congestion causes traffic to travel at slower speeds, journey times increase. This means that people spend more time away from their home and family. This has an impact on family life and wastes time. Sitting in traffic for increased periods of time can result in stress and tiredness, and unfortunately in some cases this can lead to accidents and loss of life.

Traffic congestion can have an **economic impact** as travel times are increased, which makes transport more expensive. The extra fuel and driver costs to bring products to shops have to be added to the price of goods and services. Commuters use extra fuel, which increases the demand for it. As petrol is a finite resource, this causes its price to continue to rise.

Traffic congestion also has an **environmental impact** as the increase in exhaust fumes leads to air and noise pollution. This can have an adverse effect on people's health in cities, and these areas often see an increase in the number of respiratory problems such as asthma.

Reducing traffic congestion

A number of measures can improve the movement of traffic in built-up areas:

- **Restricted on-street parking** and **multi-storey car parks** can reduce the amount of traffic blocking streets
- Systems such as **one-way streets** and **traffic lights** can help to control the flow of traffic to ease congestion
- Busy town centres can be bypassed by building a **ring road** to divert traffic away

The availability of **reliable and cheap public transport** is a key factor in reducing traffic congestion. If people have alternative methods of transport that are reliable and cheap, they will be less likely to use their car.

6.3 Increased exhaust fumes from traffic congestion lead to air pollution

- **Bus lanes** make it quicker and easier to travel by bus, which means more people use the bus service
- **Bicycle lanes** and schemes such as the **'bike to work' programme** (where an employee can buy a bike through their employer at a tax-free rate) encourage more people to travel by bicycle
- **Park and ride facilities** can be developed to encourage out of town commuters to use public transport when visiting the city

6.4 The Luas light-rail system in Dublin has helped to improve traffic flow in the city

6.5 Cycling is a cheap, reliable and environmentally friendly way to travel

QUICK QUESTIONS

1. Name two causes of traffic congestion.
2. What does the term *rush hour* mean?
3. What are the effects of traffic congestion?
4. Name three ways that traffic congestion can be reduced. (Timed activity: 3 min; 3 SRPs)
5. What is the 'bike to work' scheme?

CASE STUDY 6.1
Traffic congestion – Dublin

Dublin is the most heavily populated county in Ireland. In 2014, there were 1.3 million people living in the county. As it is the **economic centre** of Ireland, many people also commute to Dublin from surrounding areas to work and study.

- According to the National Transport Authority, 38 per cent of all private cars and 30 per cent of all goods vehicles are registered in the Greater Dublin Area. **Population growth** in the Greater Dublin Area and an **increase in the number of people who own cars** in recent years have led to traffic congestion in the Dublin region.

- As the map in Figure 6.6 shows, many roads servicing the Dublin region converge (meet) near the city centre. The city centre is the **CBD**. Many people commute to this area each day. This causes **traffic bottlenecks** since large volumes of traffic merge in the area during rush hour.

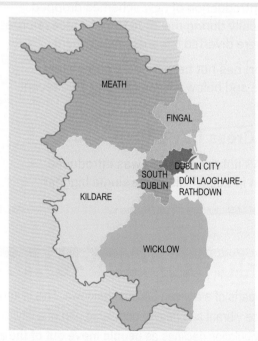

6.6 The Greater Dublin Area (GDA) includes Dublin city and the six county councils of Fingal, Dún Laoghaire-Rathdown, South Dublin, Kildare, Meath and Wicklow

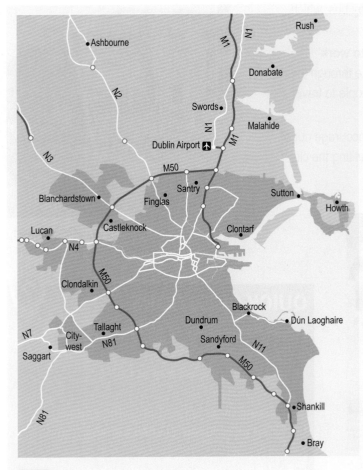

6.7 The road network of the Dublin region

transformation of the service since it began. The new project began work in September 2013 creating an extension to the two LUAS lines already established in the city. It is estimated that the works will be completed and the lines in operation by 2017. This scheme will see an extension of the LUAS Green Line from St Stephen's Green to O'Connell Street, allowing an interchange opportunity between the green and red LUAS lines at Abbey Street. This will add 13 new stops, eight of which will be in city centre locations. This is the **largest government investment in transport** at the moment, with the figure standing at €368 million. The LUAS lines are an important transport network in Dublin city, with 80,000 passengers daily.

The Dublin bike rental scheme

This project was introduced in the city in 2009. It is a **self-service bike rental scheme**. Fifty bike stations, which can each accommodate 30 bikes, were placed around the city, with an initial investment of 550 bikes. Registered users can use the service for €10 per year, and the bike usage is free for the first 30 minutes and 50 cents thereafter. A French advertising company pays for and maintains the bikes in return for free advertising space in the city. In the first year the scheme had 47,000 users and was described by Dublin City Council as a success. It is considered to be **one of the most successful shared bike rental schemes in Europe**, and there are plans to add another 287 new bikes.

Several schemes were introduced during the Celtic Tiger era in the city to combat traffic congestion, such as improvements in the **public transport network** (LUAS, Port Tunnel, Quality Bus Corridors) to divert traffic away from the city centre. The rate of introduction of new schemes dropped dramatically during the 2008 to 2013 recession, as funds were diverted towards employment.

Transport has not been ignored completely, however, and below we will examine two recent schemes.

LUAS Cross City project

The LUAS light-rail system was introduced to Dublin in 2004. This is the single biggest

GEOTERMS

A **traffic bottleneck** is a point where traffic becomes congested, causing it to slow down or stop.

Urban problem 2: Urban decay

Over time, parts of a city can become rundown. This is known as urban decay. Urban decay happens when a once vibrant and heavily populated part of a city, such as Dublin's inner city, experiences **decline**. Population declines as **people move out of the area** to more attractive locations, such as the suburbs. Economic activity also declines as **businesses relocate** to new areas of the city. This results in high unemployment in the area. High unemployment and population decline can lead to the area falling into **disrepair**. There are many environmental, economic and social problems associated with urban decay:

- **Derelict buildings** are boarded up and are often vandalised, making the landscape unattractive.
- **Unemployment levels remain high** as the declining area fails to attract new businesses.
- **Education levels are often low**, which also contributes to high unemployment.
- High unemployment can lead to increased levels of **crime and drug use**.

Absence of community

One of the biggest social problems associated with urban decay is the loss of a sense of community for the people still living in the area. As people move out of the area and the population declines, residents are left feeling isolated. Their **community breaks down** as people they know leave the area. Absence of community means that people can feel abandoned and excluded.

6.8 Parts of Limerick city have become rundown

CASE STUDY 6.2
Urban decay – Ballymun

Ballymun is on the north side of Dublin city, near Dublin Airport. A number of local authority flats were built in Ballymun in the 1960s. These were **built to rehouse many residents of Dublin's inner city**. At the time of construction, the flats were considered to be one of the best examples of social housing in Europe. There was a total of 36 high-storey blocks of flats with over 3,000 dwellings. Some of the blocks were 15 storeys high – these were known as the Ballymun tower blocks. A number of problems led to the decay of Ballymun:

- There was a **lack of amenities** in the area, with few shops and recreational facilities. In addition, there was a **lack of green spaces and trees**.
- The flats were **poorly maintained** – the lifts were unreliable, often breaking down. As the flats were **badly insulated**, they were cold and hard to heat.
- People who had been moved from the inner city felt displaced. They were isolated from family and friends. There was an **absence of community** for many who relocated to the Ballymun flats.
- The area experienced **high unemployment**. The level of education was low, with many children leaving school at a young age.
- There were high levels of **crime**, **drug use** and **alcohol abuse** in the area. Within a short space of time, Ballymun became rundown and neglected, and it had a poor image.

Later in this chapter we will look at how Ballymun has been **renewed and regenerated** (see page 124–25).

6.9 There were seven tower blocks in Ballymun, which were 15 storeys high

GEOTERMS

Urban regeneration is the improvement of an area through the creation of new facilities.

QUICK QUESTIONS ?

1. What does the term *urban decay* mean?
2. Describe three problems associated with urban decay.
3. In what decade were the Ballymun flats built?
4. What were the reasons behind building the Ballymun flats?
5. What led to urban decay in Ballymun? (Timed activity: 5 min; 5 SRPs)

6.10 Ballymun became rundown and neglected

Urban problem 3: Urban sprawl

As towns and cities grow, they spread outwards into the surrounding countryside. The **uncontrolled growth of urban areas** is known as urban sprawl. This results in rural land at the edge of towns and cities being **rezoned** for residential use. Residential areas outside the city or town develop. These are known as suburbs. Due to the rapid increase in car ownership people can now live in the suburbs and commute to the CBD to work or study.

Suburbs grow as people move out from inner city areas or to accommodate population growth. Suburbs usually have low population densities. The majority of housing in suburbs consists of individual houses with gardens, which results in a low density of housing.

As people leave the inner city for the suburbs, the city can take on the **shape of a doughnut**. The city appears empty in the middle, with the majority of people living in the suburbs and satellite towns surrounding the city.

6.11 Many US cities, such as Chicago, have experienced urban sprawl

Urban sprawl issues

There are a number of **environmental** and **cultural** issues associated with urban sprawl.

Environmental issues

- If commuters rely on cars rather than public transport, air pollution becomes a problem. Many commuters in US cities such as Los Angeles rely on cars. As a result, **air and noise pollution** is a major problem in these areas.

- The building of new developments in rural areas can **damage wildlife**. Natural hedgerows are rich in wildlife. When these are removed to make way for development, the habitat of wildlife is destroyed. Wetlands, such as marshes and **fens**,

GEOTERMS

- To **zone** land is to designate it for specific use: commercial, transport, residential, industrial or recreational.
- To **rezone** land is to change its use, for example from industrial to residential.
- **Fens** are a marshy lowland area.

6.12 Hedgerows are a habitat for wildlife

are natural habitats for wildlife and plants. These are also damaged by development and construction of new buildings and transport links.

- The construction of housing estates on river floodplains can lead to **flooding**. The development itself can be at risk. It can also increase the risk of flooding up and downstream from the development. Flooding can have a devastating effect on homes and businesses (e.g. lands on the floodplain of the River Shannon after Storm Desmond in 2015).

6.13 Flooding has become a major problem in some Irish urban areas

Cultural issues

- New developments are often given names that are unrelated to the local area. This has a cultural impact since **traditional place names and townlands** can be lost.
- The construction of new roads and housing can **damage ancient monuments and historic sites**. For example, in Dublin the remains of Carrickmines Castle were destroyed during construction of the M50 motorway. Similarly, the landscape of the historic Tara-Skryne Valley was damaged by the construction of the M3 motorway.

6.14 The site of Carrickmines Castle before the M50 motorway was constructed

CASE STUDY 6.3
Urban sprawl – Los Angeles

Los Angeles is the **second largest urban area in the USA**. There are more than 15 million people living in the region. Greater Los Angeles covers an area of 8,000 km². Downtown Los Angeles is the CBD of the region. The main roadways (called freeways) and the Metro rail system meet in this area. Downtown Los Angeles is home to a large retail area. It has many skyscrapers, where multinational corporations (MNCs) have their offices.

Los Angeles **expanded rapidly** in the 1900s. The post-war boom of the 1950s continued this expansion of the city as more people owned cars.

This enabled them to live in the suburbs that grew up around the city and commute to work. This caused the city to expand into the once rural San Fernando Valley. As the city expanded, many neighbouring towns and small cities were

EXAM HINTS

Paris, which you studied in *Horizons* Book 1, Chapter 15: European core region: The Paris Basin, can also be used as an example of a city in the developed world that has experienced urban sprawl.

6.15 There are over 8 million cars in Los Angeles

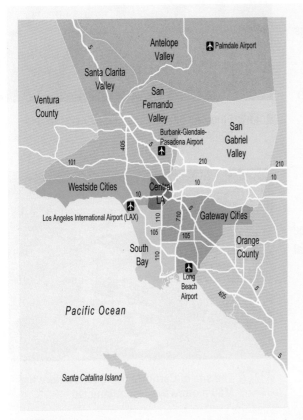

6.16 Los Angeles

Pollution

Many people live in the suburbs of Los Angeles and commute up to four hours a day to the CBD. People are reluctant to use the public transport system, preferring to commute by car. Millions of vehicles use the roads around Los Angeles every day, leading to **severe air pollution, noise pollution** and **traffic congestion**. The city has been ranked as one of the most polluted in the world.

Solutions

In recent years, measures taken to reduce pollution include the introduction of **electric and hybrid cars**, use of **low emission vehicles** and the development of the **public transport system**.

Other solutions include urban infill, green belts, and new towns:

- **Urban infill** could be introduced by the city council to encourage developers to revitalise the inner city area with new buildings or renovate the old ones rather than continuing to build on the city's urban fringe.
- **Green belts** could also be introduced. These are areas of parkland that allow urban dwellers to interact with nature, and they help to improve the environmental health of the area. Green belts help to limit urban sprawl as building on these areas is restricted.
- **New towns** are also constructed to prevent urban sprawl. They are self contained towns with their own community and not just another section of a vast city. New towns allow people to feel as if there is a sense of community in the area, a neighbourhood support system that prevents people from feeling socially isolated.

absorbed. Today, the city is divided into over 80 districts and neighbourhoods – many of these are towns and cities that were absorbed by the expanding city.

Urban sprawl is evident in the Greater Los Angeles area. Many people live in the suburbs of Los Angeles and commute to the CBD for work. Los Angeles has a well-developed road network, with some of the largest urban roadways in the world, creating a **complex road system**. As people leave the inner city for the suburbs, the city can take on the shape of a doughnut. The city appears empty in the middle, with the majority of people living in the suburbs and satellite towns surrounding the city. The inner city that is left behind can suffer from **urban decay**.

GEOTERMS

- **Electric cars** are battery powered.
- **Hybrid cars** use two or more sources of power.
- **Lower emission cars** emit lower levels of pollution.
- A **green belt** is an area of wood, parks or fields surrounding a community in an urban area.

QUICK QUESTIONS

1. What is meant by the term *urban sprawl*?
2. Why can some cities be described as being like doughnuts?
3. Describe two environmental issues associated with urban sprawl.
4. Describe two cultural issues associated with urban sprawl.
5. Write about the effects of urban sprawl on a city you have examined. (Timed activity: 7 min; 7 SRPs)

Heritage in urban areas

Many urban areas are rich in heritage. **Historic buildings**, **monuments** and **areas of archaeological interest** give cities and towns their unique character. Therefore, heritage should be preserved to protect the identity and character of urban areas. In Ireland the **Heritage Act** was introduced in **1995**. This Act ensures that heritage factors are taken into account when new developments are being planned. Lists of protected buildings and monuments are available to developers so that historic structures are considered during planning. The Heritage Council works to protect, preserve and enhance our heritage. The council has placed 28 heritage officers in local authorities across Ireland. The role of the Heritage Officer is to provide support, information and advice at a local level.

An example of the need for the Heritage Act was during the discovery of Viking remains at **Wood Quay** in Dublin city in the 1970s. The construction of the Dublin Corporation Civic Offices destroyed most of this rich archaeological site before archaeologists had a chance to finish excavating the site. The Viking remains that were saved are now in the National History Museum in Dublin.

6.17 Wood Quay in Dublin

Urban problem 4: Environmental quality in urban areas

The environmental quality in urban areas refers to the quality of **air**, **water** and **climate** in towns and cities.

Air quality

Air pollution can affect the health and well-being of people and nature. It is important to prevent and reduce the impact of harmful air emissions on human health and the environment. Air quality in urban areas can be polluted by **burning fossil fuels**, such as coal and gas. Air quality in built-up areas can also be damaged by **car emissions**.

Fossil fuels

The burning of fossil fuels releases harmful gases into the air. This can cause **acid rain** and **smog**.

- Acid rain can have harmful effects on water, soil and human health. It can also damage buildings, statues and monuments by **accelerating the weathering process**.

- Smog occurs when large quantities of smoke mix with fog. In the past, smog was a big problem in urban industrial areas. Smog can have **harmful effects on human health**. Many cities have reduced smog by banning black coal and allowing only smokeless fuel to be used. For example, smog levels in London and Dublin were successfully reduced by introducing air pollution laws.

6.18 Acid rain can damage buildings and statues, especially those made of limestone and marble

Global warming is caused by the build-up of excessive greenhouse gases, such as carbon dioxide, in the atmosphere. These gases are created by the burning of fossil fuels and car emissions.

- Global warming will cause sea levels to rise up to 59 cm by the end of the century. A rise in sea levels threatens to cause **flooding** of low-lying coastal regions and islands, some of which are heavily populated. This will have serious consequences for many urban areas.

- Global warming has also led to an increase in the occurrence and intensity of **hurricanes**, **tsunamis** and **storms**. The 2011 tsunami in Japan, which was caused by an earthquake, is an example of the devastation that urban areas can suffer as a result of these natural forces.

6.19 Coastal cities such as New Orleans are susceptible to flooding

Car emissions

One of the biggest threats to the air quality in urban areas is emissions from road traffic.

- The burning of car fuel emits **harmful pollutants** into the air. These pollutants include nitrogen oxides and benzene. They are extremely harmful to human health and to the environment.

- Many people in Ireland rely on their car to commute to work. In addition, 90 per cent of all commercial transport is by road. Recent technological advances mean that individual cars now have lower emissions. However, there has been an **increase in the number of vehicles on Irish roads**, which has cancelled this out.

GEOTERMS

- **Fossil fuels** are fuels formed by natural processes. They include coal, peat, gas and petrol.
- The **Kyoto Protocol** is an international protocol that aims to reduce global warming.
- **Global warming** is a rise in the average temperature of the Earth's atmosphere and oceans.

Under the **Kyoto Protocol**, we must monitor levels of harmful pollutants such as nitrogen oxides. Since 2010, local authorities have been required to take action to reduce levels if they exceed set targets. This protocol will end in 2020 and the Durban agreement, which was agreed in 2011, will come into action. For the first time it will involve all countries committing to cut their carbon emissions.

Water quality

The water we use comes from a number of sources, including rivers, lakes, springs and streams. Water is taken from these sources and passed through treatment plants before consumption. In order to have a high quality supply of water, the quality of water in these sources must be good.

A number of factors can impact on the quality of our water sources:

- They can become contaminated by overflow liquids from **slurry pits** and **septic tanks**.
- **High rainfall** can cause flooding, which can result in discoloured and contaminated water.
- A **breakdown in the treatment process** can also result in poor quality or contaminated water.
- The treatment process can be affected by **lack of proper equipment** or equipment that has not been **cleaned** properly.
- **Power cuts** can also interrupt the treatment process.

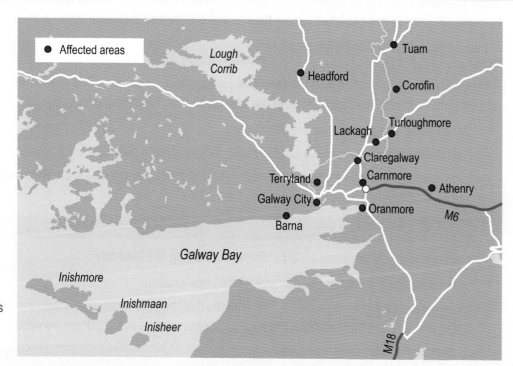

6.20 Some of the areas affected by the domestic water crisis in Galway

In 2007, Galway city and a number of its surrounding towns suffered a domestic water crisis. The water supply had become contaminated by **cryptosporidium**, a parasitic bug. This caused an outbreak of stomach illness among residents. The map in Figure 6.20 shows some of the areas affected.

- The water source for the Galway area is Lough Corrib, the second largest lake in Ireland. The lake had become contaminated by the cryptosporidium parasite. This parasite comes from animal and human waste. **Raw sewage** from nearby towns was one of the sources of the contamination. Another source was **overflow liquids from farm slurry pits and septic tanks**. These may have made their way into the water supply when the River Clare flooded earlier that year.

- There was a **breakdown in the treatment process** at one of two water treatment plants in Terryland. The plant was built in the 1940s and did not have the filtering technology to remove the parasite.

- As a result of the contamination, residents had to boil tap water before using it to cook or clean. They had to buy bottled water for drinking. This was a **huge inconvenience and expense** for families and businesses.

Measures

Sewage treatment facilities in the towns around Lough Corrib were updated to ensure that untreated sewage was not entering the water source. **Water treatment facilities** were updated with new equipment and filtration systems.

Conclusion

This example highlights the impact that poor environmental quality can have on human health.

QUICK QUESTIONS

1. Why is it important to preserve heritage in urban areas?
2. What does the term *environmental quality* mean?
3. Name two causes of air pollution in urban areas.
4. What is the Kyoto Protocol?
5. Name two factors that can impact on the quality of our water supply. (Timed activity: 4 min; 4 SRPs)

Urban planning strategies

Earlier in this chapter, we learned that **urban decay** and **urban sprawl** are two of the issues facing urban planners. Planning strategies can be used to tackle these issues. **Urban redevelopment and renewal** are used to combat urban decay. **New towns** are created to reduce urban sprawl.

Urban redevelopment

Redevelopment involves **changing the land use (or function) of an area**. The most common type of redevelopment involves changing the land use of an area from residential to commercial:

- Derelict buildings and houses are demolished.
- New buildings are constructed and used mainly for commercial purposes, such as office and retail.
- Local residents are rehoused in new towns or in the suburbs. An example is the **redevelopment of Dublin's docklands**, which started in the late 1990s.

Urban renewal

Urban renewal involves **updating an area without changing the land use**:

- Derelict buildings are refurbished or replaced by new houses.
- Services and facilities are provided. This ensures that the public transport network is adequate. It also ensures that there are facilities such as shops, schools and childcare services.

New towns

New towns are sometimes specially developed to **facilitate growth of urban area** and **reduce urban sprawl**.

- New towns are usually developed on the outskirts of large urban areas. They offer an alternative to congested inner cities and suburbs.
- New purpose-built towns control urban sprawl by taking some of the **overspill** population from the city.
- New towns are carefully planned so they have good transport links to the nearby city.
- They also have industrial areas and services, such as industrial estates, shopping centres and parks. An example is **Tallaght** to the south-west of Dublin city.

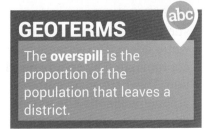

GEOTERMS

The **overspill** is the proportion of the population that leaves a district.

CASE STUDY 6.5

Urban renewal – Ballymun

In Case Study 6.2, we examined how Ballymun suffered from **urban decay** in the 1970s and 1980s. Following that decay, the area became rundown and neglected and had a poor image. They were a number of social and environmental problems associated with the decay of the area. Review Case Study 6.2 to learn more.

Renewal strategy

Ballymun Regeneration Limited (BRL) was set up in 1997 to plan and implement a regeneration programme for Ballymun. The programme aimed to **renew the town with new housing**. Under the plan, the Ballymun flats were demolished and replaced with 5,000 new homes.

Another aim was to **improve the facilities** for the 30,000 residents of the area. A town centre with retail and commercial services is at the centre of the regeneration programme. Local services such as sport and civic centres were developed.

The key aims of the renewal were:

- The provision of well-built **homes** with a good **social mix**
- The creation of **neighbourhoods** with community buildings, childcare facilities and parks
- A **town centre** with commercial activity, such as banks and leisure facilities
- The creation of **job opportunities** and a vibrant **local economy**
- The development of **transport services**
- **Community consultation** and involvement

6.21 New low-density housing and recreational facilities in Ballymun

The Ballymun Regeneration Project reached completion in 2014. The winding down of the BRL was marked by a tree-planting ceremony in 2013 with the Minister for Housing and Planning.

CASE STUDY 6.6
The development of Tallaght

6.22 Tallaght town centre

Tallaght is an example of a **new town**. It was developed to reduce **urban sprawl** in Dublin. In 1967, the Wright Report recommended the development of three new towns in western Dublin to accommodate the city's growing population – Tallaght, Lucan and Blanchardstown.

- Until the late 1960s, Tallaght was a small rural village. It was developed to house some of the city's overspill population. Since then, the **population has grown rapidly** to almost 80,000 people.
- Initially, Tallaght lacked a town centre and adequate services. However, a **new town centre** and **services** were developed. Services include an Institute of Technology, a hospital, a theatre and shopping centres. Industrial estates provide employment for local residents.
- The town has excellent **transport links**. It is connected to the city by the Luas tram line and a good road network. The M50 and N81 roads provide access for cars and commercial vehicles.

QUICK QUESTIONS

1. What planning strategies can be used to tackle urban decay?
2. What does urban renewal involve?
3. What planning strategy can help to reduce urban sprawl?
4. Describe how the Ballymun area has been renewed. (Timed activity: 5 min; 5 SRPs)
5. Define the term *new town* and give an example of one.

Developing world cities

Urbanisation is happening very quickly in developing world cities. Cities in the South grow at a very different pace to cities in the North. They also grow in a different way. The problems of urban growth experienced by developing world cities are very different to those experienced by the cities in the North.

Overcrowding

Developing world cities experience **rapid population growth**. Birth rates are high in developing countries. Also, large numbers of people migrate from rural to urban areas.

People **migrate from rural to urban areas** for a number of reasons:

- To find employment
- To seek a better quality of life
- To benefit from government policies and investment in urban areas
- To avail of better services and credit facilities in urban areas

Inward migration and high birth rates can lead to **overpopulation** and **overcrowding** in urban areas. This puts pressure on services and leads to the development of poor areas, known as **shanty towns**.

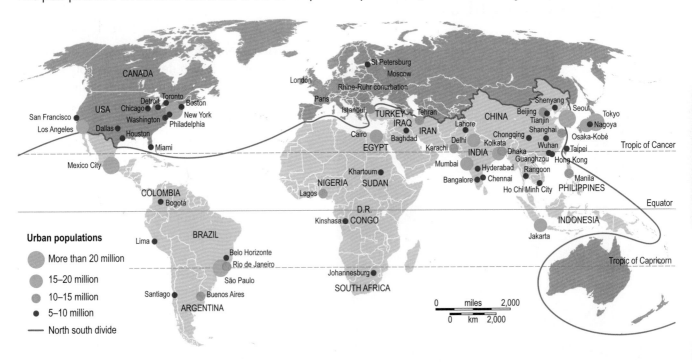

6.23 The major urban areas of the world

Pressure on services

Services in developing world cities are under extreme pressure. Overcrowding puts pressure on the **water supply**, **sewage facilities**, **waste disposal services**, **medical services**, **roads** and **electricity**. The lack of basic services leads to disease, illness and high mortality rates.

Shanty towns

A shanty town is a large urban slum that grows in an unplanned way on the outskirts of a city. The quality of housing is poor in shanty towns, with many people living in temporary shacks. Dwellings are small and overcrowded.

There are many **social and environmental problems** associated with shanty towns:

- People in shanty towns live with many types of **pollution**. Air pollution from road traffic and industrial activity causes widespread health issues. Waste disposal facilities are poor so rubbish builds up on streets. Sewage facilities are very basic, with toilet waste often flowing through open drains. This leads to illness and disease.

- Slums are characterised by **high unemployment** and **poverty**. Many people living in slums live below the poverty line. Poverty and unemployment leads to people working in the informal or **hidden economy**, where work conditions are extremely poor. There is a lack of food and clean water, so many people are **malnourished**.

- Inadequate sanitation and a lack of clean water cause **illness** and **disease**. As a consequence, many people die young, leaving behind orphaned children. Some parents abandon children if they are unable to take of care of them. Abandoned or orphaned children become **street children**, living alone on the streets. Many are lured into the sex industry. Some parents are forced to sell their children into the sex trafficking trade to survive.

- Shanty towns have high rates of **crime** and **drug use**. They are often overrun by criminal gangs who operate the drug and sex trafficking trades.

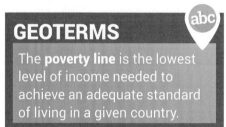

GEOTERMS

The **poverty line** is the lowest level of income needed to achieve an adequate standard of living in a given country.

6.24 The quality of housing is very poor in shanty towns

CASE STUDY 6.7
Overcrowding – Kolkata, India

Kolkata (formerly known as Calcutta) has a population of over 15 million people. It is one of the largest urban areas in the world. Kolkata is a **rapidly growing city** with an annual population growth of 4 per cent. This rapid growth has led to a number of **social and environmental problems**.

- The population of Kolkata has grown rapidly due to a **very high birth rate and inward migration**. People migrate from the rural areas of Bangladesh to seek work and to avail of better services in the city. Kolkata is a densely populated city. It has a population density of 25,000 people per km². In poorer parts of the city, there are up to 150,000 people per km².

- **Overcrowding** puts pressure on services and leads to the development of shanty towns. There are over four million people living in Kolkata's shanty towns. Buildings are crammed together and there is very little open space.

Pressure on services

Kolkata's services and resources are under extreme pressure. Because of rapid growth, many parts of Kolkata have grown in an unplanned way. This means that services are inadequate.

- **Access to clean water** is limited, with up to 40 families sharing just one tap in some areas.

- **Sanitation** is poor, especially in the shanty towns. Open drains carry domestic waste and untreated sewage. These are often washed into people's homes by heavy rain. Very basic sewage facilities lead to the spread of illness and disease.
- **Waste disposal** services are lacking in many parts of Kolkata. This results in a build-up of waste on the streets, which attracts rodents and further contributes to the spread of disease.
- **Medical services** are inadequate and many people die of curable illnesses such as cholera, typhoid and diarrhoea.
- There is no **electricity** supply to many of the poorer parts of Kolkata.
- There are no **roads** in many of the rapidly growing areas. **Public transport** is generally limited and roads are overcrowded.

City of contrasts

The city centre area of Kolkata is home to wealthy residents of the city. Employment in the city centre is high. Many people work in modern office blocks and retail outlets. Facilities and housing in this area are of a high quality. In contrast to this, the shanty towns, known locally as *bustees*, are home to the poor of Kolkata. The quality of housing is poor. Many people live in **temporary houses** made of plastic, tin or cardboard. Some people are pavement dwellers who live on the street with **no shelter**. Houses are **small and overcrowded** and are built **close together**. **Poor sanitation** and **lack of clean water** mean that many people suffer illness and disease.

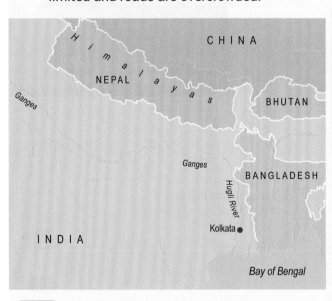

6.25 Kolkata is situated on the River Hugli

QUICK QUESTIONS

1. Why do developing world cities experience rapid population growth?
2. Name three services that are under pressure in developing world cities.
3. What is a shanty town?
4. Describe two problems faced by people living in shanty towns. (Timed activity: 6 min; 6 SRPs)
5. What is a shanty town in Kolkata known as locally?

EXAM HINTS

This is linked to *Horizons* Book 1 Chapter 17: Continental/subcontinental region: India

The future of urbanism

In the future, new cities will grow and existing cities will become more heavily populated. In 2015 there were 536 cities with a population of 1 million or more. Urban planners need to tackle the issues of urban sprawl, urban decay and inadequate services to ensure a good quality of life for future city dwellers. Cities of the future must also be sustainable and have less impact on the environment.

Cities of the future

Cities and large urban areas will need to be well-planned with good services in the future:

- The problem of **urban sprawl** will need to be reversed by intensive land use. This involves developing well-planned housing with excellent transport links and services.
- Developing a good public transport network will ease **traffic congestion** and **air pollution**.

- Urban planning and **land-zoning policies** will help to ensure that the distance between residential and industrial areas is minimised. Good housing policies will be necessary to ensure that **social integration** is achieved.
- **Counter-urbanisation** means that regional growth centres will be independent from the main urban centre of the region. For example, commuter towns close to Dublin, such as Navan and Drogheda, will be self-contained urban areas with their own CBD and services.
- **Communities** will be more involved in planning and development of services for their area.

6.26 Many European cities such as Munich have become more people-friendly

GEOTERMS

Counter-urbanisation is the idea that regional growth centres will become independent of the main urban centre.

Sustainable cities

It is important that cities of the future are **sustainable** and have a **minimal impact on the environment**:

- Cities will need to become **more people-friendly** to become sustainable. This involves renewing areas of decay, such as inner city areas, to encourage people to live in the city centre again. The development of parks, pedestrian zones and recreational facilities makes city centres more people-friendly.
- **Good public transport links** and **pollution controls** improve the environment of urban centres.
- The development of residential areas with **good transport links** and **recreational areas** is vital to reduce pollution. Well-planned suburbs with **green belts** in between must be developed.
- **Energy-efficient homes** and **waste-reduction programmes** contribute to the development of more sustainable cities.

QUICK QUESTIONS

1. What issues must urban planners tackle to ensure a good quality of life for future city dwellers?
2. How can the issue of urban sprawl be tackled in the future?
3. What can good housing policies help to achieve?
4. How can city centre areas be made more people-friendly? (Timed activity: 3 min; 3 SRPs)
5. Define the term *green belt*.

QUESTIONS

Ordinary Level – Long Questions

Traffic in urban areas

1. (i) Name one city where traffic congestion is a problem.
   (ii) Explain the reasons why traffic congestion occurs in this city.
   (iii) Describe one solution to traffic congestion.
   2015, Section 2, Q11B, 40 marks

Developing world city

2. (i) Name one city in the developing world.
   (ii) Describe and explain reasons for the rapid growth of this city.
   2015, Section 2, Q12B, 30 marks

The marking scheme for a question like this on an Ordinary Level paper is as follows:

Developing world city named	**3 marks**
Description and explanation: 9 SRPs @ 3 m each	**27 marks**
Total	**30 marks**

Travel and work

Region	On foot	Bicycle	Bus & train	Motor cycle	Car	Lorry & van	Work from home
West	7.9	1.4	2.1	0.2	68.3	9.7	10.4
Dublin	12.8	5.0	19.9	0.9	52.2	3.5	5.7
South East	9.1	0.9	1.3	0.3	69.3	8.9	10.2

Amended from CSO figures

3. The above table shows the means by which people travel to work in a number of Irish regions (%). The percentage of people working from home is also included. Examine the table and answer each of the following questions.

   (i) What was the most popular means of travelling to work?

   (ii) Which region had the greatest total percentage of people travelling to work on foot and by bicycle?

   (iii) Explain briefly why the Dublin region had the highest percentage of people travelling to work by bus and train.

   (iv) List two problems that may be experienced in urban areas where a high percentage of people travel to work by car.

   (v) List two ways authorities in urban areas attempt to reduce the number of people travelling to work by car.

   2014, Section 2, Q11A, 30 marks

Developing world city

4. (i) Name one city in the developing world.

   (ii) Explain the problems experienced in this named city.

   (iii) Describe one solution to these problems.

   2014, Section 2, Q11C, 40 marks

World cities

City	Population (millions)
Seoul	10
London	8
Manila	12
Istanbul	14

Amended from CIA World Factbook

5. Examine the data above showing the population of some of the most populous cities of the world in 2012.

   (i) Using graph paper, draw a suitable graph to illustrate this data.

   (ii) Explain briefly one problem associated with large cities.

   2014, Section 2, Q12A, 30 marks

Developing world cities

6. Describe and explain the problems caused by the rapid growth of a developing world city that you have studied.

   2014, Section 2, Q11C, 30 marks

Ireland's urban population

Town	Population
Saggart, South Dublin	2,100
Ballymahon, Co. Longford	1,500
Newcastle, South Dublin	2,600
Courtown Harbour, Co. Wexford	2,800

Amended from CSO figures

7. Examine the data showing the population of a selection of Irish towns in 2011.

   (i) Using graph paper, draw a suitable graph to illustrate this data.

   (ii) State two reasons for the growth of Irish towns.

   2013, Section 2, Q12A, 30 marks

Traffic congestion

8. Describe and explain the measures being taken in towns and cities to solve the problems of traffic congestion.

   2013, Section 2,Q12B 30 marks

> The marking scheme for a question like this on an Ordinary Level paper is as follows:
>
> Explanation of measure:
>
> | | |
> |---|---|
> | 10 SRPs @ 3 m each | **30 marks** |
> | **Total** | **30 marks** |

Dynamics of settlement

9. Examine the aerial photograph of Carrick-on-Shannon accompanying this paper (see page 107).

   (i) Using the usual notation (right background etc.), give two locations on the aerial photograph where traffic congestion could be a problem in Carrick-on-Shannon.

   (ii) Select one of the locations chosen in part (i) and, using evidence from the aerial photograph, explain why traffic congestion might occur at this location.

   (iii) Examine in detail one possible solution to this traffic congestion.

   2012, Section 2, Q11B, 30 marks

Higher Level – Long Questions

Urban problems

12. Discuss how the growth of urban centres can lead to any two of the following problems, with reference to examples that you have studied.

    ○ Traffic congestion
    ○ Urban decay
    ○ Urban sprawl

    2015, Section 2, Q10B, 30 marks

Urban problems

10. (i) Name a developing or a developed city that you have studied.

    (ii) Explain two problems arising from the growth of the city named in part (i).

    (iii) Describe two solutions to these problems.

    2012, Section 2, Q11C, 40 marks

Urban sprawl

11. (i) Explain two causes of urban sprawl in any city that you have studied.

    (ii) Explain two problems caused by this urban sprawl.

    2012, Section 2, Q12B, 40 marks

> The marking scheme for a question like this on an Ordinary Level paper is as follows:
>
> | | |
> |---|---|
> | City named | **4 marks** |
> | 2 problems explained: | |
> | Each problem 3 SRPs @ 3 m each | **18 marks** |
> | 2 solutions explained: | |
> | Each solution 3 SRPs @ 3 m each | **18 marks** |
> | **Total** | **40 marks** |

Urban growth

13. Examine the table below showing the fastest growing towns in Ireland and answer the following questions.

    (i) Calculate the increase in the total population of Newcastle, between 2006 and 2011.

    (ii) Calculate X, the percentage change in Courtown Harbour's population, between 2006 and 2011.

Town	Region	Population 2006	Population 2011	% Population change 2006–2011
Saggart	South Dublin	868	2,144	147
Courtown Harbour	Wexford	1,421	2,857	**X**
Newcastle	South Dublin	1,506	2,659	77
Carrigtwohill	Cork	2,782	4,551	64
Ballymahon	Longford	963	1,563	62

Amended from CSO

(iii) State two reasons for the rapid growth of towns in South Dublin, between 2006 and 2011.

(iv) Explain briefly one problem caused by the rapid growth of Irish towns.

(v) Explain briefly one reason why the Census of Population is important for urban planning.

2013, Section 2, Q10A, 20 marks

Future urbanisation

14. Discuss two issues facing cities in the future in the developed world.

2013, Section 2, Q12C, 30 marks

The marking scheme for a question like this on a Higher Level paper is as follows:

2 issues named @ 2 m each	**4 marks**
Issue 1 explained: 7 SRPs @ 2 m each	**14 marks**
Issue 2 explained: 6 SRPs @ 2 m each	**12 marks**
Total	**30 marks**

Rapid population growth

15. 'Authorities in the developing world cities have attempted to overcome the problems of rapid urban growth.'

Examine the above statement with reference to example(s) you have studied.

2012, Section 2, Q10B, 30 marks

Transport and traffic

16. Examine the table below showing new vehicles registered by taxation class from January to August, 2008 to 2010. Answer the following questions.

Taxation class	2008	2009	2010
Private	137,566	49,142	73,689
Goods vehicle	27,200	7,744	8,462
Tractors	3,579	1,583	1,081
Motor cycles	2,508	1,553	1,048
Other	2,751	1,058	630
Total	**173,604**	**61,080**	**84,910**

Amended from CSO

(i) How many private vehicles were registered from January to August in 2009?

(ii) What was the percentage decrease in goods vehicles registered from January to August between 2008 and 2009?

(iii) Briefly explain one reason for this decrease.

(iv) State two causes of traffic congestion.

(v) Briefly explain one way authorities attempt to solve the problem of traffic congestion.

2012, Section 2, Q11A, 20 marks

HOT TOPICS IN THE EXAMS

1. Traffic congestion
2. Problems of rapid growth of developing world cities
3. Urban sprawl

 Chapter 5 Urban settlement and planning issues

Mind map

Urban problems

Urban decay
- City rundown, e.g. inner city Dublin
- Unattractive landscape
- High unemployment and population decline
- Vandalism, crime and drug use
- Absence of community

Case study: Ballymun
- 1960s, rehoused inner city residents
- 36 blocks of flats, poorly maintained
- Lack of amenities, green spaces
- Absence of community
- High unemployment, crime
- Neglected, poor image

Urban planning strategies
- Urban decay – urban redevelopment and renewal
- Urban sprawl – new towns

Case study: Ballymun renewal
- BRL 1997, build low-density housing, job creation and social mix
- Aims: new housing and improved facilities
- Community consultation

Heritage issues
- Heritage preservation: protect urban areas' identity and character
- Heritage Act 1995, Heritage Council, Heritage Officer
- Wood Quay

Environmental quality in urban areas
- Air quality and pollution: Kyoto Protocol/Durban agreement
- Water: treated for consumption
- Global warming; flooding, hurricanes, tsunamis and storms

Urban sprawl
- Rural land – rezoned residential
- Suburbs – low population densities, commuters to CBD
- Doughnut-shaped city

Issues
- Environmental: air pollution, damage to wildlife, flooding
- Cultural: loss of placenames, destruction of historic sites

Case study: Los Angeles
- USA's 2nd largest urban area – 15 million people
- Greater LA: 8,000 km² – large road network
- One of the world's most polluted cities
- Electric/hybrid/low-emission cars, public transport development
- Doughnut shaped, urban infill, green belts, new towns

The future of urbanism
- 2015, 536 cities with 1 million+
- Urban sprawl. urban decay, inadequate services

Cities of the future
- Well-planned. excellent services and public transport
- Social integration, counterurbanisation, community involvement

Sustainability
- People-friendly: renewal, parks and recreation
- Good public transport and pollution controls
- Green belts, energy efficient homes and waste reduction

Developing world cities
- Urbanisation rapid – North and South growth different
- Overcrowding: inward migration and high birth rate
- Pressure or services – disease, illness, high mortality rates
- Shanty towns: pollution, unemployment, poverty, crime

Case study: Kolkata, India
- Population: 15 million+
- One of the world's largest urban areas
- High birth rate, inward migration, overcrowding
- Inadequate services – illlness and disease
- City centre wealthy, bustees poor
- Lack of clean water, waste collection, poor electrical supply

Traffic movement and congestion
- Roads around urban centres
- Slow, queues, increased journey times
- Inadequate public transport

Causes
- Volume: commuters to CBD, more cars
- Inadequate public transport

Effects
- Social
- Economic
- Environmental

Solutions
- Restricted on-street parking, multi-storey car parks
- One-way streets, traffic lights, ring roads
- Adequate public transport
- Bicycle lanes and schemes

Case study: Dublin
- 1.3 million people
- Economic centre of Ireland – commuters
- Increased car ownership – traffic
- Public transport improvements
  - St Stephen's Green Area traffic management scheme
  - The LUAS Cross City project

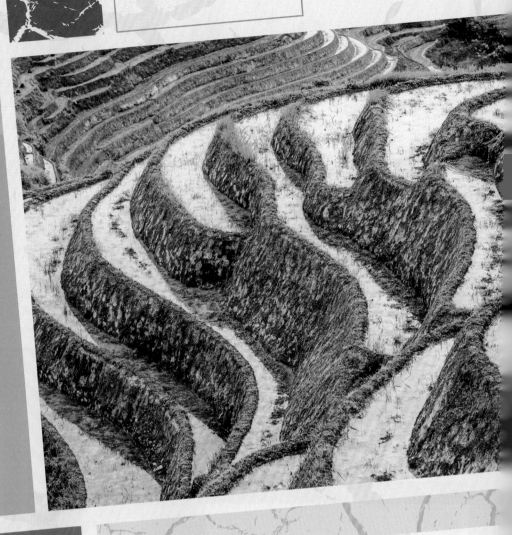

OPTION

7

Geoecology

7

Soils

By the end of this chapter, students will have studied:

- ◎ The different components of soil
- ◎ A typical soil profile
- ◎ The characteristics that are used to differentiate soil types

NOTE

This section should be allowed at least four class periods (40 minutes). Essay preparation is an important part of the option sections.

Introduction

Soil is the thin layer of **loose weathered and eroded material** that covers the Earth's surface. It is one of the Earth's most important natural resources. Soil is made up of both **organic** and **inorganic** materials. **Climate** is one of the most important factors in the formation of soil.

INTERESTING FACTS

It takes approximately 400 years to create 1 cm of soil.

General composition of all soil types

All soils are made of the following components but in different amounts. This gives rise to many different soil types around the world.

Mineral matter

Mineral matter is the **broken-down material of the parent rock**. It is the largest component of most soil types and can make up to 45 per cent of the soil. The parent rock was broken down into mineral matter by **denudation**. The mineral matter may have been derived from the area or transported by the agents of erosion: rivers, sea, wind or ice. Some minerals are soluble. These are very important, as they help nourish plants growing in the area. The particle size can vary depending on the parent rock type: for example, sandstone has very large particles, whereas clay has very small particles.

GEOTERMS

- o **Parent rock** is the bedrock of the area.
- o **Denudation** is the collective name for weathering and erosion.

Organic matter

Organic matter was once the **living material** of the plant, such as leaves and flowers, as well as the remains of animals. On average, organic matter makes up only about 5 per cent of the soil, but it is essential for soil fertility. Dead plant material is known as plant litter. As the material decays it is broken down by **bacteria and micro-organisms** into a thick, black, sticky substance called **humus**. Humus is rich in nutrients and is

GEOTERMS

Aeration is the introduction of air.

essential for plant growth. It also gives soils a dark brown appearance and because of its sticky nature helps to bind soil particles and hold moisture.

Living organisms can be anything from micro-organisms, such as bacteria and fungi, to earthworms. They live in the soil and help with the breakdown of organic matter, aerating and mixing the soil.

Water

Water is essential in the soil to help with plant growth. It is found in the pore spaces in the soil. **Water helps to dissolve minerals** so that plants can take them in through their roots. It usually makes up about a quarter of the soil's volume, but this is is very weather dependent. In desert regions, for example, soils have very little water content, whereas in boggy areas the soil can be saturated with water.

Air

Air is also found in the pore spaces between the soil particles. It **supplies oxygen and nitrogen**, essential for plant growth. It usually makes up about a quarter of the soil's volume but it is more plentiful in large grained soils such as sandy soils.

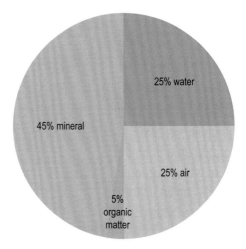

7.1 The main components of soil

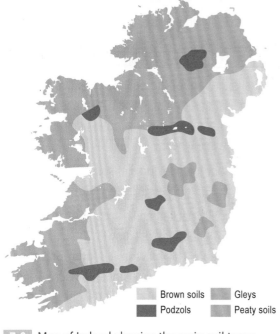

Brown soils Gleys
Podzols Peaty soils

7.2 Map of Ireland showing the main soil types

Soil profile

A soil profile is a vertical section cut through the soil, showing the layers that are present. There are normally three layers, or **horizons**, to a soil.

A horizon

The A horizon is the top layer of the soil and is also called **topsoil**. It is dark brown in colour due to the high humus content. It is also the layer where most biological activity takes place.

B horizon

The B horizon is located just below the topsoil and is also called the **subsoil**. It is lighter in colour than the A horizon due to a lack of humus content. This is the layer in which leached materials accumulate and where an impermeable layer called a **hardpan** can be created.

C horizon

The C horizon is the bottom layer of the soil profile and **contains the parent rock**.

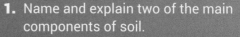

Soil characteristics

All of the following soil characteristics have a huge impact on the fertility of soils.

Texture

Texture is the **feel of the soil**, whether it is coarse or fine. This is dependent on the amount of clay, sand and silt particles in the soil. All these particles are different sizes, and so the amount of water they absorb and nutrients they retain differs. They also affect the ease to which roots can penetrate the different soil types.

There are four main textures of soils.

- **Clay soils:** these soils contain more than 50 per cent clay particles, which are extremely small and tightly packed and are not visible to the naked eye. They have a high nutrient content and are good for plant growth. They are sticky and do not allow air and water to pass through them freely. This can result in **poor drainage** of clay soils. They are **prone to waterlogging** in wintertime and become dry and cracked during the summer months. Clay soils can be difficult to plough, and plant roots find it hard to penetrate them. Therefore they are better for pastoral farming.

- **Silty soils:** these soils contain particles that are slightly bigger than clay particles and are just visible to the naked eye; they are often powdery to the touch. They have over 50 per cent silt particles and can be **badly drained** but do not suffer from waterlogging.

- **Sandy soils:** these soils contain the largest particles, which are visible to the naked eye. Sandy soils contain more than 70 per cent sand and **lack humus content**. They therefore have poor sticking ability. However, they are loose soils that are easy to cultivate, and they warm up quickly in the spring, which aids early planting. They are **free-draining soils**, as they have large pore spaces, and rarely suffer from waterlogging.

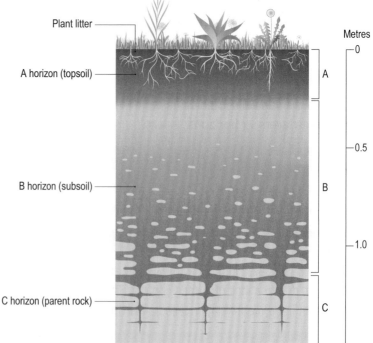

7.3 Soil profile

Leaching can be a problem in these soils as minerals and nutrients can easily be washed from the A horizon to the B horizon. To combat this, sandy soils need to be fertilised and irrigated.

- **Loamy soils:** these soils contain equal amounts of all three particles. Loamy soils are brown and crumbly in texture. They have a **high humus content** and are free from waterlogging and drying out in the summer. They are easily cultivated soils and are most suitable for farming and gardening.

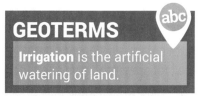
GEOTERMS abc
Irrigation is the artificial watering of land.

7.4a Sandy soil

7.4b Clay soil

7.4c Loamy soil

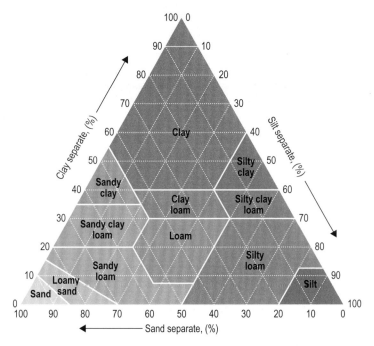
7.5 Soil textures

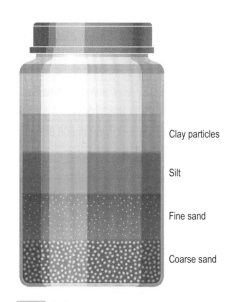
7.6 Soil sample test

Experiment to test soil texture

1. Take a sample of soil and place it in a jar with a screw top.
2. Three-quarters fill the jar with water.
3. Shake the jar for a couple of seconds, until all the material is well mixed.
4. Leave to settle overnight.
5. In the morning the soil sample will have divided into several visible layers, with the largest sand particles at the bottom and the finest clay particles at the top. Now try to determine your soil sample using Figure 7.5.

Colour

Soil can vary in colour from dark brown to light grey or yellow, depending on the amount of organic matter in it. The colour of the soil depends mainly on the parent material and the processes that have affected the soil.

- **Dark brown soils** tend to be very fertile, as they have a high humus content. They are also said to be warm soils as they attract heat, which in turn helps seed germination. Examples include **brown earths**.

- **Grey soils** tend to be infertile, as they have been leached of their humus and nutrient content. They can often be poorly draining soils or suffer from waterlogging. Examples include **podzols**.

- **Red soils** are found in tropical or equatorial regions. They owe their red colour to the presence of iron oxide (rust) in the soil. Temperatures and rainfall are high in these regions, and the soils experience rapid rates of chemical weathering. Examples include **tropical red soils**.

7.7 Tropical red soil

GEOTERMS abc

Seed germination is the growing of seeds.

Structure

Structure indicates how the soil particles are held together. Small clumps of soil bound together by humus and water are called **peds**. They can tell us a lot about the structure of the soil. The ped structure controls the amount of air and water that can be contained in the soil. The following are some of the most common soil structures.

1. **Crumb soils:** in these soils the peds have a rounded shape. They are fertile soils as air and water can pass through them easily. They are considered the best soils for cultivation. Examples are **loamy soils**.

2. **Blocky soils:** these soils have close-fitting, roughly cube-shaped particles. Examples are **sandy soils**.

3. **Platy soils:** these soils have peds with a flat and overlapping structure that can prevent the free movement of water. They are generally infertile. Examples are **clay soils**.

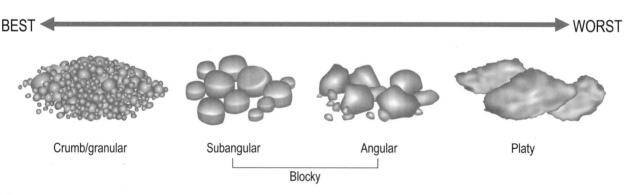

BEST ← → WORST

| Crumb/granular | Subangular | Angular | Platy |

Blocky

7.8 Common ped shapes

Water content and retention properties

The amount of water that soils can hold depends on their **structure, humus content and texture**. Humus helps to bind soil particles together, and so it is able to hold more moisture than soils lacking in humus, such as sandy soils. Clay and soils with a platy structure are able to hold large quantities of water, which often leads to waterlogging of these soil types during wet weather conditions. Sandy soils are often dry, as they have little ability to hold water, but loamy soils with their crumb structure appear to be the best to hold some moisture but not to become waterlogged. In waterlogged conditions many bacteria and fungi cannot live, therefore there is little decay of organic material.

It is vital for plant growth that soils are able to hold some moisture. If not, water stress occurs and the plants begin to wilt. **Water is essential in the soil** to allow plants to absorb minerals in a soluble form. Water also allows the development of horizons in the soil and slows the rate of soil erosion by binding the particles together.

GEOTERMS (abc)

Water stress is the need for more water than there is available.

Organic content

The organic material of soils is made up of any living matter. **Plant litter** – dead plant material, such as leaves, bark and twigs, that has fallen to the ground – and decomposing materials add nutrients to the soil in the form of **humus**. Bacteria and fungi help the decomposition of the decaying matter. Earthworms and other insects help to mix humus into the soil and also aerate it with their burrows. Soils with a high humus content tend to be dark brown in colour with a good crumb structure. A sticky jelly-like substance, humus helps to bind the soil particles together, allowing them to hold moisture. Humus also absorbs minerals that could be washed out of the soil during heavy rainfall. Brown earths in Ireland are an example of a soil rich in humus.

Soil pH

Soil pH indicates how **acidic or alkaline** the soil is. This can have a huge effect on the type of organisms and plants that can live in the soil. Most fertile soils contain a pH of 6.5. Soils that are more acidic than this, such as peat soils, have a lower pH number. They can sustain very few living organisms or plants. Lime is sometimes added to reduce the acidity level of the soil. Alkaline soils contain a high level of calcium and often develop in areas of chalk or limestone. These soils can be associated with desert or drought conditions due to the permeable nature of the underlying bedrock.

7.10 Alkaline soils often develop in areas of limestone

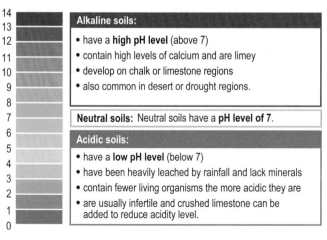

Alkaline soils:
- have a **high pH level** (above 7)
- contain high levels of calcium and are limey
- develop on chalk or limestone regions
- also common in desert or drought regions.

Neutral soils: Neutral soils have a **pH level of 7**.

Acidic soils:
- have a **low pH level** (below 7)
- have been heavily leached by rainfall and lack minerals
- contain fewer living organisms the more acidic they are
- are usually infertile and crushed limestone can be added to reduce acidity level.

7.9 The pH of soil

QUICK QUESTIONS

1. What does the term *crumb structure* refer to?
2. What are the main differences between sandy and loamy soils? (Timed activity: 2 min; 2 SRPs)
3. Why is lime added to acidic soils?
4. Why is water important in soils?

QUESTIONS

Higher Level – Long Questions
Geoecology

1. Examine the influence of mineral matter, air, water and organic matter on soil development.

    2015, Section 2, Q16, 80 marks

2. Discuss how soil development is influenced by any three of the following factors:
    - Mineral matter
    - Air
    - Water
    - Organic matter

    2013, Section 2, Q18, 80 marks

The marking scheme for a question like this on a Higher Level paper is as follows:

3 aspects identified @ 4 m each	**12 marks**
Discussion: 8 SRPs @ 2 m each per aspect	**48 marks**
Overall coherence	**20 marks**
Total	**80 marks**
4 aspects identified @ 3 m each	**12 marks**
Discussion: 6 SRPs @ 2 m each per aspect	**48 marks**
Overall coherence	**20 marks**
Total	**80 marks**

EXAM HINTS

All questions are worth 80 marks and require an essay-style answer. Your answer should include:

- An introduction: lay out all the material that will be covered later in the essay.
- Three to four paragraphs: each should focus on a new aspect of the answer; there should be six to eight SRPs in each paragraph.
- A conclusion: draw together all the information that was discussed in the essay.

EXAM HINTS

The 2007 Chief Examiner's report mentioned that some students failed to go into enough detail on a specific soil type. They gave only a general account of soils.

HOT TOPICS IN THE EXAMS

Components of soils

Chapter 8   Soil characteristics

Mind map

Soil
- Layer of loose weathered material, natural resource, organic and inorganic materials

Soils

General composition

Mineral matter
- Largest component of soil
- From denudation of parent rock
- Helps nourish plants

Organic matter
- Plants and animals
- Humus, very fertile, binds soil
- Insects, bacteria and fungi (living organisms):
  - Break down organic matter
  - Aerate and mix the soil

Water
- Aids plant growth
- Helps dissolve minerals
- Is weather dependent

Air
- Supplies oxygen and nitrogen

Soil profile

A horizon
- Topsoil
- Dark brown
- Most fertile, biological activity

B horizon
- Subsoil
- Lighter in colour
- Lacks humus, hardpan created

C horizon
- Parent rock

Soil characteristics

Texture (feel)
- Clay: tightly packed, high nutrient content, poor drainage, waterlogging
- Silty: poor drainage but no waterlogging
- Sandy: free draining, leaching, require fertilisers
- Loamy: even quantities, best soil

Colour
- Dark brown: high humus content, warm
- Grey: leached, poor quality
- Red: tropical regions, iron oxide

Structure
- Peds:
  - Crumb: fertile
  - Blocky: sandy soils
  - Platy: infertile, prevent movement of water

Water content and retention
- Dissolves minerals
- Allows development of horizons
- Slows rate of soil erosion
- Bacteria and fungi cannot live without it
- Essential for soils, absorbs minerals, develops horizons

Organic content
- Humus binds soil,
- Burrows aerate soil

Soil pH
- 6.5 pH, for most fertile soils
- Lime reduces acidity

8 Soil characteristics

SYLLABUS LINK

Soil characteristics are affected by their immediate environment and by a combination of processes operating in that environment, including human interference.

NOTE

This section should be allowed at least 10 class periods (40 minutes). Essay preparation is an important part of the option sections.

EXAM HINTS

The material in this chapter has appeared on the exam papers every year since 2006.

Introduction

Soil is a valuable **natural resource** and is the basic building block for most living things on this planet. Soils develop differently across the world because of the range of climatic factors that interact with them. Therefore many different soil types emerge. All of these soils have one thing in common: if they are not managed properly they will become sterile. Human interaction, climate change and population increases have had a major impact on the soils of the world.

Soil-forming factors

Many factors either working together or alone have a huge impact on the formation of soil.

Some of the most important are listed below.

Parent material

This is normally the **original bedrock** of the area from which minerals in the soil are derived. It can affect the soil's colour, pH, texture and ability to hold water. Parent material can also be material that was transported to the region after glaciation or fluvial, coastal or aeolian (wind) action. Weathering of loose parent material is more rapid than weathering of solid rock. The majority of Irish soils developed from glacial deposits. Soils of different parent rocks develop different characteristics:

- Soils derived from **sandstone** are sandy and free draining.
- Soils derived from **limestone** are rich in calcium.

NOTE

This section links to *Horizons* Book 1 Chapter 5: The rock cycle.

GEOTERMS

- **Fluvial** relates to something produced by or found in a river.
- **Metamorphic** rocks were once igneous/sedimentary rocks but were changed by great heat or pressure.
- **Igneous** rocks are formed when magma cools and solidifies.

- Soils derived from **shale** have a high clay content and are poorly drained.
- Soils derived from **metamorphic** and **igneous rocks** tend to be acidic due to their mineral make-up.

Climate

The climate of a region has a major influence on the type of soil that will develop there. **Precipitation and temperature** are the main agents that control the rate of weathering and biological activity in a region and, in turn, the development of soil.

- In **hot climates**, for example equatorial regions, weathering (mainly chemical) of soils is rapid, as is the decomposition of organic matter. Therefore deep fertile soils are abundant.

- In **wet climates**, for example monsoon regions, soils are prone to leaching and waterlogging.

- In **cold climates**, for example tundra regions, weathering (mainly mechanical) and biological activity are restricted. Thin, infertile soils develop as a result.

- In **dry climates**, for example the Sahel region, drought influences the upward movement of water, causing salinisation and calcification.

8.1 Soil waterlogged from the monsoon rains

Zonal soils are created in areas where particular climatic conditions, as mentioned above, have allowed them to develop. For example, the zonal soils of Ireland are brown earths, which have developed under a cool temperate oceanic climate.

Topography

The lie of the land, or its **relief**, has a major impact on the types of soils that develop in the area.

- **Higher altitude regions** tend to have soils that are heavily leached. However, because of their sloping nature, run-off is evident and the soils tend to be well drained. Soil erosion is another problem on very steep slopes.

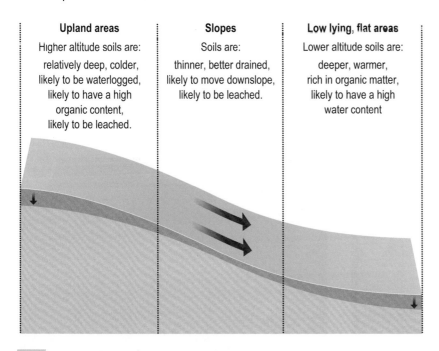

Upland areas	Slopes	Low lying, flat areas
Higher altitude soils are:	Soils are:	Lower altitude soils are:
relatively deep, colder, likely to be waterlogged, likely to have a high organic content, likely to be leached.	thinner, better drained, likely to move downslope, likely to be leached.	deeper, warmer, rich in organic matter, likely to have a high water content

8.2 Topographical influences on soil

GEOTERMS

- **Aspect** is the direction in which a slope is facing. North-facing slopes are colder and south-facing slopes are warmer.

- **Calcification** is the build-up of calcium in the ground, which can be caused by irrigation in an area. This layer of calcite is impermeable. Plant roots are unable to penetrate it and it can lead to crop failure.

- **Salinisation** is the build-up of dissolved salts in the land. It can be caused by irrigation. This layer of salt is poisonous and prevents crop growth.

- **Lower altitude regions** tend to have deeper fertile soils, but these areas can be prone to waterlogging.
- As **altitude** increases, so does precipitation. Temperatures decrease and so, in turn, does the length of the growing season. **Biological activity** on higher slopes is also decreased due to the drop in temperatures, making less humus available for the soils that develop there. **Aspect** can also be important in the formation of soil. Different soil types can develop on the cold north-facing slopes than on the more productive warmer south-facing slopes.

Biological activity

Living organisms have a huge impact on the **decomposition** of organic material or plant litter and the **formation of fertile soil**. Bacteria and fungi are needed for the formation of nutrient-rich humus. Rabbits, foxes, earthworms and insects are needed to aerate, mix and drain the soil found in the A and B horizons. Their burrows are also helpful in bringing water and air further into the soil. Vegetation is needed by the soil as plant litter adds fertile organic matter. The roots and foliage of the plants help to bind the soil and prevent erosion. The leaves and branches of trees add a protective cover and prevent raindrop erosion in wet climates.

Human interference

People can play a huge part in the enrichment or destruction of this precious natural resource. Farmers can add **fertilisers**, such as lime, to soils to improve their fertility. **Irrigation** and **drainage** schemes can be implemented in areas that suffer from water problems. Unfortunately, **deforestation** and the destruction of vegetation continue to remove organic matter from soils and also remove the foliage that protects the soil from raindrop and aeolian erosion.

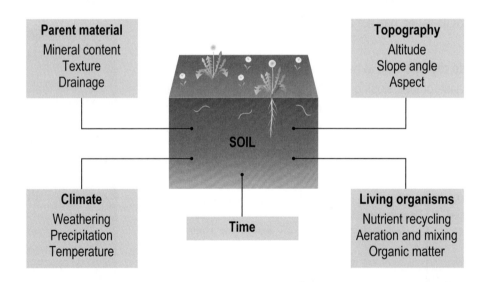

Parent material
Mineral content
Texture
Drainage

Topography
Altitude
Slope angle
Aspect

SOIL

Climate
Weathering
Precipitation
Temperature

Time

Living organisms
Nutrient recycling
Aeration and mixing
Organic matter

8.3 Soil-forming factors

GEOTERMS

Deforestation is the clearance of forests. This is usually due to logging (where wood is cut down for fuel or for the timber industry) or 'slash and burn' clearances (where forests are cleared for farm land).

QUICK QUESTIONS

1. What are the two types of parent material?
2. Where do deeper fertile soils form and why?
3. How do living organisms contribute to soil formation? (Timed activity: 6 min; 6 SRPs)
4. Why would farmers add lime to their fields?
5. Suggest why soils would form quicker in areas of softer parent material.

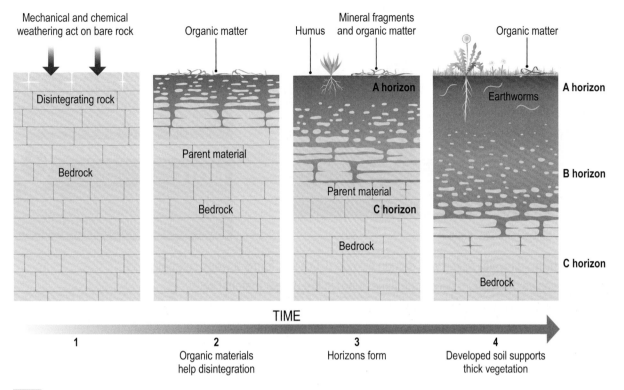

Mechanical and chemical weathering act on bare rock

Disintegrating rock

Bedrock

Organic matter

Parent material

Bedrock

Humus

Mineral fragments and organic matter

A horizon

Parent material

C horizon

Bedrock

Organic matter

Earthworms

A horizon

B horizon

C horizon

Bedrock

TIME

1

2
Organic materials help disintegration

3
Horizons form

4
Developed soil supports thick vegetation

8.4 The formation of soil over time

Time

Soil takes a long time to form: approximately 400 years to create 1 cm of soil. Most soils in Ireland's upland areas are around 10,000 years old, as original soils were removed during glaciations. In lowland areas soils are much older. Soils develop quicker in areas of softer parent material, such as sandstone, than in harder areas, such as granite.

Soil processes

Not all soils are the same. They undergo different biological, physical and chemical processes, which result in them developing different characteristics. Some of the most common processes active in soils today are described below.

Weathering

The parent material of the soil is broken down into mineral matter by the processes of physical and chemical weathering.

- **Mechanical (physical) weathering** involves the processes of freeze-thaw action (frost shattering) and exfoliation (onion layer weathering), which result in the parent material being shattered and exposed to further weathering. It is broken down into pieces of scree, but the mineral make-up of the pieces of rock have not changed. This type of weathering is most common in climates of extremes.
  - **Freeze-thaw action** is most common not only in extreme climates but also in upland areas, where temperatures regularly go above and below freezing.
  - **Exfoliation** is most common in desert regions, where there is a large diurnal temperature range.
- **Chemical weathering** is the decomposition of the parent material through chemical processes that alter the soil's characteristics.

- **Carbonation:** rainwater mixes with carbon dioxide (CO_2) and forms a weak carbonic acid, which dissolves the calcium carbonate (limestone) in the parent material soil.
- **Hydrolysis:** the process whereby parent material in soil that is derived from granite is broken down into kaolin clay by the breakdown of the rock's natural cement feldspar.
- **Oxidation:** the process whereby iron in the soil once exposed to oxygen in the air turns into iron oxide, which is a reddish-brown colour. Tropical red soils are an example of this.

Erosion

Agents of erosion can both help and hinder the formation of soils.

- **Rivers** deposit **fertile alluvial soils** on their floodplains. These soils are made of fine particles of clay and silt and make for rich farming areas.
- **Winds** (aeolian) deposit **fertile loess soils** across the Northern European Plain but in areas of severe drought they can harm soils as they remove the fertile top layers.
- **Glaciers** deposited rich layers of boulder clay thousands of years ago, such as in the Golden Vale, Co. Tipperary. Again these glaciers have also been responsible for the removal of soil, especially in the West of Ireland, and the formation of sandy infertile outwash plains in the Curragh, Co. Kildare.

Leaching

Leaching is the process whereby **soluble minerals and nutrients are washed out of reach of plant roots** in the A horizon after heavy rainfall. It is most common in upland areas. The minerals gather and form an impermeable layer – a **hardpan** – between the A and B horizons and because of this, waterlogging of the soil can also occur. **This can make the soil infertile.** Leaching of pesticides and fertilizers from the soil can pollute nearby water sources.

Metres

Humus

Water soaks down through soil

Hardpan

Parent material

A horizon

B horizon

C horizon

8.6 Leaching can lead to waterlogging. How did this occur?

Podzolisation

Podzolisation is a **severe form of leaching**. Podzols form under coniferous trees, mainly in upland areas where there is a lack of organic material. These areas often experience heavy rainfall. As the water seeps through the soil it can become very **acidic**, with a pH of 4.5 due to the acidic nature of the trees' organic material. This causes problems for the soil, as the acidic water can dissolve many of the nutrients found there, making them **infertile**. The A horizon is often an ash-grey in colour, as it is washed of its nutrients with the exception of quartz the mineral found in granite. **Hardpans** can develop in these soils and waterlogging can also be a problem, as hardpans are impermeable.

Laterisation

Laterisation is another type of **extreme leaching**, but it is found in tropical and equatorial regions. High temperatures and heavy rainfall contribute to rapid chemical weathering and leaching in these regions. Only large concentrations of iron and aluminum oxides remain in these soils and when exposed to the air they undergo oxidation (rusting). This gives the soils their reddish-brown colour. **Latosols** or **tropical red soils** develop.

Humification

Humification is the process that causes the **breakdown and decomposition of organic matter** in the soil into fertile humus. It is a gel-like substance that increases the soil's ability to hold water. The organic matter is broken down by micro-organisms such as bacteria and fungi. Oxygen and rainwater are also needed for humification to take place. During this process, **nutrients are converted into soluble form** so that they can be easily absorbed by plant roots. In areas of high temperatures and high rainfall, humification is accelerated: for example in tropical regions. In Ireland it is quite slow and can take up to 10 years. In cold climates the process can stop altogether, and dead plant and animal material can lie preserved in permafrost.

Calcification

Calcification occurs in areas that suffer from low levels of precipitation, for example in the interiors of continents. Evaporation is higher than precipitation and water is drawn up through the soil by capillary action. A **layer of calcium carbonate** collects close to the soil surface: in the A horizon it helps to make the soil fertile and encourage plant growth, but if the soils bake in direct sunlight the layer of calcium cannot be penetrated, making the soils infertile. Such soils are alkaline, with a pH of above 7. **Chernozem** or 'black earths' of the prairies in the USA are an example.

Salinisation

In hot climates, such as deserts or semi-desert regions, water is drawn up through the soil by **capillary action**. The water contains dissolved salts. The water evaporates, leaving behind a layer of salt. This eventually forms

GEOTERMS
o **Capillary action** is the upward movement of water.
o **Permafrost** is the top layer of soil in a boreal or tundra climate that remains frozen for most of the year.

QUICK QUESTIONS
1. What is the main difference between mechanical/physical and chemical weathering?
2. What are podzols? (Timed activity: 8 min; 4 SRPs)
3. Why is the humification process faster in equatorial regions than in Ireland?
4. What is the difference between calcification and salinisation?
5. How can irrigation cause salinisation?

8.7 An example of salinisation

a **hard toxic white crust** on the surface of the soil that poisons plants, making the land sterile. Irrigation water can also cause salinisation. It introduces extra water to the area, causing the water table to rise. This in turn brings dissolved salts to the surface, killing plants. It is a major problem in heavily **irrigated areas** of the world, such as California in the USA.

Classifications of soils

Climate has a major influence on the formation of soils and soil-forming processes.

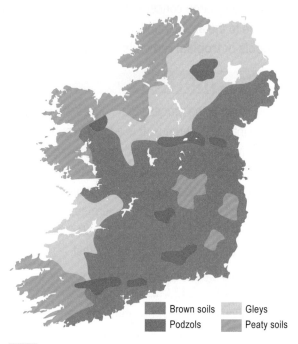

- Different soils are created in different climatic regions of the world. These are called **zonal soils**, as they occupy a large zone or region of the Earth's surface. They are mature soils and have well-developed soil profiles that have formed over a long period of time. One of the zonal soil types in Ireland, associated with the cool temperate oceanic climate, is **brown earth**.

- Within the world's climatic zones, there can be variations in local factors such as relief and climate. These can have a major impact on drainage, parent material and vegetation in the area. These factors in turn can affect the soil, leading to variations between it and the major soil of the region. As a result, **intrazonal soils** can develop. These are zonal soils that display slightly altered characteristics. **Peaty soils** are an example of an intrazonal soil in Ireland. They were once brown earths that have remained waterlogged.

Brown soils	Gleys
Podzols	Peaty soils

8.8 The main soil types found in Ireland

- **Azonal soils** develop when soils are too immature to have developed fully into zonal soils. These soils do not have well-developed soil profiles and were only recently deposited by agents of erosion, such as wind, sea, ice or rivers. An example of an azonal soil is volcanic or alluvial soils.

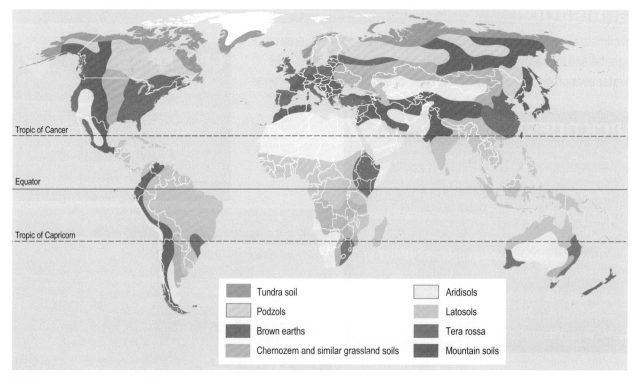

Tundra soil	Aridisols
Podzols	Latosols
Brown earths	Tera rossa
Chernozem and similar grassland soils	Mountain soils

8.9 Global pattern of zonal soils

How zonal soils are related to climate and vegetation zones

Zonal soil	Climate zone	Vegetation zone
Tundra soil	Tundra	Tundra
Podzols	Cold temperate continental	Coniferous forest (taiga)
Brown earths	Cool temperate oceanic	Deciduous forest
Chernozems/grassland soils	Warm temperate rainy and steppe	Grasslands
Aridisols (desert and semi-desert soils)	Desert/semi-desert	Desert/semi-desert
Terra rossa	Mainly warm temperate oceanic	Mainly Mediterranean
Latosols/tropical red soils	Equatorial/tropical	Rainforest
Mountain soils	Mountain climate	Mountain vegetation

Table 8.1 List of main zonal soils

Irish soil type: Brown earths

- Brown earths are zonal soils that develop in regions that were once covered by deciduous forest, such as oak and ash. These regions are normally located between latitudes 40 N to 60 N and have **cool temperate oceanic climates**, with temperature ranges from 5 to 17°C and approximately 1,500 mm of rainfall per year. There is also a long growing season due to these mild weather conditions. Brown earths are the most common soil type found in Ireland. They are loamy soils that developed from the **glacial till** deposited in the region at the end of the last ice age.

- Brown earths are **very fertile** with high levels of humification. This is due to a large volume of decaying foliage (leaf fall) found in these areas, especially in autumn. Therefore brown earths have a **high humus and nutrient content**. They are dark brown in colour and there can be little visible difference between the A and B horizons, as both are very fertile. Owing to moderate temperatures, biological activity can take place for at least nine months of the year in these soils. Micro-organisms and earthworms are needed to help break down the organic matter and mix it in the soil. Insect burrows can also be used to aerate the soil and allow water to pass freely through it.

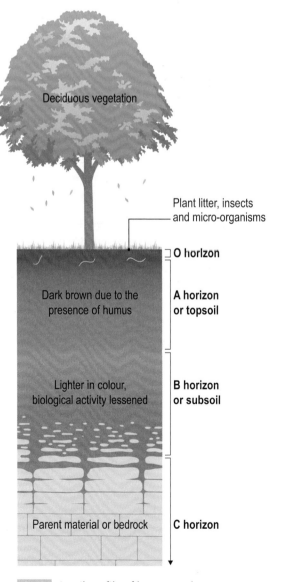

Deciduous vegetation

Plant litter, insects and micro-organisms

O horizon

Dark brown due to the presence of humus — A horizon or topsoil

Lighter in colour, biological activity lessened — B horizon or subsoil

Parent material or bedrock — C horizon

8.10 A soil profile of brown earth

EXAM HINTS

The exam papers often ask you to focus on a study of one named soil type in your answer. Brown earths could be examined under the three headings 'inorganic (parent) material', 'organic material' and 'limited leaching'.

GEOTERMS

Till is the material deposited by a glacier.

- Brown earths develop in areas of moderate rainfall and are not heavily leached; therefore they are **free draining** as hardpans have not developed. Brown earths have a good crumb structure because of the presence of humus, which binds the soil particles (peds) together. These normally have four horizons and are slightly acidic, with a pH level of between 5 and 7.

- Brown earths are **suitable for farming** both tillage and pasture as long as crop rotation is carried out. The soils are easily worked all year round and are highly productive. Fertility of these soils can be maintained with the addition of lime, artificial fertilisers and manure.

- Three variations in brown earths have occurred in Ireland:

  ○ **Acidic brown earths:** these occur on land over 500 m above sea level with bedrocks of sandstone or granite. They have a low pH and are very acidic due to increased rainfall.

  ○ **Podzolic brown earths:** these are brown earths that have become slightly leached, so they are paler in colour. These are found on limestone lowland areas that are covered in boulder clay. They cover 22 per cent of the country.

  ○ **Shallow brown earths:** these soils are no more than 50 cm deep and are found in limestone areas such as the Burren in Co. Clare. They can also be referred to as **rendzina soils**.

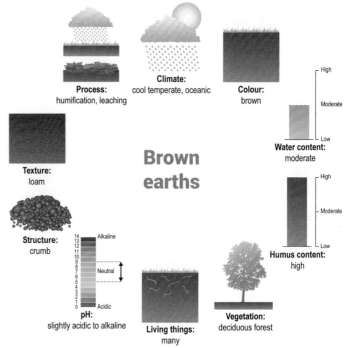

8.11 The main characteristics of brown earths

NOTE

This section links to Chapter 14: Irish core region: The Dublin region in *Horizons* Book 1.

Subcontinental soil: Aridisols

The subcontinental region that we have studied is **India**. One of the soil types found in the north-west of this region, especially near to the Thar Desert, is **aridisol**. We will examine this soil type in more detail in Chapter 9, as it is the soil type of the Sahel, but the main characteristics of aridisols are as follows:

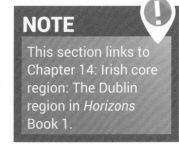

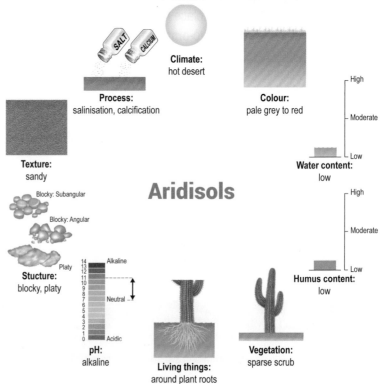

8.12 The main characteristics of aridisols

- They occur in **hot, dry conditions**.
- They are **poorly developed**.
- They are **light grey** in colour.
- Their **humus is limited** due to the nearly complete absence of vegetation.
- They contain abundant nutrients so **rapid growth** can occur in these soils **after rainfall**.
- **Salinisation** is a problem.

Human interference with soil characteristics

Soil is a valuable natural resource but only if it is managed properly. Vegetation cover helps to protect the soil but when this is removed the soil is open to **erosion by water, wind and ice**. The rate of soil erosion in the world today is accelerated by the impact of climate change on vulnerable areas of the planet. These areas experience extremes of **drought and flooding**.

Humans are one of the biggest threats to the world's soils through mismanagement, extensive forest clearances and poor farming practices. **Overgrazing, overcropping and deforestation** are three of the main causes of extensive soil erosion across the world. These practices can damage soil structure and change soil characteristics. Soil erosion is a worldwide problem, as up to 10 million hectares of soil lose some of its fertility annually.

The Burren, Ireland

The Burren in Co. Clare is a region that suffers from poor-quality soil, but this was not always the case. Given the extensive megalithic tombs from Neolithic times and settlement features from the Celtic period in the area, it is safe to assume that this region was once able to sustain a higher population density than today. It also appears to have been farmed successfully in the past.

8.13 Soil erosion can be caused by overgrazing, overcropping and deforestation

Degradation of soil resources in this region has occurred. It is believed that this happened due to two main factors: climatic and human. The region experiences a higher than average level of rainfall than the rest of Ireland, leaving the soil open to raindrop and gully erosion. The farmers of the area are also believed to have overgrazed and overcultivated the land over thousands of years, leaving the soil and underlying limestone rock exposed to the harsh elements of the region.

8.14 A megalithic tomb in the Burren, Co. Clare. Why do you think this landscape was unable to sustain a large population?

Gujarat and Rajasthan, India

In north-west India the regions of Gujarat and Rajasthan are under threat from **soil erosion** as sands from the nearby Thar Desert are blown into the area. People of the region are dying of starvation as drought-stricken fields are unable to produce crops. Monsoon rains did not reach the area for many years until the floods that affected Pakistan and nearby regions of India in 2010. In 2015 further monsoon rains killed 50 people in the Gujarat region and created dangerous landslides in the Darjeeling tea-growing region of India.

Rajasthan was once a relatively prosperous area with a largely rural society. The ecological balance of the region was upset as deforestation increased to make way for settlement and farming. Cash crops were introduced to the region by the Indian Government to earn badly needed foreign income. Unfortunately this led to **monoculture** and the further degradation of the region's soils.

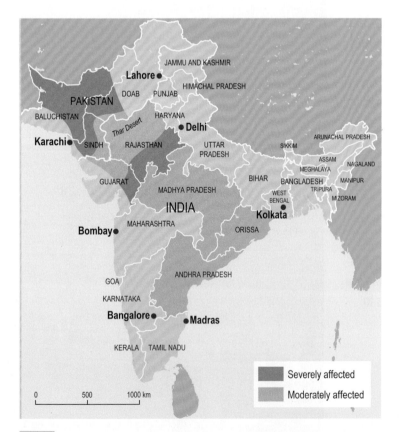

8.15 The regions of India affected by soil erosion and desertification

GEOTERMS abc

- **Gully erosion** is when fast-moving water concentrates on a small area and carves out channels in the land.
- **Soil degradation** is destruction caused to the quality of soil.
- **Monoculture** is when the same crop is grown every year.

CASE STUDY 8.1
Desertification and the Sahel

Desertification is the **spreading of the deserts**. Its impact has increased in recent years because of climate change and human interaction with regions.

- Climate change has caused world **rainfall levels to decrease** by one-third in the last 20 years.

- Rising temperatures have led to **higher rates of evaporation**.

- **Droughts** have occurred, for example in 1968 and 1973 in the Sahel and other parts of Africa.

- Cattle dung was once used to fertilise the land. It is now used as a fuel because of lack of trees in the area. Owing to **lack of humus** in the ground and **expensive fertilisers**, the soil quickly lost its nutrients and became sterile. The lands were abandoned and open to desertification.

- Competition for grazing lands and the need for more land to harvest the same amount of crops led to **vegetation being removed from marginal land**, and these areas were also brought under cultivation. Local people are also being pushed to more marginal lands to grow crops to support their own families. These lands are the most vulnerable to desertification. Once sand has encroached on farmland in these areas it cannot be brought back under cultivation again.

- A **high birth rate** and a **falling death rate** has led to a 2 per cent population growth per year. Therefore parts of the Sahel are overpopulated, which is placing extra pressures on the limited natural resources of the area such as food and fuel.

The Sahel is a **semi-arid region of Africa** located directly south of the Sahara Desert and runs for approximately 4,000 km. It takes in many countries, including large parts of Mali, Chad and Sudan. The Sahel was originally a grassland savannah biome and it is now being converted into a **hot desert biome**. The region experiences both extremes of heat and a more temperate climate throughout the year with rains falling as a monsoon between May and October, the growing season. The Sahel supports a nomadic pastoral-based society.

- From the 1960s onwards rain in the Sahel has decreased and the area suffers from drought conditions.

- Seasonal rains are becoming less reliable and in the last 20 years alone they have reduced by 30 per cent.

- Soils are unable to support vegetation. The area has become increasingly barren as the

EXAM HINTS

This is linked to the case study on the Sahel in Chapter 2: Overpopulation

8.16 Cracked earth due to drought. What has happened to the soil?

8.17 A farmer with his herd of zebu cattle. What problems will this farmer encounter in the Sahel?

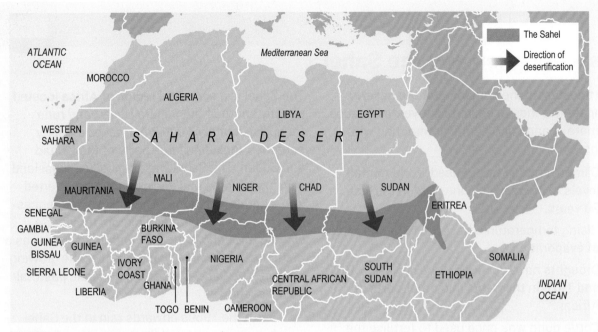

8.18 The Sahel region of Africa

prevailing winds have blown away the region's topsoil.

- The Sahara Desert is spreading at a rate of 5 to 10 km per year into this vulnerable area.

Human interaction has also contributed to desertification in the Sahel in the following ways.

Overgrazing

From the 1930s to the 1970s, the Sahel region of Africa received wetter weather than usual and people were attracted to the region.

- The population of the region increased by one-third due to **high birth rates**. The number of cattle in the Sahel doubled, as the local people of the area measure their wealth by the number of cattle a person owns. Therefore **overgrazing** of the region took place as the Sahel contained more animals than it had the potential to sustain. The vegetation cover was lost and the soil became exposed to the elements. It was now open to **aeolian and raindrop erosion**.
- The nomadic practices of the people of the region changed as they began to **settle in one area**. Herders were also encouraged by the African Government to remain longer in one area and wells were created as drinking holes for cattle. Farmers also began to practise a more sedentary style of farming by fencing off areas to allow cattle to graze the land more intensively as the **fallow year was abandoned**. This groundwater took centuries

to accumulate and was being used up at an alarming rate. As rainfall in the Sahel had decreased, the groundwater was not being replenished. Wells of the areas dried up as the region's water table dropped. The ground

GEOTERMS

- A **prevailing** wind is a wind that is most common to that region.
- A **savannah** is a mix of grass with sparse woodland.
- A **biome** is a major world region that has its own unique climate, soil type, flora and fauna.
- A **monsoon** is a period of seasonal heavy rainfall.

EXAM HINTS

If the exam question looks for two ways in which soils have been eroded, overgrazing and overcropping could be examined under one heading as 'poor farm practices' and 'deforestation' under the other.

INTERESTING FACTS

The word Sahel means 'shore' in Arabic.

around the wells has also been open to compaction by the presence of many animals.

- Large numbers of animals in the region also helped to compact the soil, making it harder for rainwater to infiltrate the land. This increased **surface run-off** and, in turn, increased **soil erosion** in the area.

Overcropping

As the population of the Sahel increased, so did demand for food. For example, in the last 50 years the area devoted to crops has trebled. This has caused continuous farming of the land.

- The **fallow year** was abandoned to increase the production of food in the short term – the soil was not left to rest or not fertilised properly. For example, in Niger if groundnuts (peanuts) are grown for 3 years in a row the soil must be left fallow for the following 6 years if they hope for it to replenish its nutrients properly.

- In the 1960s, countries of the Sahel received cheap loans, which they cannot now repay. They are regarded as a **highly indebted poor country** (HIPC). For such countries to qualify for debt relief they must put more of their land under **cash crops**, such was cotton. Huge plantations have been set up in the region to produce these crops. The crops are then sold on the world market to pay off national debts.

- This growth of cash crops has led to **monoculture** in the region and the **degradation of the Sahel's soil**.

- This has caused local farmers to cultivate more marginal lands to feed their own families. The soil of these areas are not mature and lose their nutrients very quickly, becoming barren and leading to **crop failure and desertification**.

Deforestation

Trees, small bushes and scrub vegetation are cut down in the Sahel region for firewood, building materials and to make way for agriculture. In Mali alone half a million hectares of trees have been cleared.

- The demand for wood in the Sahel increased as the population of the region also

8.19 Overgrazing contributes to soil erosion in the Sahel region

increased. Trees are being cut down by the **slash and burn** method 30 times faster than they are being replaced. The people of this region do not have the resources to replant the trees.

- **Trees are invaluable** to this region as they act as barriers to prevent wind and raindrop erosion. Their roots help to bind the soil and prevent further erosion. The leaf litter continually fertilises the soil and when the tree dies it adds valuable nutrients to the soil. Trees also absorb water during periods of heavy rainfall.

GEOTERMS

- **Fallow** is the stage in crop rotation when the land is not used to grow crops.
- **Slash and burn** is cutting down trees and burning their stumps and surrounding vegetation.

EXAM HINTS

Reference can be made to the texture, colour and structure of the soils in the Sahel and how desertification, farming practices and climate change have affected them in exam answers on this section.

Soil conservation

If managed properly, soil is a **sustainable resource**. There are methods that can be put in place to prevent soil erosion. The method chosen should be appropriate to the technology and skills base available in the region.

Contour ploughing

Contour ploughing is done in line with the contours of the field across rather than up and down. During heavy rainfall the water is trapped in the furrows and has time to soak in, **reducing soil erosion** in the area. Soil and vegetation quality is also improved due to increased water infiltration. Soil erosion in an area can be reduced by up to 50 per cent by contour ploughing. Ploughing should not be carried out in dry weather, to reduce the risk of wind erosion of loose soil. It is more dangerous than traditional ploughing but new hydraulic equipment on tractors is making it safer, and it is used widely in Europe and Midwest USA.

Terracing

This is put in place in areas that are too steep for contour ploughing. A series of small walls is built along a hill slope, similar to steps of a stairs and behind it the land is flattened and planted. There is a lip or bund at the edge of each step that traps water and allows it time to soak or percolate into the soil. This **prevents gully erosion and leaching** in the area by surface run-off. The building and maintenance of these terraces is labour intensive, but they are used widely in upland areas of China and Vietnam. It prevents monsoon rains from severely degrading the soil resources of the regions.

8.20 Terracing on steep slopes in China

Shelter belts and strip farming

Trees or shelter belts are planted as a **barrier around fields** to prevent sands blowing across crops and destroying them. The trees break the force of the wind and their roots help to bind the soil. Studies have shown in West Africa that their presence can increase crop yields by up to 20 per cent. If fruit trees are planted, they are another source of humus and food. Some of the trees can be trimmed and thinned to provide firewood, but full deforestation of an area should be carried out in a sustainable fashion, by cutting and replanting trees (**afforestation**) at a sustainable rate.

The field in the centre of the shelter belts or windbreakers can be divided up into widely spaced rows and planted; the gaps are filled with a different crop. This allows the entire field to be under cultivation at once, but the soil does not become exhausted as the crops use different minerals and nutrients from the ground.

Farmers are encouraged to plant different crops in the same areas of the field every three years so that different minerals are removed from the ground. During the fourth year the field is left fallow (no crops, just grass) and this allows time for the minerals in the soil to regenerate. This process helps to keep the soil healthy and fertile.

Stone lines

Lines of stones are evenly placed along upland fields to **prevent surface run-off** removing the top layer of soil. The rain gathers behind the stone, allowing it time to percolate into the soil and nourish the plants in the area. It also helps to feed the water table below ground and prevent long-term soil erosion of the area. It is most effective on gentle slopes. The stone lines take up 2 per cent of the land but can increase crop yields by 50 per cent. They are used extensively in Burkina Faso and are made of raw materials found locally. The stones lines also help to trap seeds and organic material that can decay and add valuable nutrients to the soil.

8.21 Stone lines

New breeds of animals

Smaller, better quality breeds of animals decrease the number of animals in a region and **reduce the risk of overgrazing**. These breeds produce more milk and meat, which means that fewer animals are required.

QUICK QUESTIONS

1. What are the main threats to soils of the world today?
2. What are the main causes of soil erosion in the Rajasthan region of India?
3. What problems did increased numbers of cattle have on the Sahel region of Africa?
4. What is monoculture and how did the introduction of cash crops accelerate monoculture?
5. Name and explain two methods of soil conservation. (Timed activity: 10 min; 10 SRPs)

QUESTIONS

Higher Level – Long Questions
Geoecology

EXAM HINTS

All questions are worth 80 marks and require an essay-style answer. Your answer should include:

- An introduction: lay out all the material that will be covered later in the essay.
- Three to four paragraphs: each should focus on a new aspect of the answer; there should be six to eight SRPs in each paragraph.
- A conclusion: draw together all the information that was discussed in the essay.

1. Explain how soil characteristics impact on soil development.

   2014, Section 3, Q16, 80 marks

The marking scheme for a question like this on a Higher Level paper is as follows:

3 aspects identified @ 4 m each	**12 marks**
Discussion: 8 SRPs @ 2 m each per aspect	**48 marks**
Overall coherence	**20 marks**
Total	**80 marks**
4 aspects identified @ 3 m each	**12 marks**
Discussion: 6 SRPs @ 2 m each per aspect	**48 marks**
Overall coherence	**20 marks**
Total	**80 marks**

2. Soil profiles are the result of the operation of soil forming processes. Discuss.

   2014, Section 3, Q17, 80 marks

3. Examine how desertification and conservation have impacted on soil characteristics.

   2013, Section 3, Q16, 80 marks

4. Explain how weathering, leaching and podzolisation have impacted on the characteristics of soil.

   2012, Section 3, Q16, 80 marks

5. Discuss how human activities can accelerate soil erosion.

   2012, Section 3, Q17, 80 marks

EXAM HINTS

The 2007 Chief Examiner's report mentioned that some students failed to go into enough detail on a specific soil type. They gave only a general account of soils.

HOT TOPICS IN THE EXAMS

1. The Sahel
2. Soil-forming processes
3. A detailed account of one soil type, e.g. brown earths

Chapter 7 Soils
Chapter 9 Biomes
Chapter 10 Human interaction with biomes

Mind map

Aridisols (subcontinental soil)

- Hot dry conditions
- Poorly developed
- Light grey
- Limited humus
- Rapid growth after rainfall

Soil processes

Weathering
- Physical: exfoliation and freeze-thaw
- Chemical: carbonation, hydrolysis, oxidation

Erosion
- Breakdown and removal of soils, water, ice, air
- Deposition of fertile soils

Leaching
- Washing nutrients out of reach of roots

Podzolisation
- Severe leaching under coniferous trees, hardpan

Laterisation
- Extreme leaching, tropical regions, formation of tropical red soils/latosols

Humification
- Creation of humus

Calcification
- Capillary action brings calcium carbonate to the surface, beneficial to plants

Salinisation
- Salts brought to the surface, harmful

Brown earths (Irish soil)

- Zonal soils under deciduous forest
- Cool temperate oceanic climate
- Most common Irish soil type
- Fertile, dark brown, high humus
- Crumb structure, loamy, slightly acidic, easily worked, productive
- Biological activity, aerate and mix, 9 mth
- Acidic brown earths: low pH
- Podzolic brown earths: leached
- Shallow brown earths

Classification of soils

Zonal soils
- Well-developed soils linked to a climatic region

Intrazonal soils
- Variations in local factors leads to slightly altered zonal soils

Azonal soils
- Immature soils that are not fully developed, recently deposited

Soil characteristics

Soil-forming factors

Parent material
- Natural resource
- Original bedrock
- Material transported by agents

Climate
- Precipitation and temperature

Topography
- Higher altitude poor, thin
- Lower altitude good, deep
- Aspect north cold, south warm

Biological activity
- Humus formation
- Animals aerate and mix
- Vegetation, roots bind soil – plant litter

Human interference
- Add fertilisers, drainage and irrigation schemes
- Or remove organic matter/foliage protection

Time
- 400 years for 1 cm

The Sahel

Soil erosion
- Semi-arid, south of Sahara, nomadic society, drought

Overgrazing
- Population increased by one-third
- Cattle = wealth, pressure on soil
- Wells, compacted soil

Overcropping
- HIPC, cash crops, monoculture
- No fertiliser, dung used as fuel, no fallow year

Deforestation
- Firewood, building material
- Don't have resources to replant
- Aeolian erosion

Desertification
- Rainfall decreased by one-third
- Higher evaporation
- Droughts 1968 and 1973
- Marginal lands used
- Spreading of deserts onto farms
- Rapid population growth
- 5–10 km per year

Soil conservation
- Contour ploughing: across field, allows infiltration
- Terracing: steeper hills, bunds, soaks, prevents gully erosion
- Shelter belts and strip farming: trees barrier around field, different crops In strips
- Stone lines: appropriate technology, prevents leaching
- New breeds of animals: healthier, need fewer

9 Biomes

 SYLLABUS LINK

The pattern of world climates has given rise to distinctive biomes. These biomes are world regions characterised by groups of plants and animals adapted to specific conditions of climate, soil and biotic interrelationships.

By the end of this chapter, students will have studied:

◉ The nine main biomes of the world
◉ The origins of the desert biome
◉ The main characteristics of the desert biome
◉ How climate, soil type, flora and fauna of the desert biome are interrelated

Introduction

A biome is a major world region that has its own unique climate, soil type, flora and fauna. The overall controlling factor of any biome is **climate**. It controls the distribution and the location of all biomes. There are **nine main biomes** in the world today and all aspects of the biomes are interrelated. Many biomes around the world have been altered by human activities.

NOTE

This section should be allowed at least eight class periods (40 minutes).

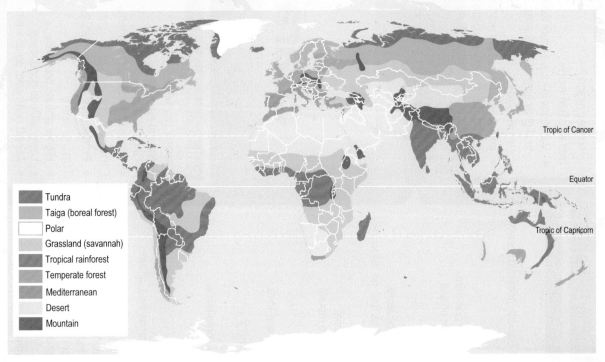

Legend:
- Tundra
- Taiga (boreal forest)
- Polar
- Grassland (savannah)
- Tropical rainforest
- Temperate forest
- Mediterranean
- Desert
- Mountain

Tropic of Cancer
Equator
Tropic of Capricorn

9.1 The major biomes of the world

EXAM HINTS

Biomes are a very popular topic on the exam paper.

 INTERESTING FACTS

Traditionally a biome is named after the original vegetation of the region. For example, Taiga is named after the taiga forests located there.

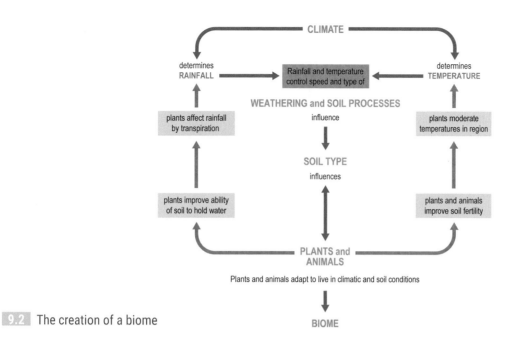

```
                              CLIMATE
        ┌────────────────────────┴────────────────────────┐
        ▼                        ▲   │   ▲                 ▼
   determines          ┌─────────────────────────┐    determines
   RAINFALL    ───────▶│ Rainfall and temperature │◀─  TEMPERATURE
        ▲              │ control speed and type of │        ▲
        │              └─────────────────────────┘         │
┌──────────────────┐     WEATHERING and SOIL PROCESSES  ┌──────────────────┐
│ plants affect    │              influence             │ plants moderate  │
│ rainfall         │                 │                  │ temperatures in  │
│ by transpiration │                 ▼                  │ region           │
└──────────────────┘             SOIL TYPE              └──────────────────┘
        ▲                        influences                     ▲
        │                            ▲                          │
┌──────────────────┐                 │                  ┌──────────────────┐
│ plants improve   │                 ▼                  │ plants and       │
│ ability of soil  │                                    │ animals improve  │
│ to hold water    │                                    │ soil fertility   │
└──────────────────┘                                    └──────────────────┘
        ▲              PLANTS and                               ▲
        └──────────────ANIMALS──────────────────────────────────┘

        Plants and animals adapt to live in climatic and soil conditions
                                 │
                                 ▼
                               BIOME
```

9.2 The creation of a biome

Desert biome

A desert biome can be defined as 'an arid region that is characterised by little or no rainfall, in which vegetation is scarce or absent, unless it has specially adapted' (*Dictionary of Physical Geography*). Many of the world's deserts are located between 15° and 30° north and south of the equator. An example is the Sahara.

- **Not all deserts are sandy.** Sandy deserts account for only 10 per cent of the world's deserts. Most are bare rock.

- **Not all deserts are hot.** For example, the Gobi Desert is cold, with temperatures in the winter falling to as low as −40°C. Desert regions experience a large diurnal temperature range, which can be up to 30°C. This is why geographers often say 'night is the winter of the desert'. Desert regions can experience temperatures of up to 45°C when the sun is high in the sky and its rays are concentrated on a small area of land, giving great heat. Deserts have no cloud cover. This causes high temperatures during the day but rapid heat loss during the night.

- **All deserts are dry**, some receiving as little as 1 cm of rainfall a year. The rainfall is unpredictable and can often occur in short, heavy downpours called 'desert storms'. Most of this much needed moisture can be lost through evaporation and the inability of the rain to infiltrate the hard soil. Rapid run-off can lead to flash flooding and **gully erosion**. Evaporation rates in deserts can often be higher than precipitation levels. Cold deserts are also dry, as precipitation is often in solid form, such as snow, and if temperatures do not reach **ablation** levels, the snow will not provide water for plants and animals to use.

9.3 A desert region

GEOTERMS

- **Diurnal temperature variation** is the change in temperature over a 24-hour period, from the high temperatures during the day to the cool temperatures at night.
- **Gullying** is when heavy rainfall run-off erodes small channels into the soil surface.
- **Ablation** is the temperature point that needs to be reached for ice to melt.

- There are three main types of desert:
  - **Extremely arid:** almost no precipitation over a 12-month period
  - **Arid:** less than 250 mm annually
  - **Semi-arid:** 250–500 mm annually

We will focus on the **hot desert biome** in this section.

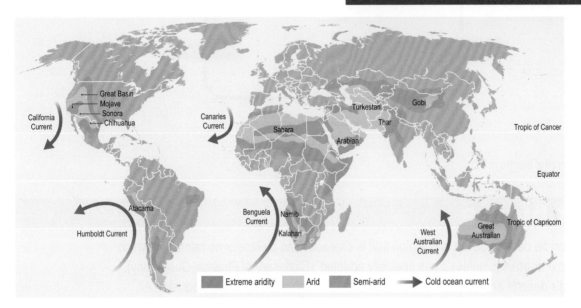

9.4 The desert biomes of the world including cold ocean currents

The main characteristics of the hot desert biome

Climate

Dry trade winds

Most deserts of the world are **located between 15° ad 30° north and south of the equator**. They have low levels of rainfall, with a maximum of 250 mm per year, and high evaporation rates because of the effects of the global wind patterns on the region.

- Warm air rises at the equator; warm air can hold moisture.
- As it continues to rise, it cools and condenses, forming **convectional rain** over equatorial regions.
- At approximately 30° north and south of the equator (horse latitudes) the air has been cooled. It starts to fall, as cold air is heavier than warm air.
- As it descends, the air becomes a **warm, dry wind** that blows over these areas, bringing desert conditions as it absorbs rather than releases moisture. The region also experiences **clear,**

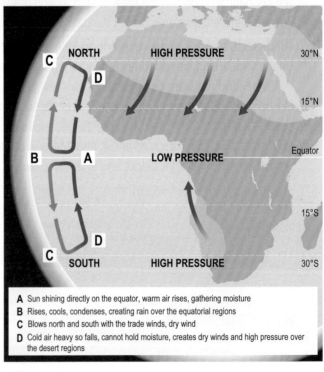

A Sun shining directly on the equator, warm air rises, gathering moisture
B Rises, cools, condenses, creating rain over the equatorial regions
C Blows north and south with the trade winds, dry wind
D Cold air heavy so falls, cannot hold moisture, creates dry winds and high pressure over the desert regions

9.5 High-pressure belts and trade winds

cloudless skies and **maximum sunshine** (90 per cent), as the sun is directly overhead, with **low humidity** levels (10 per cent).

- The cycle continues as air moves from this high-pressure system found at the horse latitudes to the low-pressure system of the equator as part of the **trade wind system**.

Rain-shadow effect

Some of the world's deserts occur on the **western edges of continents**.

- As **moisture-laden winds** move inland from the ocean, they have to rise over coastal mountains. This causes the air to cool and condense, forming rain.

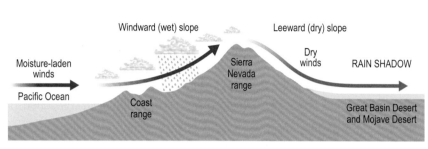

- All the winds' moisture is lost on the **windward side** of the mountain range.

9.6 Relief rainfall and the rain-shadow effect

- The winds then blow over the **leeward side** of the mountain range as dry winds. Desert conditions can develop here, as can be seen in the Mojave Desert, USA. This is referred to as the **rain-shadow effect**.

Influence of cold ocean currents

As mentioned above, some deserts form on the western edges of continents. This is also due to the influence of cold ocean currents.

- As moisture-laden coastal winds move in over cold ocean currents (the Canaries Current, for example), they are **cooled**.
- Cold air cannot hold much moisture, so any moisture is lost at sea in the form of **coastal fog**.
- The air then blows inland as **dry, warm prevailing winds** that take up any moisture in the area, creating desert conditions over the regions in which they blow.

Continentality

Some deserts form in the interior of continents.

- Moisture-laden winds blow in from the oceans and by the time they reach the interior of the continents they have lost most of their moisture.
- Then they are warmed by the sunshine and blow as **warm, dry winds** in these regions, adding to the desert conditions experienced there. An example of this is the Sahara Desert in Africa.

If rains do come to the hot desert biome they are short, heavy, unpredictable downpours that do not have time to infiltrate the soil. They often create **flash flooding** in localised areas.

9.7 The rocky Mojave Desert in California

QUICK QUESTIONS

1. Define the term *desert biome*.
2. What are the main characteristics of a desert region?
3. How can a cold desert such as the Gobi Desert also suffer from drought?
4. How can cold ocean currents create desert conditions?
5. Draw a labelled diagram of relief rainfall. (Timed activity: 3 min)

Soil

Characteristics

The dominant soil type of the desert region is **aridisols**. These are dry soils that occur in regions of very low precipitation levels. The texture of the soil type ranges from fine and sandy to coarse and gravelly. These soils originated in mountainous regions thousands of years ago.

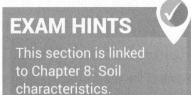

EXAM HINTS

This section is linked to Chapter 8: Soil characteristics.

- The **coarser-grained** aridisols are found close to the lower slopes of the mountains. These are unable to hold moisture and tend to be infertile. These soils originated from rocks that had undergone the weathering process of exfoliation. Extremes in temperature caused the rocks in the region to rapidly expand and contract on a frequent basis, until eventually pieces of rock broke off to become sand particles, the main component of aridisols.

- The **finer-grained** materials have been moved further on to lowland basins by torrential downpours and dry winds. Here there is deep soil cover, but these soils do not favour the growth of a wide variety of plants.

Few desert regions have deep soil cover, as most are rocky or stony.

Lack of vegetation

Aridisols are **poorly developed** and there is no noticeable A horizon due to little organic matter in the region. Both the A and B horizons have a **high mineral content**, giving the soil its light grey colour. The lack of humus in the region also limits the activity of micro-organisms.

Lack of rainfall

Aridisols can be productive soils, as they have abundant nutrients. This is evident **after heavy downpours, when rapid plant growth** occurs. Intensive evaporation in the desert region, however, means that the water does not last long.

9.8 An oasis in a desert

Soil-forming factors

Owing to a lack of rainfall in desert regions, **capillary action** is active on groundwater of the region. Dissolved minerals are present in the groundwater. As it reaches the surface, rapid evaporation occurs, leaving behind a layer of minerals, hindering the growth of plants in the desert.

- Extensive **salt pans** can form if **salinisation** occurs, bringing dissolved salts to the surface. Salt is poisonous to plants, which means nothing can grow in a salt pan.

- If **calcification** occurs, a layer of calcium forms on the surface. As it dries out, it forms a **hardpan** of calcite. This can become impermeable, making it impossible for plant roots to penetrate it.

INTERESTING FACTS

Aridisols show their fertile nature when they burst into life where they have access to a supply of water. A good example of such a water supply is a spring at an oasis.

9.9 Salt pans

Flora (vegetation)

Vegetation in the desert regions is **sparse**, mainly due to a shortage of water, high evaporation rates and a lack of fertile humus in the soil. Plant life in the regions has had to adapt to extremes of heat and drought. **Productivity levels in deserts are low**. The plants are also well spread out to prevent competition for limited resources. The following are the adaptations that have occurred over thousands of years to help plants cope in this harsh environment.

Life cycle

Desert plants have adapted their life cycle to make the most of the **short periods of rainfall** available in the region. Seeds of these fast-growing plants (called **ephemerals**) can lie dormant for many years, protected by a waxy coating. Once the rains arrive, these seeds burst into life, germinating, flowering and producing seeds. This can happen in 2 to 3 weeks following heavy rains, as they have a very short life cycle. An example is the creosote bush of North America. Ephemerals make up to 40 per cent of desert plants.

Succulents

Succulents are plants that have developed various ways to store precious water found in the desert. These plants, such as the cactus, have adapted different ways of storing water.

- They have **fleshy interior**, which acts like a sponge in times of rainfall to soak up extra water.

- The cactus has **grooves** on its trunk that allow it to expand to store more water. These grooves also act as vertical channels, bringing water directly to the root system below. Water can also be stored in **roots** and **underground bulbs**.

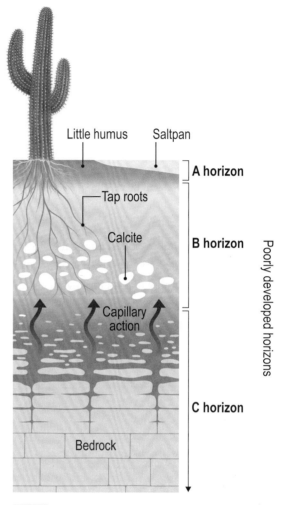

Little humus   Saltpan

A horizon

Tap roots

Calcite

B horizon

Capillary action

C horizon

Bedrock

Poorly developed horizons

9.10 A soil profile of soils found in desert regions – aridisols

9.11 The creosote bush of the North American deserts

9.12 A cactus is a succulent plant

- The cactus has also developed **waxy leaves and stems** that prevent moisture loss.
- They have a thick coating of thin hairs called **trichomes** that traps air around the plant, preventing increased evaporation by moving air.

Root systems

Two root systems have developed in plants of the desert region to help them to adapt to shortages of water.

NOTE

This paragraph can be used to explain how the plants adapt to the depth of soil.

- **Radial roots:** this is the root system used by the cactus. It has shallow roots that are close to the surface and spread out in a radial pattern for great distances around the plant to create a large moisture-collecting area.
- **Tap roots:** this is the root system used by the mesquite bush. It puts all its energy into creating one long root, in some cases up to 50 m long. The tap root is able to penetrate the soil and reach the water table below.

Defensive systems

Many desert plants have developed defensive systems to prevent attack from birds and animals. For example, the cactus has developed **spiky leaves** to prevent its fleshy interior from being eaten. The creosote bush gives off an **unpleasant taste and smell** to deter animals.

QUICK QUESTIONS

1. Why are horizons poorly developed in aridisols?
2. What conditions are needed for salinisation to occur?
3. Define the term *ephemerals*.
4. Describe in detail one example of plants adapting to aridisols in a hot desert biome. (Timed activity: 8 min; 8 SRPs)
5. List four ways that plants have adapted to the unique climatic conditions in a hot desert biome.

INTERESTING FACTS

Some plants, such as the desert dandelion, only bloom at night to avoid the scorching daytime temperatures.

Fauna (animals)

There are few large animals in the desert region, as they are unable to store enough water or withstand the high temperatures. However, like plants, some animals have adapted to deal with the extremes of this biome.

Behaviour

Desert animals have adapted their behaviour to cope with the extremes of the desert climate.

- Some animals, such as the elf owl, are active only at night (**nocturnal**), when temperatures are lower.
- Other animals, such as the desert tortoise, live in **burrows under the ground**, where temperatures are lower (adapting to soil, which is easy to burrow).
- Some animals, such as desert toads, **hibernate** for long periods of time (8 or 9 months of the year) until the desert storms come. Then they mate and lay fertilised eggs within 24 h, and within 2 weeks a new batch of toads emerge.
- Insects and animals such as the jackrabbit follow the **shadows** of larger objects, such as cacti, during the day to keep cool.

9.13 A jackrabbit using the shade to avoid the scorching desert temperatures

Body-form evolution

To survive the desert heat, some animals have evolved characteristics that help them to cope with the extremes of the hot desert climate.

- The desert fox has evolved **paler fur** than its relatives. This has the added advantage of camouflage as well as preventing the animal from taking in too much heat by reflecting the sun's rays (adapting to the colour of the soil).
- Animals have also evolved **long body parts** to help them release heat from their bodies. The jackrabbit and the desert fox have very long ears containing many blood vessels that dilate to release heat, cooling the animal down under the hot desert sun.

9.14 The long ears of the desert fox release heat

9.15 Camels are known as the 'ships of the desert'

The **camel** has adapted in many ways to cope with the desert climate:

- **Fat stores** in its humps, which can be converted into water in times of drought
- **Pads of tough skin** on its knees and belly to enable it to lie on the hot sand (adapting to the soil type)
- **Long eyelashes** to protect the camel's eyes from sandstorms (adapting to the soil type)
- **Wide padded feet** to allow the camel to walk on soft sand without sinking (adapting to the soil type)
- A **tough-skinned mouth** to enable the camel to eat thorny desert plants

Body-function evolution

Desert animals have evolved some rather unusual traits to survive the hot desert biome.

- The desert toad has evolved horns on its hind feet to act as **digging tools** for building burrows to escape the desert sun (adapting to soil type).
- Some animals, such as the desert gazelle and reptiles, preserve water in their bodies by producing **uric acid** instead of urine.
- Other animals, such as the collared lizard, have evolved **waterproof skin** to prevent moisture loss from their bodies.
- Birds of the desert, such as the roadrunner, preserve energy by **not flying**.

INTERESTING FACTS

Camels can drink up to a 100 litres of water at a time and do not sweat, in order to conserve their water supplies.

QUICK QUESTIONS

1. Why can few large animals survive in the desert?
2. What does the term *nocturnal* mean?
3. In what ways has the camel adapted to the harsh climate of the desert region?
4. Why do the desert tortoise and the desert toad burrow underground?
5. Examine the main characteristics of aridisols and explain how this has shaped certain animal adaptations in the hot desert biome? (Timed activity: 3 min; 3 SRPs)

QUESTIONS

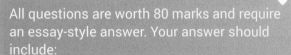

EXAM HINTS ✓

All questions are worth 80 marks and require an essay-style answer. Your answer should include:

- An introduction: lay out all the material that will be covered later in the essay.
- Three to four paragraphs: each should focus on a new aspect of the answer; there should be six to eight SRPs in each paragraph.
- A conclusion: draw together all the information that was discussed in the essay.

1. Examine, with reference to one biome that you have studied, how plants and animals have adapted to specific climatic and soil conditions.

   2015, Section 3, Q18, 80 marks

2. With reference to one biome that you have studied, account for the type of climate experienced in this biome and explain how this climate impacts on soil and vegetation within the biome.

   2013, Section 3, Q17, 80 marks

The marking scheme for a question like this on a Higher Level paper is as follows:	
3 aspects identified @ 4 m each	**12 marks**
Discussion: 8 SRPs @ 2 m each per aspect	**48 marks**
Overall coherence	**20 marks**
Total	**80 marks**
4 aspects identified @ 3 m each	**12 marks**
Discussion: 6 SRPs @ 2 m each per aspect	**48 marks**
Overall coherence	**20 marks**
Total	**80 marks**

3. Examine the characteristics of any one biome that you have studied under three of the following headings:
   - Climate
   - Soils
   - Flora
   - Fauna

   2011, Section 3, Q17, 80 marks

4. Examine the influence of climate on the characteristics of one biome that you have studied.

   2010, Section 3, Q16, 80 marks

5. Describe and explain the main characteristics of one biome that you have studied.

   2008, Section 3, Q18, 80 marks

6. Describe how plant and animal life adapt to soil and climatic conditions in a biome which you have studied.

   2007, Section 3, Q18, 80 marks

7. Examine the main characteristics of a biome that you have studied.

   2006, Section 3, Q17, 80 marks

EXAM HINTS ✓

The 2007 and 2012 Chief Examiner's report mentioned that students did not refer to the question asked and some failed to deal with adaptations of plant and animal life in detail as they concentrated too much on climate.

HOT TOPICS IN THE EXAMS

1. Soil and climatic influences on flora and fauna
2. The main characteristics of a hot desert biome, i.e. soil, climate, flora and fauna

 Chapter 8 Soil characteristics

Mind map

Biomes

Climate

Dry trade winds
- Equator warm air rises = rain
- 30°N/S cools, falls, dry warm air = desert
- Part of trade wind system

Rain-shadow effect
- Warm, moist coastal winds
- Rise over coastal mountains, lose rain
- Desert conditions form on leeward side

Influence of cold ocean currents
- Warm air over sea picks up moisture
- Cools over ocean currents, forms fog
- Moisture lost before winds hit land

Continentality
- Winds of interior warm and dry
- Distance from sea, winds lost moisture

Biomes
- Major world region with own unique climate, soil type, flora fauna
- 9 world biomes

Fauna

Behaviour
- Very few large animals
- Nocturnal, live in burrows
- Hibernate, follow shadows

Body-form evolution
- Jackrabbit: long ears, heat loss, pale fur
- Camel: stores fat, long eyelashes, thick skin, wide feet, tough-skinned mouth

Body-function evolution
- Toad: horns on feet for digging
- Desert gazelle: uric acid instead of urine
- Roadrunner: doesn't fly
- Collared lizard: waterproof skin

Desert biome
- Arid region with little or no rain
- Low 15–30°, mid 30–40°N and S
- 10% sandy, some cold, e.g. Gobi Desert
- Large diurnal temperature range
- Dry, 1 cm rain, desert storms
- Evaporation, inability to infiltrate soil
- Three types:
  - Extremely arid, no rain
  - Arid, less than 250 mm
  - Semi-arid, 250–500 mm

Soils

Characteristics
- Aridisols from mountains
- Coarse, infertile
- Fine, deep soils found in lowland basins

Lack of vegetation
- No A horizon, lack of humus, grey colour

Lack of rainfall
- Very productive after heavy rainfall, high evaporation levels

Soil-forming factors
- Active capillary action
- Salinisation, calcification

Flora

Life cycle
- Vegetation sparse, limited resources
- Fast-growing plants, ephemerals 40%, creosote bush

Succulents
- Store water, fleshy interior, bulbs, roots, waxy leaves, e.g. cacti

Root systems
- Radial: spread out over a large area
- Tap: long root to reach water table

Defensive systems
- Cacti: spiky leaves
- Creosote bush: unpleasant taste and smell

10 Human interaction with biomes

By the end of this chapter students will have studied:

◉ The clearing and felling of the temperate forest biome in Ireland from ancient settlers to present day

◉ Industrial development and the impact it has had on the temperate forest biome of Europe

◉ The impact of deforestation on the tropical rainforest biome of the Amazon Basin

◉ Intensive agricultural practices and the impact they have on the tropical rainforest biome of Brazil

SYLLABUS LINK

Biomes have been altered by human activities.

NOTE

This section should be allowed at least four class periods (40 minutes).

Introduction

Human activities have had a major impact on world biomes, often clearing natural vegetation for agricultural purposes, or in some cases simply replacing it. Industrial development, which started in the late-nineteenth century has also had a huge impact on the quality of the biomes of the world. These human activities have not only affected the vegetation of these biomes but also the unique animal and soil types found there, which depend on the vegetation to survive. We will now examine the impacts that these human activities have had on two world biomes: the **temperate forest biome of Europe** and the **tropical rainforest biome of Brazil**.

EXAM HINTS

This section is a very popular question on the exam paper. It is important to know about human interaction in **two** separate biomes.

CASE STUDY 10.1
Temperate forest biome

Human activity 1: Early settlement and clearing of forests in Ireland

● Forests of deciduous mixed woodland, such as oak and sycamore, are the natural vegetation of a **cool temperate climate**. This type of forest originally covered 70 per cent of Ireland.

● The Neolithic people (the first farmers) began to clear the forests approximately 5,000 years

ago to make way for **farming and settlement**.

● **Forest clearance** on a large scale increased with the introduction of the Celts and the beginning of the Iron Age in Ireland, 500 BC–AD 400. Iron tools were sharper and stronger than ever before, and deforestation in Ireland increased during this period. The Celts did exercise some management of the native forest, as under

Brehon law it was an offence to cut down any of the so-called 'nobles of the wood': oak, hazel, holly, yew, ash, Scots pine or crab-apple trees.

- **Overgrazing** of the land occurred in the west as farmers had numbers of animals that were above the carrying capacity of the land. This is why the Burren, Co. Clare, has exposed limestone; many of the overlying layers of soil were removed by denudation.

- **Deforestation** continued over the next 1,000 years as both the Vikings and the Normans made use of the forests in Ireland for constructing bridges, defensive settlements and longboats.

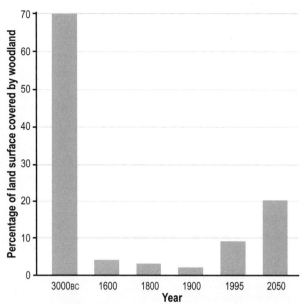

10.2 The decline of forests in Ireland from 3000 BC to (estimated) AD 2050

10.1 Woodland in Co. Kerry

- In the sixteenth century, English and Scottish planters arrived, and deforestation of the natural vegetation increased again. The planters cleared large areas of natural woodland for **agricultural use**, and **town and road construction**. The population at this time was twice what it is today, so the demand for wood was great, and it was also exported to England by the planters. Most of the Irish oak was cleared during this period. It takes 80 years for an oak tree to grow, and therefore the trees were not replaced.

- The forest clearance continued at an alarming rate, and in 1922 only **1 per cent**

of the natural forests of Ireland remained: approximately 35,000 hectares mainly located on large estates. The natural habitat of the native red deer and Irish elk had been destroyed, and some animals of the biome became extinct. For example, the wolf was wiped out in Ireland. The soils of the region were open to soil erosion because of exposure to the processes of **denudation**. The fertility of the soil was also reduced, as decaying leaf litter was removed from the region along with the trees.

- Today in areas such as Kenmare, Co. Kerry, tiny fragments of the original Irish biome remain. Here rhododendron plants native to Asia were brought in and affected the local plant species as it fought for light and space. Only **12 per cent** of Ireland is now covered in woodland. This is one of the lowest percentages in Europe, where the average is 31 per cent. The Irish Government hopes to improve this figure in the future, and by 2035 it is estimated it will reach 16 per cent.

Human activity 2: Industrial activity, causing acid rain (Industrial development in Europe)

- Industrial activity in Europe is the main cause of acid rain. Emissions, such as **sulfur dioxide** and **nitrogen oxide**, are

Chemistry Biology

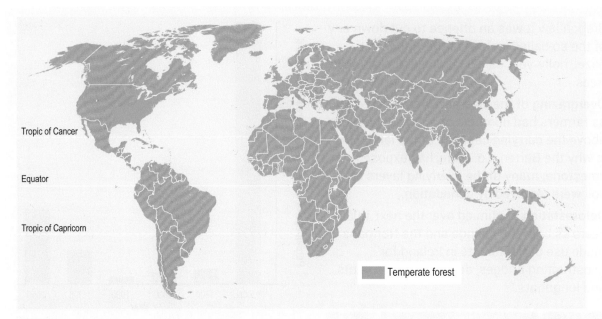

10.3 A map showing the temperate forest biome

Tropic of Cancer

Equator

Tropic of Capricorn

█ Temperate forest

released from industries, homes and cars that burn fossil fuels. They mix with rainwater, forming a weak nitric and sulfuric acid. This then falls as acid rain, with a pH less than 5.6.

- If acid particles do not dissolve in the rainwater, they fall as acidic dust called **dry deposition**.
- Acid rain affects vegetation, fish, buildings, monuments and soil quality. It is estimated that over **50 per cent of trees** in Germany, Switzerland and the Netherlands are affected by acid rain.
- When acid rain falls on the land, it is called **acid deposition**. The **critical load** of an area is the amount of acid rain that can fall without damage to soil and vegetation; 20 per cent of forests in Europe have acid deposition above their critical load.

The impact of human activity on soil

Acid rain can affect the health of soils of the temperate forest biome in a number of ways.

- **Aluminium** concentrations in the soil increase with acid rain. This causes damage to the root hairs of plants, especially trees, so that they are unable to absorb essential nutrients. This in turn affects the health of the trees and can stunt their growth.

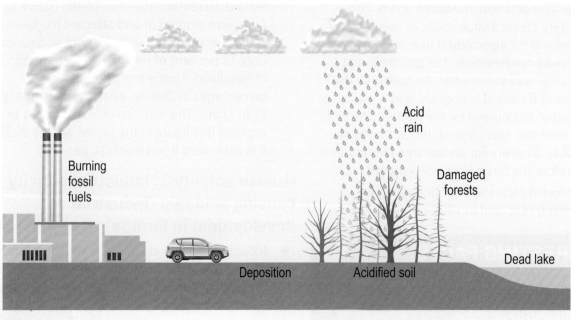

Burning fossil fuels

Acid rain

Damaged forests

Deposition   Acidified soil

Dead lake

10.4 Acid rain formation

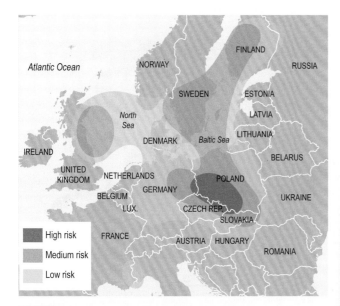

10.5 Areas of Europe affected by acid rain

High risk
Medium risk
Low risk

of growth per year. Acid rain can cause **leaf damage**, reducing the leaves' ability to photosynthesise. This then damages the tree's overall health and reproductive ability. It also leaves the plant open to attack from insects, fungi and frost.

- **Nutrient leaching** can occur as toxic metals found in acid rain, such as lead and zinc, deprive soils and, in turn, trees of the important nutrients needed for healthy plant growth. To overcome these problems, **lime** is added to the soil to neutralise the effects of acid rain. This is expensive, as it takes three tonnes of lime to neutralise a field for 20 years. It is estimated that acid rain has damaged over half of Germany's trees. Acid rain has also damaged 11,000 km of rivers and 7,500 lakes in Sweden. These have to be limed on a regular basis.

- **Seed germination** in the soil is also affected, again reducing forest growth rates and fertility levels in the soil. In Sweden this is estimated to be as high as a €495 million loss

INTERESTING FACTS

Acid rain has lowered the pH of Sweden's waterways, killing off snails and larvae that provide food for fish and frogs in the region. Fish also die from aluminium poisoning as excess amounts enter the water through acid rain.

QUICK QUESTIONS

1. How did the Celts properly manage deforestation?
2. Why did the felling of trees accelerate in the sixteenth century?
3. Name three effects of acid rain on Europe.
4. Draw a labelled diagram to explain how acid rain is formed. (Timed activity: 3 min)
5. Why is lime added to agricultural land and lakes in affected areas?

CASE STUDY 10.2
Tropical rainforest biome

The tropical rainforest biome is at its most extensive in the Amazon Basin of South America. It is the natural vegetation of the **equatorial climate**. The natural forest is referred to as *selva* and contains an immense number of plant and animal species. The felling of this tropical woodland has both local and global impacts.

Originally in the tropical rainforest biome of Brazil, the native people, such as the Yanomami tribe

of the Amazon Basin, practised **slash and burn** cultivation, and small areas of land were cleared for subsistence farming. After a couple of years, the land was exhausted and the people moved on, but because the area of land was so small, it was easily taken over by the forest again. This is referred to as **sustainable exploitation** of the forest.

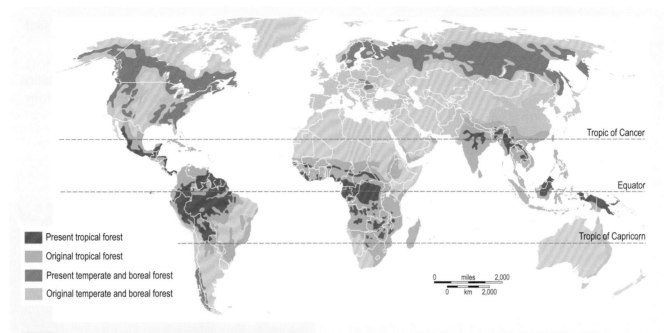

Present tropical forest
Original tropical forest
Present temperate and boreal forest
Original temperate and boreal forest

Tropic of Cancer

Equator

Tropic of Capricorn

| 0 | miles | 2,000 |
| 0 | km | 2,000 |

10.6 The distribution of world forests past and present

10.7 A member of the Yanomami tribe of the Amazon rainforest

Human activity 1: Felling of tropical rainforests (Deforestation)

- Since the 1970s, deforestation of the tropical rainforest biome has increased greatly as the global demand for **hardwoods**, such as teak and mahogany, continues. These clearances have normally been done by people outside the forest biome. Less than 2 per cent of the natural rainforest along Brazil's Atlantic coast has survived. The tropical rainforests of the world have decreased from 2.9 billion hectares in 1800 to little over 1.5 billion hectares today. Felling of tropical rainforests has increased in recent years, as farming yields higher profits per hectare than forestry.

- One of the main activities to cause large areas of deforestation in Brazil is

logging, which accounts for 3 per cent of Brazilian economic activities. The Brazilian Government wants to take advantage of mineral and timber wealth in the region. It also adds to the industrial strength of the country, as the Government receives a portion of the timber company's profits.

- **Illegal timber felling** is a problem in Brazil and accounts for 80 per cent of all timber felled in the Brazilian rainforest. It is used to produce products such as cheap plywood.

10.8 Deforestation in the Brazilian rainforest

Human Activity 2: Mining and construction (Industrial development)

- **Roads** were built, opening up the rainforest to excessive exploitation. Roads such as the Trans-Amazonian Highway cut through the forest to allow entry for logging companies to access even the most remote parts of the rainforest. These roads often divide the forest into unviable sections, and much of the wildlife of the biome's habitats is destroyed.

- **Iron ore and copper** are mined in the region, and once again large tracts of land are cleared to bring these minerals to the surface. This opencast mining scars the landscape.

- Between the 1950s and the 1960s, the Brazilian Government set about building a new capital, **Brasilia**, on the edge of the Amazon rainforest. This was to attract more people inland, away from the overcrowded coastal cities. Large-scale deforestation had to take place for the construction of the city.

- People were attracted to the area as the Government gave people **free land** to encourage them, which led to increased clearing of the forested areas. Today some 2.3 million people live in the city. Wood is still used as a fuel by many of these people.

- The construction of 125 new **hydroelectric power** (HEP) stations in the Amazon region has helped Brazil to develop its industrial activities. The region has an unlimited water supply and ideal river conditions. Large tracts

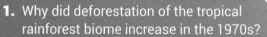

QUICK QUESTIONS

1. Why did deforestation of the tropical rainforest biome increase in the 1970s?
2. What is unsustainable exploitation?
3. Why is it important to retain the tropical rainforest biome? (Timed activity: 6 min; 6 SRPs)
4. How can building roads impact negatively on the natural habitat?
5. Give **one** example of a positive impact and **one** example of a negative impact of the construction of HEP stations in the Amazon Basin.

of forest are flooded for the construction of these HEP stations, which generate 75 per cent of Brazil's electricity.

Human activity 3: Farming (Intensive agricultural practices)

- Deforestation of the tropical rainforests in Brazil has taken place to make way for large cattle ranches and soya bean cultivation. These areas are farmed intensively by large-scale **multinational companies** (MNCs). Brazil is the world's largest exporter and producer of beef and the Government plans to double its share of the market by 2018, showing little regard for the local environment.
Soya bean is a **cash crop** used to repay international debt. The production and subsequent deforestation that took place was so extensive that in 2006 environmental groups such as Greenpeace placed a ban on buying soya beans from these areas.

- Tropical red soils (latosols) of the biome are fast becoming exhausted and open to soil **erosion**, as the fallow year has been abandoned in the search for profits.

- Large-scale use of **fertilisers** and **pesticides** to improve plant growth can increase acidity levels in the region, which can be harmful to plants and animals of the biome.

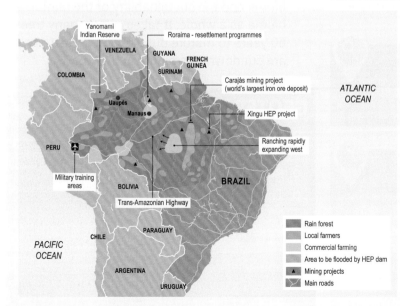

10.9 Human activities in the Amazon Basin

- Soils of the tropical rainforest can be further damaged by agricultural practices such as increased use of machinery. This can lead to **soil compaction**, making it impossible for plant roots to penetrate the soil.
- At the moment the future looks bleak as even the **Brazilian Government encourages large-scale clearances** of the tropical rainforest for agriculture: it is estimated that 40 hectares of rainforest are lost every minute to agricultural use. In Brazil alone, it is estimated that if the rate of destruction of forests continues, 40 per cent of the country's rainforests will be lost by 2050.

The impact of human activity on soil

- **Soil erosion** in the tropical rainforest biome is increasing as trees are felled and the canopy layer is removed, exposing the soil to the processes of weathering and erosion. The soil is easily eroded, as the trees' roots no longer hold the soil together.

10.10 The tropical rainforest in Brazil

EXAM HINTS

The human activities listed above can also be referred to as economic activities in an exam answer, as they all refer to the extraction and sale of natural resources for profit. Pollution can also be discussed, as it is a by-product of these industries if they are not managed properly.

- The **nutrient cycle** has been destroyed as the foliage layer (from which some of the soils' nutrients are derived) has also been removed.
- Heavy rainfall in the region exposes the soil to large-scale **leaching**, and in upland areas landslides and mudslides can be a problem.
- As loose soil and regolith move down slope under the influence of gravity, trees and their roots no longer act as a barrier in the region. The soil's upper layers can be fully removed in a process called sheet erosion or deep grooves can be cut into the soil by river channelling. This is called **gullying**.
- As the canopy layer is removed the soil can be baked and dried in the direct sunlight. These hard-baked infertile soils, referred to as **laterite soils**, are of little use for farming. Grass growing in these conditions is of poor quality. To prevent the cattle that graze on them from being of poor quality too, even more land is cleared to feed them.
- Laterite soil formation can be accelerated by the use of bulldozers and large machinery, which further **compact the soil**.
- Soil can be deposited in rivers, increasing the water level and causing **flooding** of the region. Many low-lying areas of the Amazon Basin, such as Upper Peru and Ecuador, have experienced flooding damage, which destroys vegetation and animal habitats.

The impact of human activity on biodiversity

- **Large-scale felling** is a major threat to the biome and the sustainability of the rainforest biome as a whole. It takes a mahogany tree 60 years to mature but 2,000 of these trees are cut down per minute in the world's

GEOTERMS

- The **canopy** is the topmost layer of foliage in a forest.
- **Regolith** is loose weathered material.
- The **nutrient cycle** includes all the processes by which nutrients are transferred from one organism to another. For example, the **carbon cycle** includes uptake of carbon dioxide by plants, ingestion by animals, and respiration and decay of the animals.

rainforests. This is **unsustainable exploitation** of the forest biome.

- It is important to preserve the tropical rainforests of the world as a viable biome, because they are home to over 15 million species of plant and animal, many of which have adapted especially to this biome. In 1 square kilometre alone, there are more plant and animal varieties than in the whole of Europe.

- In the tropical rainforest biome animal habitats have been destroyed, inevitably leading to the **extinction** of many species.

- People have introduced new species of plant, such as soya beans, into the biome. These plants have no natural enemies, and so could spread into the biome at an alarming rate and compete with native species. This could result in a loss of both plant and animal **biodiversity** in the tropical rainforest biome.

- One-quarter of all **pharmaceutical drugs** originated from the tropical rainforest biome. For example, quinine from the cinchona tree is used to treat malaria. If the biome continues to be destroyed at today's rate, scientists will not have time to discover all the plant species that live there. As a result, cures for many of today's biggest killers, such as AIDS and cancer, could be lost forever.

In Brazil alone, **90 tribes have been wiped out** in the Amazon rainforest due to industrial and agricultural expansion into this biome. The number of native tribes people in the region has been reduced to fewer than 250,000 in 2000 from nearly 6 million in the 1500s. The causes of this dramatic drop in numbers are varied.

- Native tribal villages were often wiped out by so-called 'white man' **diseases** that they had no natural immunity for, such as measles and the common cold.

- Others were **murdered** by cattle ranchers and loggers keen to take over the areas where they lived.

- In recent years the Brazilian Government has tried to increase the recognition of the human rights of native tribes such as the **Yanomami**, but these are hard to implement in the remote regions of the Amazon rainforest.

Deforestation of the tropical rainforest of Brazil is a problem for the world as well as the native tribes. This is because this biome is a **carbon sink**.

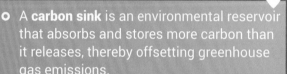
Scarlet macaw parrots in the Amazon jungle

This vast area of forest has a huge part to play in global warming and climate change. Trees take in carbon dioxide and convert it into oxygen. Drastically reducing the number of trees through deforestation increases atmospheric CO_2 and global temperatures, which could have a disastrous effect in many parts of the world, including low-lying countries such as the Netherlands and Bangladesh.

GEOTERMS

- A **carbon sink** is an environmental reservoir that absorbs and stores more carbon than it releases, thereby offsetting greenhouse gas emissions.
- **Biodiversity** is the range of organisms present in a particular ecological community or biome.

QUICK QUESTIONS

1. Define the term *cash crop*.
2. Why were Greenpeace so concerned with the production of soya beans in the Amazon Basin?
3. Write a paragraph on how human activities can impact on the soils of the region. (Timed activity: 10 min; 8/10 SRPs)
4. What impact did deforestation of the rainforest have on native tribes?
5. What is a carbon sink?

EXAM HINTS

The Sahel case study in Chapter 8: Soil characteristics can be used here instead to examine intensive agricultural practices in the hot desert biome. The human activities that impact on the biome could be studied under the headings 'deforestation', 'overcropping' and 'overgrazing'.

QUESTIONS

Higher Level – Long Questions

EXAM HINTS

All questions are worth 80 marks and require an essay-style answer. Your answer should include:

- An introduction: lay out all the material that will be covered later in the essay.

- Three to four paragraphs: each should focus on a new aspect of the answer; there should be six to eight SRPs in each paragraph.

- A conclusion: draw together all the information that was discussed in the essay.

Geoecology

1. Discuss the impact of human activity on soil.

   2015, Section 3, Q17, 80 marks

2. Biomes are altered by human activity. Discuss.

   2014, Section 3, Q18, 80 marks

The marking scheme for a question like this on a Higher Level paper is as follows:	
3 aspects identified @ 4 m each	**12 marks**
Discussion: 8 SRPs @ 2 m each per aspect	**48 marks**
Overall coherence	**20 marks**
Total	**80 marks**
4 aspects identified @ 3 m each	**12 marks**
Discussion: 6 SRPs @ 2 m each per aspect	**48 marks**
Overall coherence	**20 marks**
Total	**80 marks**

HOT TOPICS IN THE EXAMS

Two different types of human activities and how they have impacted on biomes

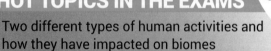

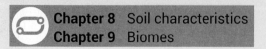
Chapter 8 Soil characteristics
Chapter 9 Biomes

EXAM HINTS

In recent years more emphasis has been placed on overall coherence marks. These marks are allocated to students that construct their answers to fit the question asked. Therefore all the information in your answer must be relevant, and every sentence must relate to the question. Your answer must be well laid out and planned before you begin writing. Using a very simple mind map will help with this.

3. Examine how any three of the activities listed below can impact on biomes:
   - Early settlement
   - The felling of tropical rainforests
   - Intensive agricultural practices
   - Industrial development

   2012, Section 3, Q18, 80 marks

4. The development of economic activities can alter biomes. Discuss this statement with reference to appropriate examples you have studied.

   2011, Section 3, Q18, 80 marks

5. Explain two ways in which human activities have impacted on soils.

   2010, Section 3, Q17, 80 marks

6. Assess how biomes have been altered by human activities.

   2009, Section 3, Q18, 80 marks

7. Examine two ways in which human activities have altered the natural characteristics of a biome that you have studied.

   2008, Section 3, Q16, 80 marks

8. Assess the impact of human activity on a biome that you have studied.

   2006, Section 3, Q18, 80 marks

Mind map

Early settlement and clearing of forests, Ireland: Temperate forest biome

- Deciduous mixed woodland
- 5,000 years, Neolithic people/Celts, farming and settlement
- West, overgrazing, Burren
- Increased 16th century English and Scottish planters, agri, roads, towns
- 1922: 1% natural forest
- Animals of biome extinct, e.g. wolf
- Open to soil erosion, loss of fertility
- 12% woodland in Ireland, lowest in Europe, 31%

Industrial development in Europe: Temperate forest biome

- Primary cause: acid rain = industrial activity
- Burn fossil fuels = weak nitric and sulfuric acid
- pH 5.6, acid deposition
- 20% EU forests above critical load
- Leaf damage
- Reduces forest growth
- Aluminium levels in soil
- Nutrient leaching
- Lime added to neutralise effects, 3 tonnes 20 years
- Damage to half of Germany's trees
- Sweden: 11,000 km rivers and 7,500 lakes
- Fish: aluminium poisoning
- Woodland animals

Human interaction with biomes

Felling tropical rainforest, Brazil: Tropical rainforest biome

- Yanomami tribe, 'slash and burn'
- Subsistence, sustainable exploitation
- 1970s deforestation increased demand for hardwoods, e.g. teak
- 1800 2.9 b, today 1.5 b hectares
- Unsustainable exploitation
- Logging: 3% Brazilian economic activities, illegal = 80% of felled trees
- Mining, e.g. iron ore, copper, wood as fuel
- Roads, unviable sections isolated
- 1950s building of capital Brasilia, large-scale deforestation, 2.3 m people
- Soil erosion, exposed, leaching, landslides and mudflows, sheet erosion, flooding
- 15 m species of plant and animal
- Carbon sink, global warming

Intensive agricultural practices, Brazil: Tropical rainforest biome

- Large cattle ranches, soya products
- MNCs, soil exhaustion, overused, fertilisers, soil compaction
- Soil erosion, denudation, nutrient cycle lost = laterite
- Habitats destroyed, new species introduced, reduces biodiversity
- 25% all pharmaceutical drugs, e.g. quinine, new cures lost, e.g. AIDS and cancer
- Native people wiped out from 6 m in 1500s to 250,000 today
- Brazilian Government encourages deforestation
- By 2050 40% rainforest destroyed

OPTION

8

Culture and identity

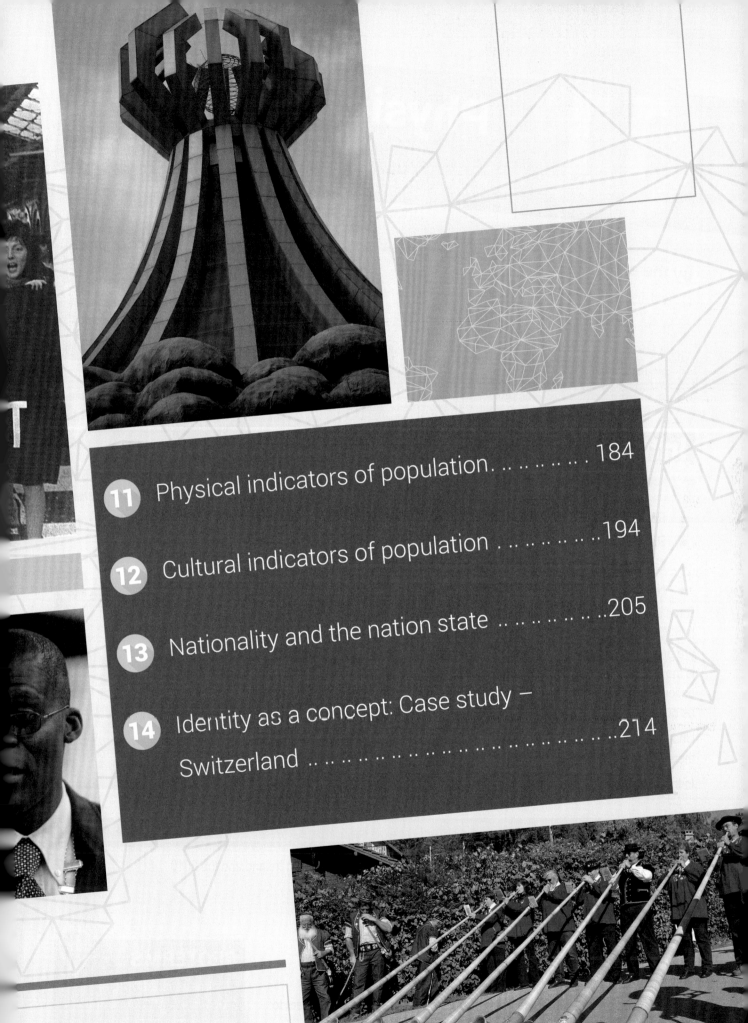

11 Physical indicators of population

SYLLABUS LINK

Populations can be examined according to physical and cultural indicators. Culture and identity are tied to ideas of ethnicity, which include race, language, religion and nationality.

By the end of this chapter, students will have studied:

- ◎ Global racial groupings
- ◎ Multi-racial societies
- ◎ Racial mixing
- ◎ Racial conflict
- ◎ The impact of colonialism and migration on racial patterns

Introduction

Elements of culture and identity

- Race
- Religion
- Language
- Nationality

NOTE

This section should be allowed at least five class periods (40 minutes).

Race is a physical characteristic – genetics decides your skin colour, your height, and so on. **Language**, **religion** and **nationality** are culturally determined – we are brought up to believe in certain things and to act in certain ways. **Ethnicity** is the result of the mixing of **physical** (race) and **social** (language, religion and nationality) features. These characteristics combined make us unique. They give us our culture and our identity.

Understanding the factors that influence race, language, religion and nationality is therefore central to explaining culture and identity.

In this chapter we will examine one of the components of ethnicity: race.

GEOTERMS

- ○ **Ethnicity** is a combination of race, language, religion and nationality.
- ○ **Race** is the categorising of a person based upon their physical characteristics such as skin colour.

Race

The forms at the top of the opposite page are taken from the 2011 census in Ireland and the 2010 census in the USA.

There are three obvious differences between the questions asked.

- The census question from Ireland mentions 'Irish' in three of the four categories.
- The US form lists a greater number of races.
- The Irish census asks about 'ethnic background'; the US census refers to 'race'.

GEOTERMS

A **census** is an official (government) count and survey of a population.

11 What is your ethnic or cultural background?

Choose ONE section from A to D, then ✓ the appropriate box.

A White

1		Irish
2		Irish Traveller
3		Any other White background

B Black or Black Irish

| 4 | | African |
| 5 | | Any other Black background |

C Asian or Asian Irish

| 6 | | Chinese |
| 7 | | Any other Asian background |

D Other, including mixed background

| 8 | | Other, write in description |

Irish census form

6. What is this person's race? Mark ✗ one or more boxes.

☐ White
☐ Black, African Am., or Negro
☐ American Indian or Alaska Native – *Print name of enrolled or principal tribe.* ↘

☐ Asian Indian   ☐ Japanese   ☐ Native Hawaiian
☐ Chinese   ☐ Korean   ☐ Guamanian or Chamorro
☐ Filipino   ☐ Vietnamese   ☐ Samoan
☐ Other Asian – *Print race, for example, Hmong, Laotian, Thai, Pakistani, Cambodian, and so on.* ↘   ☐ Other Pacific Islander – *Print race, for example, Fijian, Tongan, and so on.* ↘

☐ Some other race – *Print race.* ↘

US census form

Why do some countries ask about ethnicity and others about race on their census form? In the past, race was used as the basis for intolerance. Think of the Nazis. Asking about ethnicity rather than race is seen as a less threatening question. Ethnicity is therefore more likely to feature on a census form. America is one of only a handful of countries that specifically asks about race on a census form.

Examining race is therefore complicated in part because of past events and present fears.

🔍 **INTERESTING FACTS**

In France no direct census questions can be asked that would determine the exact ethnic, racial or religious make-up of society.

History and race

The word *race* was probably first used to mean 'breed' or 'strain'.

In the past, many people divided the world into different races. For example, in 1775 Johann Blumenbach split up the world's population into five main races. These were the Caucasian or white race, the Mongolian or yellow race, the Ethiopian or black race, the American or red race and the Malayan or brown race.

Using racial divisions like Blumenbach's, some people began to rank races. Racial divisions were used to justify social and economic inequalities. Ultimately this creation and ranking of racial groups led to racist ideologies. Hitler and the Nazis classified people into races using more than just skin colour. This led them to kill millions of people of 'inferior races', including millions from the Jewish 'race'.

Today we are understandably sensitive about putting people into racial categories. Historically, researchers have loosely divided the world into areas that correspond to different racial groups. (See Figure 11.2.)

GEOTERMS abc

An **ideology** is a body of ideas, usually political and/or economic, forming the basis of a national or sectarian society.

11.1 Hitler and the Nazis – past racist ideologies have shown how dangerous it can be to define people by race

Using Figure 11.2 below, you can see that, historically at least, race corresponded to broad geographic areas. Do you think Figure 11.2 is a good representation of racial groups today?

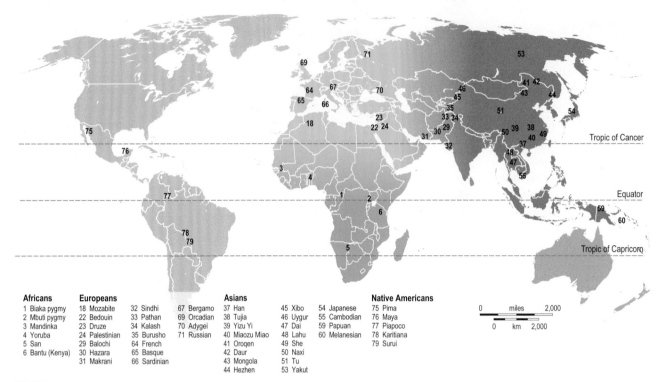

Africans	Europeans		Asians		Native Americans
1 Biaka pygmy	18 Mozabite	32 Sindhi	37 Han	45 Xibo	54 Japanese	75 Pima
2 Mbuti pygmy	22 Bedouin	33 Pathan	38 Tujia	46 Uygur	55 Cambodian	76 Maya
3 Mandinka	23 Druze	34 Kalash	39 Yizu Yi	47 Dai	59 Papuan	77 Piapoco
4 Yoruba	24 Palestinian	35 Burusho	40 Miaozu Miao	48 Lahu	60 Melanesian	78 Karitiana
5 San	29 Balochi	64 French	41 Oroqen	49 She		79 Surui
6 Bantu (Kenya)	30 Hazara	65 Basque	42 Daur	50 Naxi		
	31 Makrani	66 Sardinian	43 Mongola	51 Tu		
		67 Bergamo	44 Hezhen	53 Yakut		
		69 Orcadian				
		70 Adygei				
		71 Russian				

11.2 Map of the world showing the geographical boundaries that historically have been used to categorise populations into different racial groups: Europeans, Asians, Native Americans and Africans

Colonialism and migration: Multi-racial societies

Many countries are **multi-racial** – they have more than one race of people living within their borders.

CASE STUDY 11.1

Racial mixing: Brazil

Many of these multi-racial societies did not always exist. Instead different people from different races gradually came to live in one country. Racial mixing occurred. In Brazil the process of racial mixing was a relatively **peaceful** one.

Brazil has a population of 170 million – 91 million (53 per cent) consider themselves as white, 65 million (38 per cent) as grey/brown (meaning racially mixed), 10 million (6 per cent) as black, 761,000 (4 per cent) as yellow (Asian), and 734,000 (4 per cent) as **indigenous**.

Why? Racial mixing in Brazil is the result of a number of waves of immigration. The Portuguese colonised Brazil. With Portuguese (white) settlers also came large numbers of African (black) slaves.

When? Up to 8 million Africans were brought to Brazil between 1540 and 1850.

From 1870 to 1953, many immigrants arrived from Italy and Portugal, along with significant numbers of Germans, Spaniards, Japanese, Syrians and Lebanese. All of the above groups lived alongside the native Amerindians. In Brazil racial mixing has been achieved in relative harmony.

GEOTERMS

An **indigenous** people is the native people of the country or region.

11.3 Famous Brazilians of mixed ancestry: (a) Footballer Ronaldo (black and white), (b) model Adriana Lima (Swiss, African and Amerindian)

Effects:

Brazil is seen as a 'racial democracy' – a country in which race has not led to serious conflict.

The mixed-race nature of Brazil's population is reflected in the racial characteristics of some famous Brazilians. See Figures 11.3 a and b above.

QUICK QUESTIONS ?

1. Name the four elements of ethnicity that give rise to culture and identity.
2. In which European country is it illegal for the government to collect information on race and ethnicity?
3. Why might researchers be uncomfortable classifying people by racial categories?
4. Examine the impact of colonialism on racial patterns in Brazil. (Timed activity: 10 min; 6/8 SRPs)

CASE STUDY 11.2
Racial conflict: The USA

The USA is also a racially mixed country. Like Brazil, racial mixing in the USA was the result of colonialism and waves of immigration. Colonialism played a particularly important role in racial mixing as it gave rise to the slave trade, which brought millions of people from Africa to the USA.

What? Unlike in Brazil, racial mixing has led to a lot of conflict in the USA.

On 4 July 1776, the USA declared its independence from Britain. In the American Declaration of Independence it was stated 'That all men are created equal'. However, it was not until 1863 that slavery was abolished in the USA.

Even then not all Americans were treated equally.

Why? Right up until the 1960s black people in the USA were discriminated against. Many were:

- Not allowed to vote
- Forced to attend black-only schools
- Segregated in public places such as restaurants and on buses

Effects:

As a result of this racial discrimination, black people in the USA began to protest. From the mid-1950s black Americans demanded their **civil rights** – the right to be treated equally regardless of race. They wanted the right to vote, to go to any school and not to be forcibly **segregated**.

GEOTERMS abc

- **Civil rights:** the right to be treated equally.
- **Segregation**: not allowing different races to mix.

Looking at Figure 11.4, try to explain why you think the protesters did not want integration in schools.

11.4 White Americans protesting against the decision to allow black students into a 'white' secondary school

11.5 Martin Luther King addressing a peaceful Civil Rights march, 1963

- The American Civil Rights protests of the 1950 and 1960s were largely peaceful. Led by Martin Luther King, Civil Rights protesters used non-violence as a way of overcoming racial inequality.

- Not all protesters agreed with non-violence. Militant groups such as the Black Panthers and the Black Power movement felt it was justifiable to use violence, including murder and arson, as a way to achieve racial equality. Race riots occurred in Harlem (New York) and in the Watts district of Los Angeles in 1965, and across the country in 1968 after Martin Luther King's assassination.

- By the end of the 1960s, most of the civil rights demands had been met. The Civil Rights Law (1964) guaranteed the vote for black Americans. It also made racial discrimination in public facilities and in jobs illegal.

- On 20 January 2009, Barack Obama became the first African-American President of the USA. This event showed how tolerant and increasingly racially harmonious the USA had become since the Civil Rights protests of the 1950s and 1960s.

Look at Figure 11.7. What race were Barack Obama's mother and father?

11.6 Bobby Seale (left), and Huey Newton (right), co-founders of the Black Panther Party for Self-Defence

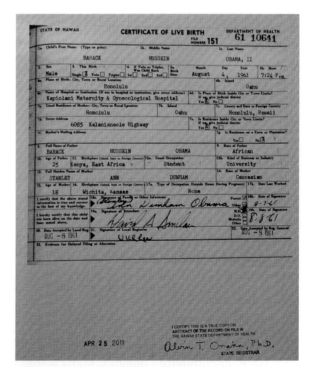

11.7 Barack Obama's birth certificate

Impact of colonialism on racial patterns

Both Brazil and the USA were colonised. The racial mixing that resulted had a massive impact on **racial patterns** in both countries.

Large numbers of white Europeans and black Africans came to live in areas they were not originally from. Racial mixing occurred. This racial mixing affected subsequent racial relations in different ways.

In Brazil the movement of slaves and colonisers to a new country ultimately resulted in a relatively harmonious society – **racial democracy**. Even if this idea of racial equality is today being questioned, Brazil's racial mixing was generally peaceful.

The pattern of **racial exclusion** and **segregation** found in the USA stemmed from the same colonial movement of slaves and colonisers that occurred in Brazil.

In one case the racial mixing, brought about by colonialism, resulted in racial harmony; in another it caused racial tension.

GEOTERMS

Colonialism is when one country is politically controlled and then economically exploited by another country.

QUICK QUESTIONS

1. Name a prominent American Civil Rights leader of the 1960s.
2. How were black Americans discriminated against during the 1950s and 1960s?
3. Outline the two different approaches that were adopted by American Civil Rights protesters during the 1950s and 1960s.
4. Examine the impact of colonialism on racial patterns in the USA. (Timed activity: 10 min; 6/8 SRPs)

Migration and racial patterns

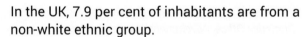
CASE STUDY 11.3
The UK

In the UK, 7.9 per cent of inhabitants are from a non-white ethnic group.

What? The UK is an example of a multi-racial European country.

Why? The UK is a multi-racial society because of the mass migration of large numbers of non-white people to Britain, especially after the Second World War, looking for a better life.

When? This migration was part of a wider pattern of movement that followed decolonisation. Many people of different races migrated from former colonies to old colonial powers such as the UK, France and Belgium.

Effects:

In the UK serious **racial difficulties** occurred as a result of this migration. These racial problems were most obvious in 1981 when the cities of London, Birmingham, Manchester, Sheffield, Leeds and Liverpool all experienced race riots. Petrol bombs were thrown at the police for the first time on mainland Britain. A report on the riots in London concluded that '... racial disadvantage ... is a fact of ... British life'.

Today most people in the UK believe that a multi-racial society is a positive development. Migration has made sure that the UK has always had a good supply of workers. Without these people, Britain's economy would suffer. The mixing of people from many different backgrounds is also celebrated because it is believed that such mixing makes a society more innovative, dynamic and vibrant.

GEOTERMS

Decolonisation is when former colonies gain political independence.

What? The arrival in Ireland of large numbers of migrants during the 1990s and 2000s has had an impact on racial patterns in Irish society.

Traditionally the flow of non-Irish nationals into Ireland was small. As a consequence racial mixing did not really occur to any great extent. For example, during the period 1980 to 1988 there was an average of 800 non-Irish persons arriving here each year.

Why? Due to a growing economy (in the Celtic Tiger era) numbers then steadily increased each year, reaching a high of 39,448 non-Irish nationals moving to Ireland in 2006. Although numbers decreased after 2006 there were nonetheless 544,357 non-Irish nationals living in Ireland by April 2011, representing 199 different nations. These non-Irish nationals made up 12 per cent of Ireland's population. (See Table 11.1.)

Effects:

The inward migration of non-Irish nationals has led to increased racial/ethnic mixing in Ireland. Most non-Irish nationals have integrated well into Irish society.

Despite integrating well, there have been problems. For example, 182 reports of racism were received by a number of organisations in the six months from July to December 2014, representing a consistent level of reporting with previous periods. The most common expressions of racism were dominated by shouting, strong language and harassment, often occurring with other forms of racist expression or behaviour such as threats, unfair treatment, refusal of service and physical assault.

Nationality	2011
Poland	122,585
UK	112,259
Lithuania	36,383
Latvia	20,593
Nigeria	17,642
Romania	17,304
India	16,986
Philippines	12,791
Germany	11,305
USA	11,015
China	10,896
Slovakia	10,801
France	9,749
Brazil	8,704
Hungary	8,034
Italy	7,656
Pakistan	6,847
Spain	6,794
Czech Republic	5,451
South Africa	4,872
Other non-Irish	85,390
Total non-Irish	**544,357**

Material compiled by the Central Statistics Office, Government of Ireland

Table 11.1 Ireland's non-Irish population by nationality, 2011

GEOTERMS

Celtic Tiger is a nickname for Ireland during the late 1990s and early to mid-2000s when the country experienced rapid economic growth.

INTERESTING FACTS

- **544,357:** The number of non-Irish nationals in Ireland in April 2011

- **320,096:** The increase in the number of non-Irish nationals since April 2002 to 2011

- **12%:** The percentage of residents who were non-Irish nationals in 2011

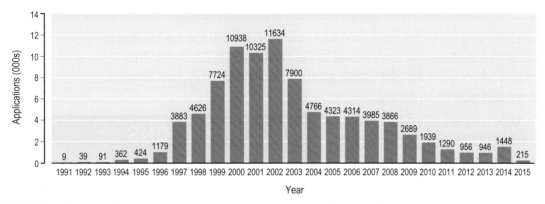

Applications for declaration as a refugee, from 1991 to the end of January 2015

Among the many non-Irish nationals who have moved to Ireland in recent years are substantial numbers of asylum seekers and refugees.

In the early 1990s there were very few applications for asylum in Ireland. This changed dramatically in the following years. By 2002 the number of applications peaked at over 11,000. Numbers then gradually declined, reaching a low of 946 applications in 2013. (See Figure 11.8.)

Integration into Irish society for refugees was, and still is, more problematic than for other non-Irish nationals. This difficulty in integrating is caused by a number of factors.

> ## GEOTERMS
>
> - An **asylum seeker** is someone who claims to be a refugee but whose claim has not yet been confirmed.
> - A **refugee** is a person who is forced to move country because of a well-founded fear of persecution for reasons of race, religion, nationality, membership of a particular social group or political opinion. Most countries agree to provide protection for a refugee.

- **Racial discrimination:** many refugees are non-white. Some experience racism.

- **Language barriers:** many refugees do not speak English.

- **Unrecognised skills or qualifications**: many refugees may have fled their home country without obtaining the necessary documentation to prove their qualifications/expertise. Even those who do have the documentation find that because they come from countries outside the European Union, their qualifications cannot be easily verified.

- Processing of applications: since the year 2000, asylum seekers in Ireland have been accommodated in various centres – guesthouses, hotels, hostels, mobile homes and at Mosney, a former holiday camp in County Meath. While housed in such centres, asylum seekers are not permitted to take up paid work or to access full-time third level education.

- By 2015 there were over 4,000 asylum seekers living in such accommodation centres. Some have to wait at these centres for many years. In 2015 the average length of stay was two years but nearly 800 asylum seekers were resident in a centre for seven or more years. This can lead to the applicant becoming de-skilled, bored, depressed and institutionalised. This impedes their ability to lead a 'normal life' if granted refugee status. Despite these difficulties, integration for refugees is possible. For example, in June 2007 Rotimi Adebari, a refugee from Nigeria, was elected Mayor of Portlaoise Town Council. He also completed a Master's degree and set up his own business.

- Once granted asylum, refugees like Rotimi Adebari are free to live and work in Ireland. Integration becomes a lot easier.

11.9 Rotimi Adebari, a former refugee who became Mayor of Portlaoise

Impact of migration on racial patterns in the UK and Ireland

- Post-war migration has had a significant impact on racial patterns in the UK. For the first time in the UK's history, a large non-white community moved to that country and settled there. This gave rise to serious racial conflict in the past. Today, although racial problems remain, Britain is considered a harmonious multi-racial society.

- The movement of large numbers of non-Irish nationals into Ireland from the late 1990s was a historically important event; Ireland's racial/ethnic composition was altered.

- Most non-Irish nationals integrated well into Irish society. Many found work, participated in community events and organisations and sent their children to local schools.

- Nonetheless there were/are issues. Refugees in particular have had a difficult time integrating and a consistent level of racist events has also been reported in recent years.

QUICK QUESTIONS

1. Name three cities in England that suffered from race riots in 1981.
2. Explain the difference between an asylum seeker and a refugee.
3. Why is it harder for a refugee to integrate into Irish society? Give three reasons.
4. Examine how migration has affected racial/ethnic patterns in the UK and Ireland. (Timed activity: 16 min; 18/24 SRPs)

QUESTIONS

Higher Level – Long Questions

Culture and identity

1. Examine the impact of colonialism and migration on ethnic/racial patterns.

   2015, Section 3, Q19, 80 marks

2. Examine the impact of colonialism on racial distribution.

   2012, Section 3, Q20, 80 marks

3. Examine how migration can impact on racial patterns.

   2011, Section 3, Q21, 80 marks

The marking scheme for a question like this on a Higher Level paper is as follows:

3 aspects identified @ 4 m each	**12 marks**
Discussion: 8 SRPs @ 2 m each per aspect	**48 marks**
Overall coherence	**20 marks**
Total	**80 marks**
4 aspects identified @ 3 m each	**12 marks**
Discussion: 6 SRPs @ 2 m each per aspect	**48 marks**
Overall coherence	**20 marks**
Total	**80 marks**

EXAM HINTS

All questions are worth 80 marks and require an essay-style answer. Your answer should include:

- An introduction: lay out all the material that will be covered later in the essay.
- Three to four paragraphs: each should focus on a new aspect of the answer; there should be six to eight SRPs in each paragraph.
- A conclusion: draw together all the information that was discussed in the essay.

HOT TOPICS IN THE EXAMS

Between 2006 and 2015 questions on the impact of migration and/or colonialism on racial/ethnic patterns were asked on seven different occasions. If answering this question, use Brazil and the USA when discussing colonialism, and Britain and Ireland when analysing migration.

Mind map

Migration and racial patterns
- UK
  - Multi-racial European country
  - Mass migration of large numbers of non-white people to Britain
  - Decolonisation
  - Migrated from former colonies to old colonial powers
  - Racial difficulties
  - Race riots
  - Today: positive development
  - Good supply of workers
  - Society: more innovative, dynamic and vibrant
- Ireland
  - Large number of non-Irish nationals arrived
  - Included asylum seekers
  - Most non-Irish nationals integrated well
  - Some integrating problems, especially for refugees

Race
- A physical characteristic
- Language, religion and nationality
- Culturally determined
- Ethnicity: mixing of physical (race) and social (language, religion and nationality) features
- Five main races

Impact of colonialism on racial patterns
- Racial mixing in USA and Brazil

Physical indicators of population

Multi-racial societies
- More than one race of people living within country

Brazil
- Waves of immigration
- Racial democracy
- Peaceful

USA
- Conflict
- 1960s black people discriminated against
- American Civil Rights protests 1950s and 1960s – peaceful
- Militant groups
  - Black Panthers
  - Black Power movement
  - Justifiable to use violence
- Civil Rights Law (1964)
- Barack Obama, first African-American President (2009)

Impact of migration on racial patterns in the UK and Ireland
- UK
  - Harmonious multi-racial society
- Ireland
  - New migrants altered racial/ethnic composition of Ireland
  - Refugees had more difficult time integrating

12 Cultural indicators of population

 SYLLABUS LINK
Culture and identity are tied to ideas of ethnicity, which include race, language, religion and nationality.

By the end of this chapter, students will have studied:
- Language as a cultural indicator
- Religion as a cultural indicator
- Everyday expressions of culture and identity

 NOTE
This section should be allowed at least five class periods (40 minutes).

Introduction

In the previous chapter, we examined how race is a physical indicator through which we can examine populations. In this chapter, we will look at populations through three cultural indicators: **language**, **religion** and **everyday expressions of culture and identity** such as music.

Language

Language families

There are thousands of different languages in the world today. They appear to have no common ancestry. No original human language has ever been discovered.

Instead it is believed that there were a number of primitive languages. It is from these primitive languages that the thousands of modern languages all come.

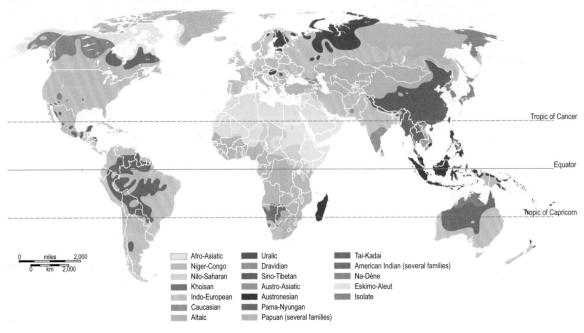

Afro-Asiatic	Uralic	Tai-Kadai
Niger-Congo	Dravidian	American Indian (several families)
Nilo-Saharan	Sino-Tibetan	Na-Déne
Khoisan	Austro-Asiatic	Eskimo-Aleut
Indo-European	Austronesian	Isolate
Caucasian	Pama-Nyungan	
Altaic	Papuan (several families)	

12.1 The major language family groups of the world

Languages are therefore seen as belonging to different language family groups. Each group is a number of languages that appear to share a common primitive language, even though today they may be very different.

- About half the world's population speaks an Indo-European language. This makes it the largest and most important language family group. As can be seen from Figure 12.1, there are many more language families.

- Gaelic, English and Polish all belong to the same Indo-European language family group. However, they are not really alike. A Polish-speaking person will not understand Gaelic simply because both languages belong to the same language group.

- As a result, each language family is further divided into different branches – languages that are even more closely related. Using the Gaelic, English and Polish example above, these languages are all placed into different language branches of the Indo-European family group.

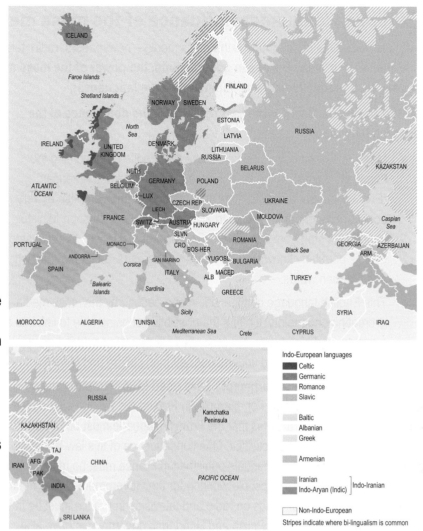

12.2 The Indo-European language family

Look at Figure 12.2. Name the languages that are today considered part of the Romance branch of the Indo-European family. What do you think links all the languages in the Romance branch?

European languages

Language is not only about communication. It is also an important part of our identity. Indeed our national identity is more often than not tied to language. For example, it would be difficult to think of someone as French, Spanish or German if they spoke only English. One of the main parts of a person's nationality (and hence identity) may well be language.

It is not hard to understand why this should be so in Europe. Historically many European countries deliberately promoted a certain language. It was easier to rule a country when one language was spoken. Language was important if a new unified country was to be established.

Today there are three main influences on the growth and development of a language – family, education and the mass media.

Whatever language is spoken at home naturally has a big influence on a person's language development. Children usually learn to speak the language of their parents.

Education also has a significant part to play. Schools not only reinforce the language skills taught at home, they also introduce students to second and other languages. For example, in Ireland, the Irish language (*Gaeilge*) is a (mainly second) language usually learned at school. In general it is not spoken at home, although there are obvious exceptions.

European languages: Influence of the mass media

The third influence on language is the mass media – newspapers, radio, television and increasingly the internet. **For many European governments, the power of the mass media is sometimes seen as having a gradually negative impact on native languages**.

This concern with the mass media is really about **the dominance of the English language**.

- Many European governments believe that English is becoming too dominant. English is the main language of the internet. American (English language) music, films and TV programmes are also all very popular throughout the world. In 2010 the German Transport Minister banned his staff from using many English words. He was trying to stop what is popularly known in Germany as *Denglish* – a blend of English and German words.

- This English language dominance, in part caused by the mass media, is creating uncertainty. It offers the possibility of being able to link into a common world language. Yet many believe that this could in turn weaken national languages and undermine (national) culture and identity.

- **Some European governments have used laws to restrict the influence of English**. For example, in France the Toubon Law was enacted in 1994. It states that the French language must be used in French Government activities. One consequence of this law is that all computer instruction manuals published in France must be made available in French to people working for the Government. It also means that 40 per cent of songs on radio and television in France must be in the French language. The Polish and Hungarian governments have also made laws that try to limit the impact of English in their countries.

- Many European governments not only attempt to restrict the influence of mass-media English on their national language, they also try to counter the dominance of English and other languages by promoting their national language abroad. A number of European countries provide assistance to various **cultural institutes** such as **Alliance Française** (France), **Goethe Institut** (Germany) and **Instituto Cervantes** (Spain).

12.3 Jacques Toubon, the French Minister of Culture who was largely responsible for the 1994 Toubon Language Law

GEOTERMS

Englishisation is a term used to describe the influence of modern American culture in an increasingly globalised world.

Minority languages – policies for survival

Some governments attempt to promote minority and/or endangered languages. Two examples of such minority language revitalisation strategies that have seen some degree of success are Irish and Welsh. In the case of Irish and Welsh it was felt that the potential loss or weakening of the language would damage cultural identity.

Gaeilge

Irish is now spoken as a first language by a minority of Irish people. There are just over 72,000 people who use Irish as a daily language. It is also a second language for many other Irish people.

The Gaeltachts are areas where Irish is used as a first language by a substantial number of the community. See *Horizons* Book 1 page 181 for a more detailed description of the Gaeltacht.

The Irish Government has tried to keep these Gaeltacht areas alive because they are seen as vital to the survival of the Irish language.

Read *Horizons* Book 1 pages 293–294 to revise how the Irish Government has supported these Gaeltacht areas and tried to promote the Irish language in general.

The Welsh language

The Welsh language declined during the twentieth century until 2001, when the census showed a slight increase in the numbers speaking and using Welsh. Today there are 575,730 people who speak or use Welsh, some 21 per cent of the total population of Wales.

The survival (and slight growth) of Welsh as a language was achieved because action was taken to encourage people to speak the language. These actions included:

12.4 Signs in Irish in a Gaeltacht area

1922	Urdd Gobaith Cymru, a Welsh-speaking children and youth group was established.
1942	The Welsh Courts Act allowed the Welsh language to be used in court.
1956	An all-Welsh speaking secondary school was established.
1967	The Welsh Language Act made it a right to have official forms in Welsh.
1977	A Welsh-language radio station, Radio Cymru, began broadcasting.
1982	An all-Welsh television channel, S4C, was created.
1993	Another Welsh Language Act created the Welsh Language Board (which promotes and facilitates the use of the Welsh language) and gave equal status to English and Welsh.
2010	A law was passed by the Welsh Assembly (parliament) making Welsh an official language in Wales.

The Welsh language survived because of the actions taken to promote it. Without the measures above, the Welsh language might have faced extinction.

Comparison of the experiences of two minority European languages – Welsh and Irish

For both languages, it was the **link between cultural identity and language** that started the revival plans. Both languages were seen as an important part of identity.

Alun Ffred Jones, the Welsh Assembly Minister for Heritage, said in 2010: 'The Welsh language is an essential part of the cultural identity and character of Wales. It helps to define who we are as a nation – in our communities, in our relationships with friends and families and as individuals.'

Many of the strategies used in Wales to save the Welsh language were also used in Ireland – the establishment of schools, radio and television stations and the use of laws to help promote the language.

As in Ireland, there are clear geographical patterns to the survival of the language in Wales.

- In both countries there are more speakers of the respective languages in the north and west. (See Figure 12.10 on page 181 and Figure 18.12b on page 293 of *Horizons* Book 1). Like Irish, Welsh is enjoying a revival in urban areas.

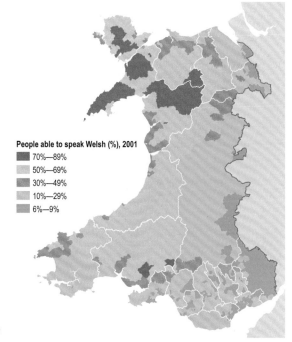

People able to speak Welsh (%), 2001
- 70%—89%
- 50%—69%
- 30%—49%
- 10%—29%
- 6%—9%

12.5 Map of Wales showing the number of people able to speak Welsh in 2001

In both cases migration has had a profound effect on the language. Many native speakers have had to leave their mainly rural homes and move to urban areas in search of work. Immigration of people unable to speak the language has also occurred.

Unlike in Ireland, no Gaeltacht-type area was established in Wales. Also, in Ireland the State has always tried to promote Irish. This governmental level of support for the Welsh language was not always possible.

The Irish and Welsh languages are examples of the outcomes of policies that were started to keep minority languages alive in Europe for mainly cultural reasons.

QUICK QUESTIONS ?

1. What is a 'language family group'?
2. State three influences on the growth and development of a language.
3. Why do many European governments have concerns about the impact of the mass media on native languages?
4. Examine the strategies that have been implemented to aid the survival of the Irish and Welsh languages. (Timed activity: 10 min; 6/8 SRPs)

Religion

Religion leaves an imprint on societies through its ability to shape people's beliefs, attitudes and behaviour. It is a major factor in the cultural and political life of most nations.

The symbols, rites, ideas and values of various religions have had a profound effect on every country. The religion of most people in a certain area therefore plays an important part in that society.

Looking at Figure 12.6, we can see that a fairly definite distribution of religions occurs in the world.

- The Christian religion dominates in North and South America, Europe and Australia. Islam is prevalent through much of North Africa and the Middle East. Hindus and Sikhs are the main religious groups in India and central Asia. Large parts of Russia and China are classified as having no dominant religion/non-religion – can you think why? Indigenous religions are important in central and southern Africa as well as the north and east of Russia and northern Canada.

- Nearly 33 per cent of the world's population is classified as Christian. This makes it the largest and most dominant faith, with Muslim and Hindu religions coming second and third, respectively.

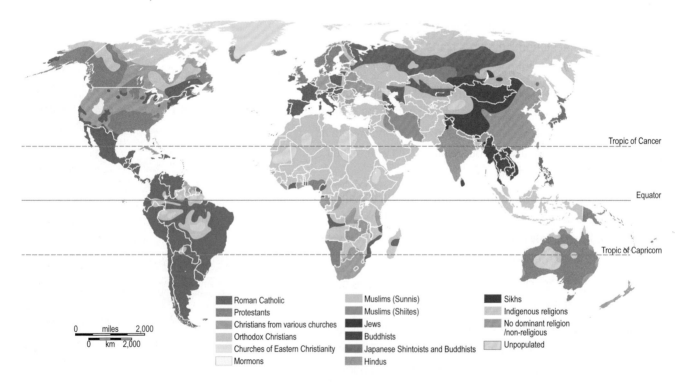

Roman Catholic
Protestants
Christians from various churches
Orthodox Christians
Churches of Eastern Christianity
Mormons

Muslims (Sunnis)
Muslims (Shiites)
Jews
Buddhists
Japanese Shintoists and Buddhists
Hindus

Sikhs
Indigenous religions
No dominant religion /non-religious
Unpopulated

12.6 The distribution of world religions

How a dominant religion can influence a society is very apparent in the case of Ireland.

- Ireland is a predominantly Christian country. To be more precise, it has been an overwhelmingly Catholic country since the foundation of the State in 1922. Although historically Ireland was a Catholic country, the birth of an independent Ireland was the start of a new relationship between the Catholic Church and the Government of Ireland. This relationship was to determine many of the social and cultural characteristics of Ireland.

- Ireland is a republic. It is a constitutional democracy and does not have a monarchy. From 1937 to 1972, Ireland's Constitution gave special recognition to the Catholic Church. Catholicism was seen in the Constitution as being more important than any other religion in Ireland. As a result of this State approval, the Catholic Church had an enormous influence on the development of Irish society and culture.

- In 1950 the Minister for Health, Noel Browne, was forced to resign. He wanted to give free hospital and healthcare to mothers and their newborn children. However, the Catholic Church thought that Browne was bringing communist ideas to Ireland. In communist countries religion was banned – the Catholic Church did not like communist ideology. Therefore it did not like Browne's ideas. As a result of his 'communist' ideas, Browne had to resign. His resignation showed how much influence the Catholic Church had in Ireland.

> **GEOTERM** abc
>
> A **constitution** is a set of general laws that are written down.

Aside from the 'mother and child' controversy, many of the rules and ideas of the Catholic Church became the basis of numerous laws in Ireland.

- Between 1935 and 1980 it was illegal to sell contraceptives in Ireland. This law was really the result of Catholic teaching, which stated that artificial contraception should not be used by Catholics.

- During the 1980s and later, there were many attempts to change the laws on divorce and abortion in Ireland. Much of the opposition to the changes came from people who believed that abortion and divorce should not be made legal because the Catholic Church thought so. Today divorce is allowed by the Irish Government because of a law passed in 1995. Abortion is still illegal.

12.7 In 1971 a group of women staged a protest against the laws on contraception in Ireland by taking a train to Belfast and bringing back illegal contraceptives to Dublin

Aside from constitutional issues, the Catholic Church contributed enormously to the functioning of the Irish State. It ran schools, hospitals and many other social services. These functions, together with its special position in the Constitution, meant that the **Catholic Church was a unifying force**. It helped to fundamentally shape Irish society through its ability to define many of the beliefs, attitudes and behaviours of the Irish people.

In the last two decades the influence of the Catholic Church in Ireland has grown weaker for a number of reasons. As a result, **Ireland is becoming a more secular (less religious) society**. Behaviour that was once seen as wrong and unlawful is now widely accepted.

As a consequence of the growing secularisation of Ireland, homosexuality was decriminalised in 1993. Same-sex civil partnerships were made possible because of a law passed in 2010. In 2015 the people of Ireland voted to change the constitution to permit same-sex marriage.

These changes would not have been possible in the past because the Catholic Church believes homosexuality is morally wrong and that marriage can only be between a man and a woman.

Religious conflict

Most religions believe that peace is good and that violence is bad. It is therefore one of the greatest ironies of human history that many wars and countless lives have been lost by people fighting for their religious beliefs.

When Britain stopped ruling India in 1947, the country had to be split into two separate nations, Pakistan and India. This had to be done because the mainly Muslim population of Pakistan hated the mainly Hindu population of India and vice versa. An estimated half a million people were killed in 1947 as people from each religion fought against each other in the initial confusion created by the creation of two new countries.

CASE STUDY 12.1
Religious conflict in Northern Ireland

Why? Religious conflict has existed in the north of Ireland for hundreds of years due to a decision taken in 1609 to have a plantation in Ulster. Approximately 80,000 English and Scottish people were given land in Northern Ireland by King James I of England. Other parts of the north of Ireland were also planted.

The English and Scottish planters who settled in Northern Ireland were Protestant. They also saw themselves as loyal to the monarchy in Britain.

Most of the native people in Northern Ireland at the time were Catholic. They were angry that their land was taken by outsiders and most did not like the British monarchy.

12.8 Map of the areas planted in Ulster, 1609

■ Assigned to Scottish undertakers	Assigned to servitors and Irish
Assigned to English undertakers	Assigned to Trinity College and selected individuals
Not part of official plantation	Londonderry plantation

Effects:

From the anger and distrust created by the plantations came hundreds of years of conflict. **Religion played a central part in the conflict.**

It was used to determine which 'side' you were on. Catholics and Protestants therefore remained hostile to each other.

In 1922, Northern Ireland was established as a state separate from the rest of Ireland (the Irish Free State). The new Northern Irish state was controlled by the Protestant majority.

In the twentieth century, this hatred between the two religious groups erupted into renewed violence during and after the 1960s.

In 1967, the Northern Ireland Civil Rights Association (NICRA) was established. It wanted Catholics in Northern Ireland to be treated the same as Protestants. Catholics wanted equality. They demanded an end to many of the corrupt political practices that existed in Northern Ireland. These included **gerrymandering** and the requirement that to vote in local elections a person had to own property (many Catholics did not own property).

Unfortunately, their demands were ignored. Sectarian violence erupted between the two groups. In order to try to stop the violence the British Government sent the British army in. The arrival of the army in 1970 led to more conflict.

GEOTERMS

Gerrymandering: a way of distorting an election result by manipulating geographic boundaries so that one group will do better than another.

According to the mural shown in Figure 12.9, what were the marchers demanding?

Out of this situation the Provisional IRA was born. The IRA waged a 'war', called The Troubles, against Britain until 1994. Thousands died. To the IRA, they were fighting to unify Northern Ireland and the Republic of Ireland. They believed that this would help end discrimination against Catholics. To others, including the Protestant population of the north, the IRA was a terrorist organisation that murdered many innocent people.

In 1998 the Good Friday Agreement was signed. Under this agreement Protestants and Catholics agreed to share power in Northern Ireland. The war in the north of Ireland that was so closely tied to religion ended. Catholics and Protestants could live peacefully together in Northern Ireland.

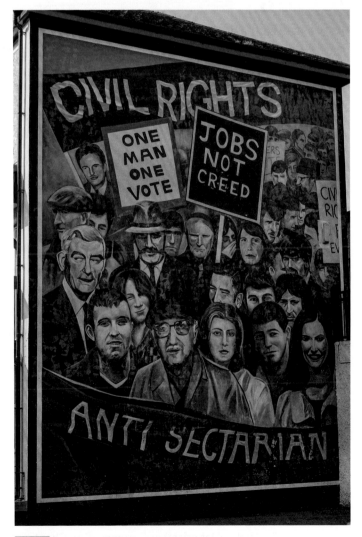

12.9 A wall mural in Northern Ireland depicting a Civil Rights march from the 1960s

QUICK QUESTIONS ?

1. Name the largest and most dominant religion in the world.
2. What was the Mother and Child controversy?
3. Why was there religious conflict in Northern Ireland during and after the 1960s?
4. 'Religion can be a divisive as well as a unifying force'. Discuss with reference to Ireland and Northern Ireland. (Timed activity: 15 min; 9/12 SRPs.)

12.10 The end of religious conflict – Ian Paisley (Free Presbyterian) and Martin McGuinness (Catholic) agreed to work together to run the government of Northern Ireland in 2007

Everyday expressions of culture and identity

We live in an **increasingly globalised world**. Much of the technology, information, food and music that we are exposed to each day is similar to that in many (especially developed) countries. Nonetheless most of us have some understanding of what it means to be Irish. The same is true for most other European citizens in relation to their own identity.

The persistence of national identity in a globalising world is due in part to everyday expressions of culture and identity.

In Ireland these everyday expressions include: sport – Gaelic football and hurling; music and dance – traditional Irish music and céilí dancing; Festivals – St Patrick's Day.

- Founded in 1884, the **Gaelic Athletic Association/Cumann Lúthchleas Gael (GAA)** is a 32-county sporting and cultural organisation that has a presence on all five continents. It is Ireland's largest sporting organisation. The GAA is one of the largest amateur sporting associations in the world. It plays an influential role in defining Irish culture.

- Traditional Irish music and dance are characterised by instruments such as the bodhrán, harp and fiddle and by céilí dancing. **Comhaltas Ceoltóirí Éireann**, established in 1951, is the largest group involved in the preservation and promotion of Irish traditional music. It is a non-profit cultural movement with hundreds of local branches around the world. It runs the definitive system of competitions for Irish music, called the 'Fleadh Cheoil', every year.

- From the Galway Races to the Kilkenny Arts festival, Ireland hosts many such cultural events each year. St Patrick's Day, 17 March, has become a secular celebration of Irish culture in general and is marked in most large towns in Ireland with a parade. Since 1995 a **St Patrick's Festival** has been held in Dublin. It lasts a number of days and attempts to develop a major annual international festival around the Irish national holiday.

In England these everyday expressions might include cricket, Yorkshire pudding and St George's Day. Other examples from elsewhere in Europe could include French cuisine, bullfighting in Spain and the Munich Beer Festival (Oktoberfest) in Germany. See Chapter 14 for everyday expressions of Swiss culture.

Everyday expressions of culture and identity are, however, not just restricted to such obviously national events or traditions.

- **Soccer** is a sport that promotes the national identity of many people in different countries even though it might not be a 'native' sport.

- The **Eurovision Song Contest**, which started in 1956, now attracts over 100 million viewers each year. Despite the strong feelings of national identity that it creates, many of the songs are not sung in national languages. In this instance popular national identity and culture can be promoted using foreign languages.

- Some events attempt to promote cultural identity by emphasising the connections between different cultures. The **Inter-Celtic Festival** held in Lorient in France every year encourages Celtic music from many different countries and regions. Different national cultures are expressed by emphasising a common Celtic history.

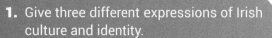

QUICK QUESTIONS

1. Give three different expressions of Irish culture and identity.
2. Why are expressions of culture and identity arguably more important in an increasingly globalised world?
3. 'Everyday expressions of culture and identity are not just restricted to national events or traditions.' Using examples, explain what this statement means.
4. Examine how people express their culture and identity in everyday life. (Timed activity: 10 min; 6/8 SRPs.)

QUESTIONS

Higher Level – Long Questions
Culture and identity

1. Examine the importance of religion as a cultural indicator.

    2014, Section 3, Q19, 80 marks

2. Examine how people express their culture and identity in everyday life.

    2013, Section 3, Q20, 80 marks

The marking scheme for a question like this on a Higher Level paper is as follows:

3 aspects identified @ 4 m each	**12 marks**
Discussion: 8 SRPs @ 2 m each per aspect	**48 marks**
Overall coherence	**20 marks**
Total	**80 marks**
4 aspects identified @ 3 m each	**12 marks**
Discussion: 6 SRPs @ 2 m each per aspect	**48 marks**
Overall coherence	**20 marks**
Total	**80 marks**

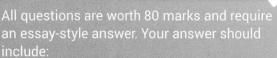

EXAM HINTS

All questions are worth 80 marks and require an essay-style answer. Your answer should include:

- An introduction: lay out all the material that will be covered later in the essay.
- Three to four paragraphs: each should focus on a new aspect of the answer; there should be six to eight SRPs in each paragraph.
- A conclusion: draw together all the information that was discussed in the essay.

HOT TOPICS IN THE EXAMS

Language and/or religion as a cultural indicator – as factors that help shape societies.

Chapter 12	Concept of a region in *Horizons* Book 1
Chapter 18	Complexities of regions in *Horizons* Book 1

Mind map

Cultural indicators of population

European languages
- Important part of our identity
- Three main influences on growth and development of a language:
  - Family
  - Education – schools introduce second/other languages
  - Mass media

Everyday expressions of culture and identity
- Increasingly globalised world
- Persistence of national identity
- Ireland
  - Gaelic football/hurling
  - Traditional Irish music and céilí
  - St Patrick's Day

Religious conflict
- Religious beliefs: many wars and countless lives lost by fighting
- Pakistan and India:
  - Muslim population of Pakistan
  - Hindu population of India

Language families
- No original human language
- Number of primitive languages
- Different language family groups
- Indo-European language
- Gaelic, English and Polish – branches

Relationship between Church and State in Ireland
- Constitutional democracy
- Predominantly Christian country
- Church-State relationship determined many social and cultural characteristics
- Catholic Church – a unifying force
- Ireland becoming a less religious society

Northern Ireland
- Ulster Plantation
- Protestant planters: loyal to the monarchy in Britain
- Native Catholics: angry that their land was taken by outsiders
- Catholics and Protestants hostile to each other
- Renewed violence during and after 1960s
- NICRA – Catholics wanted equality
- Gerrymandering
- Sectarian violence erupted between the two groups
- Provisional IRA – The Troubles
- 1998: Good Friday Agreement
- Protestants and Catholics agreed to share power

Religion
- Ability to shape people's beliefs, attitudes and behaviour
- Major factor in cultural and political life of most nations
- 33% of world population Christian
- Largest and most dominant faith
- Muslim and Hindu religions second and third largest

Influence of the mass media
- Gradually negative impact on native languages
- Dominance of the English language
  - Main language of the internet
  - Weakens national languages
  - Undermines (national) culture and identity
- Laws to restrict the influence of English
  - Toubon Law (France)
- Cultural institutes
  - Alliance Française, Goethe Institut, Instituto Cervantes

Minority languages – policies for survival
- Promote minority and/or endangered languages
- Gaeilge
  - Gaeltachts
  - Irish is used as a first language
  - Government has tried to keep these Gaeltacht areas
  - Vital to survival of the language
- Welsh
  - Welsh Language Act
  - Welsh language radio station
  - Welsh television channel
  - Welsh Language Board
  - Actions taken to promote the use of Welsh helped survival
- Comparison of the experiences of Welsh and Irish
- Link between cultural identity and language started revival plans
- Important part of being Welsh or Irish
- Geographical patterns to the survival of the language
- Migration has had a profound effect
- State has always tried to promote Irish
- Governmental support for Welsh language not always possible

Nationality and the nation state

13

 SYLLABUS LINK

Nationality and the nation state are political entities placed on the physical and cultural landscape

By the end of this chapter, students will have studied:

◎ Nation states as political entities on the physical and cultural landscape

◎ The complexity of relationships between political structures and cultural groups

Introduction

Today there are over 190 countries or states in the world. Most have the following characteristics:

- A defined territory
- A permanent population
- A government
- The capacity to enter into relations with the other states

NOTE

This section should be allowed at least 10 class periods (40 minutes).

Physical and political boundaries

To create a country you must define its territory – a boundary/border must be created. In creating a border, four steps are usually taken.

1. **Delimit:** a boundary is drawn on a map.

2. **Define:** a written agreement like a treaty setting up the border is signed.

3. **Demarcate:** the border is physically marked using some visible means.

4. **Administrate:** once established, some procedure may be put in place to control and police a border.

There are two general types of borders – physical and political.

- **Physical borders** follow natural features such as rivers or mountains. For example, the Pyrenees acts as a natural border between Spain and France, and the River Rhine is part of the boundary between France and Germany. These physical features are used as borders because they usually divide people and are obvious and convenient to use.

13.1 The border between North and South Korea

- **Political borders** do not necessarily ignore natural physical features, although frequently they do. An obvious political boundary is found in the division between North and South Korea. After the Second World War, the Korean peninsula was split in two along a line of latitude (38th). The border was redrawn in 1953 and now roughly follows the 38th parallel.

Many disputes arise between countries over borders. These inter-state disputes can be split into two general types.

- **Natural resources:** conflict occurs over natural resources that lie near or on a border.
- **Location:** in this case states may argue over where the border is.

Such disputes may be concerned with delimitation – where the boundary is drawn on official maps, aerial and satellite images – or/and with demarcation – the physical objects that make a boundary, such as rivers, fences and walls.

Borders that use the physical landscape may be more obvious than political borders but both nonetheless give rise to inter-state disputes. These disputes vary in intensity from managed or dormant to violent or militarised.

Current examples of inter-state border disputes include:

- **Spratly Islands:** China, Taiwan, Vietnam, Brunei and Malaysia claim all or parts of the Spratly Islands. There are two reasons for the conflict:
   - They are seen by all the countries involved as important in establishing international boundaries (a demarcation dispute).
   - The islands may contain significant reserves of oil and gas (natural resources dispute).

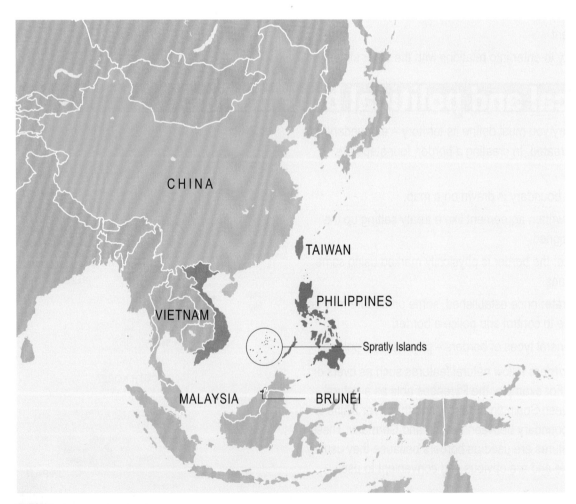

13.2 The Spratly Islands

- **Calero Island:** This demarcation dispute involves the north-western section of the Calero Island on the San Juan river that marks the Nicaragua–Costa Rica border. Both countries dispute the ownership of a piece of the Calero Island. In 2010 Costa Rica's President said the presence of Nicaraguan troops on part of Calero Island was 'the invasion of one nation to another'. The International Court of Justice provisionally ruled in 2011 that Costa Rica and Nicaragua should stop sending or maintaining civilians, security forces or police in the disputed border area.

13.3 Calero Island

QUICK QUESTIONS

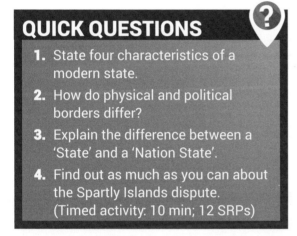

1. State four characteristics of a modern state.
2. How do physical and political borders differ?
3. Explain the difference between a 'State' and a 'Nation State'.
4. Find out as much as you can about the Spartly Islands dispute.
   (Timed activity: 10 min; 12 SRPs)

Nation states

Much of Europe during the nineteenth century was divided into various empires. These empires contained many groups of people who did not share a common culture or identity. The Austro-Hungarian Empire, for example, which existed from 1867 to 1918, had over 10 officially recognised languages that reflected the many ethnic groups within its borders. What united empires like Austro-Hungary was the allegiance of the people to the monarch.

During the nineteenth and early twentieth centuries many of these multi-ethnic empires were overthrown. New ways of organising countries were introduced. Many believed that a country should have people of a similar culture and identity living together. The idea of a nation state was born.

The growth of nation states has not occurred without difficulties.

How does a nation state deal with a group of people who are not part of the nation state but feel they should be? Such excluded groups typically live in another state. This in turn can create problems for the host state as it tries to cope with a large number of people who do not feel any attachment to the nation or state they live in.

Most difficult of all, perhaps, is deciding how a large number of people who believe that they are a nation, but have no state, should be treated.

GEOTERMS

A **nation** is a population that is united by a common culture and identity. A **state** is when people come together to rule a certain area. When people of a similar culture and identity (a nation) decide to politically control a certain geographic area (state), a **nation state** is created.

13.4 Ethnic groups within the Austro-Hungarian Empire

Conflict between political structures and cultural groups

Most of the conflict between political structures and cultural groups involves the **exclusion** of people from their **chosen nation state** and their inclusion in another state. Conflict can range from democratic protest to violence.

CASE STUDY 13.1
Excluded and living in the wrong state: Nationalists and the partition of Ireland

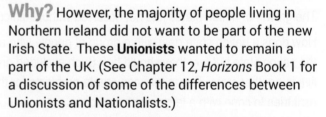

When? In **1920** the Government of Ireland Act laid the legal basis for a border that would divide, or **partition**, the island of Ireland. The border became a reality in **1922** when Northern Ireland decided to remain a part of the UK while the Irish Free State became a new independent country.

Many people living in Northern Ireland wanted to be part of the Irish Free State (later called the Republic of Ireland). These **Nationalists** shared a common culture and identity with the inhabitants of the new Irish State.

Why? However, the majority of people living in Northern Ireland did not want to be part of the new Irish State. These **Unionists** wanted to remain a part of the UK. (See Chapter 12, *Horizons* Book 1 for a discussion of some of the differences between Unionists and Nationalists.)

The boundary that was drawn measured 499 km. It defined Northern Ireland as consisting of the parliamentary counties of Antrim, Armagh, Down, Fermanagh, Londonderry and Tyrone and the parliamentary boroughs of Belfast and Londonderry.

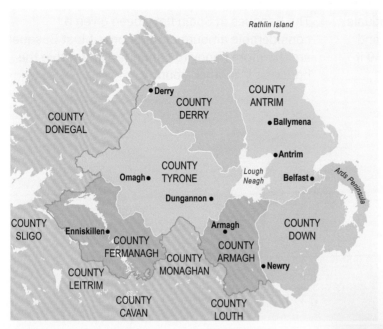

13.5 Northern Ireland

the seeds of a troubled period in Irish history. (See Chapter 12, *Horizons* Book 1 for a description of this conflict.)

Some Nationalists sought to peacefully and democratically change and improve conditions for Nationalists. The most important of these groups was the Social Democratic and Labour Party (SDLP). As leader of the SDLP, John Hume received a Nobel Peace Prize in 1998 for his work in Northern Ireland.

By contrast, the IRA sought to unite Northern Ireland and the Republic of Ireland through violent means. It believed that this was the only solution to nationalist problems.

It was a political border that followed no significant physical features.

Effects:

The purpose of the border was to ensure that many Unionists would not have to live in southern Ireland. While it did achieve this, it also ensured that many Nationalist areas ended up in Northern Ireland. **The border therefore excluded the Nationalist population in Northern Ireland from their preferred nation state.** This was to sow

13.6 John Hume, former leader of the SDLP and Nobel Peace Prize winner

CASE STUDY 13.2
No nation state: The Basques

What? Like nationalists in Northern Ireland, many Basques do not identify with the nation states they live in. Unlike Northern Ireland nationalists, there is no state in existence with which the Basques share a common culture and identity. The Basques are a **nation without a state**. Many Basques would like to see the **establishment of a Basque nation state**.

Where? The Basque homeland is an area located in the western Pyrenees. The Basque people consider themselves to be a separate nation because of their language, culture and traditions. However, the Basque homeland is

located within the borders of two nation states – Spain and France.

When? From 1937 to 1975 the Spanish dictator, Franco, attempted to repress the Basque culture. He banned the speaking of the Basque language, Euskera, in public and tried to keep the Basque areas of Spain poor.

Effects:

As a result, one extreme Basque group, Euskadi Ta Askatasuna, or ETA (Basque Homeland and Freedom), attempted to establish an independent Basque state through the use of violence.

ETA has been blamed for killing 829 individuals since 1968, as well as injuring thousands and undertaking dozens of kidnappings. In 2010 it declared a permanent ceasefire.

The Basques in Spain have been given a considerable amount of autonomy. Most Basques are therefore happy to continue living within the borders of 'another' country.

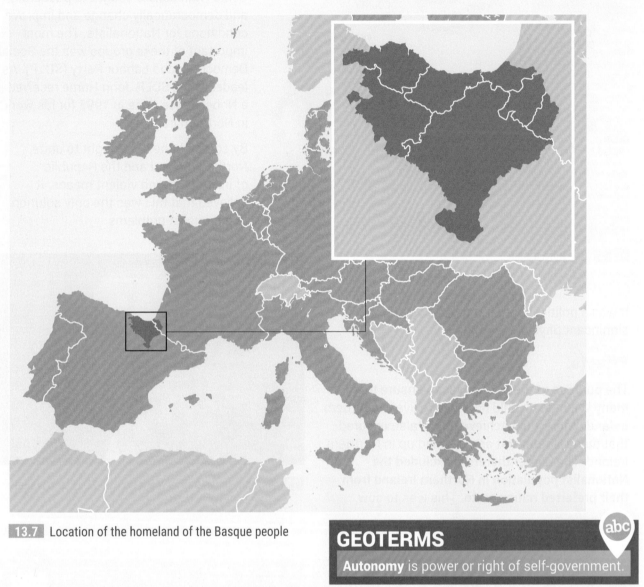

13.7 Location of the homeland of the Basque people

GEOTERMS

Autonomy is power or right of self-government.

CASE STUDY 13.3

No nation state: The Kurds

What? The Kurds are a largely Sunni Muslim people with their own language and culture. They live in an area that is split between a number of different countries – Turkey, Iraq, Iran, Armenia and Syria. This area is generally known as Kurdistan – the land of the Kurds.

When? The breakup of the multi-ethnic Ottoman Empire in the early twentieth century led to the creation of many new nation states. A new nation state named Kurdistan was proposed but was never realised. The subsequent division of the Kurdish people across a number of different countries was caused by complex political factors.

Effects:

In Turkey the Kurdish language was forbidden, as was the wearing of traditional Kurdish costumes

13.8 Kurdistan

Fig 13.9 Memorial to the victims of the 1988 Halabja gas attack

in cities. Kurds in Turkey have differed in their approaches to dealing with their situation.

The Democratic Regions Party (DBP) is a Kurdish political party that wants greater autonomy for the mainly Kurdish areas in Turkey. The DBP believes this can be achieved peacefully. In 2015 the DBP was represented by another political party, the Peoples' Democratic Party (HDP), in the Turkish general election. The HDP won 80 seats in the election.

The Kurdistan Workers' Party, commonly known as PKK, is a Kurdish militant organisation. From 1984 to 2013 the PKK waged an armed struggle against the Turkish state for cultural and political rights and self-determination for the Kurds in Turkey. In 2013 the PKK declared a ceasefire and moved its fighters to the Kurdistan Region of northern Iraq.

There are between four and five million Kurds in Iraq (roughly 20 per cent of the Iraqi population). Iraqi Kurds were repressed after supporting Iran in the 1980–88 Iran-Iraq war. In 1988 thousands of Kurds died when the Kurdish town of Halabja came under poison gas attack by the Iraqi army.

In 2014 an independence referendum for Iraqi Kurdistan was postponed.

QUICK QUESTIONS

1. Why did the partition of Ireland lead to conflict?
2. 'The Basques are a nation without a state.' Explain this statement.
3. How have the Kurds in Turkey attempted to resolve the problems created by not having their own nation state?
4. Examine the effects of political boundaries on cultural groups. (Timed activity: 10 min; 6/8 SRPs)

QUESTIONS

Higher Level – Long Questions
Culture and identity

EXAM HINTS

All questions are worth 80 marks and require an essay-style answer. Your answer should include:

- An introduction: lay out all the material that will be covered later in the essay.
- Three to four paragraphs: each should focus on a new aspect of the answer; there should be six to eight SRPs in each paragraph.
- A conclusion: draw together all the information that was discussed in the essay.

1. Examine the effects of political and/or physical boundaries on cultural groups.

    2015, Section 3, Q21, 80 marks

2. The existence of different cultural groups within state borders can lead to conflict. Discuss.

    2014, Section 3, Q20, 80 marks

3. Many cultural groups do not have a nation state of their own. Discuss.

    2013, Section 3, Q19, 80 marks

4. Conflicts can occur between national governments and cultural groups. Discuss.

    2012, Section 3, Q19, 80 marks

5. Examine the effects of political boundaries on cultural groups.

    2011, Section 3, Q20, 80 marks

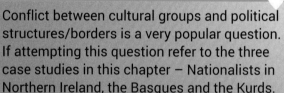

The marking scheme for a question like this on a Higher Level paper is as follows:

3 aspects identified @ 4 m each	**12 marks**
Discussion: 8 SRPs @ 2 m each per aspect	**48 marks**
Overall coherence	**20 marks**
Total	**80 marks**
4 aspects identified @ 3 m each	**12 marks**
Discussion: 6 SRPs @ 2 m each per aspect	**48 marks**
Overall coherence	**20 marks**
Total	**80 marks**

HOT TOPICS IN THE EXAMS

Conflict between cultural groups and political structures/borders is a very popular question. If attempting this question refer to the three case studies in this chapter – Nationalists in Northern Ireland, the Basques and the Kurds.

Mind map

Border disputes
- Natural resources
- Location
  - Spratly Islands: demarcation and natural resources dispute
  - Calero Island: demarcation dispute

Nationality and the nation state

Conflict between political structures and cultural groups
- **Exclusion: Partition of Ireland**
  - 1920 Government of Ireland Act
  - Unionists wanted to remain a part of the UK
  - Political border followed no significant physical features
  - Many Nationalist areas ended up in Northern Ireland
  - Excluded Nationalist population in Northern Ireland from their preferred nation state
  - John Hume (SDLP)
  - IRA
- **No nation state: The Basques**
  - Nation without a state
  - Many Basques would like a Basque nation state
  - Basque homeland located within Spanish and French borders
  - Spanish dictator, Franco, attempted to repress Basque culture
  - Banned *Euskera*
  - ETA
  - Autonomy
- **No nation state: The Kurds**
  - Sunni Muslim
  - Live in an area split between a number of different countries
  - Multi-ethnic Ottoman Empire broke up
  - Democratic Regions Party
  - Kurdistan Workers' Party

Physical and political boundaries
- Define territory
  - Delimit: boundary drawn on a map
  - Define: written agreement, e.g. treaty setting up the border signed
  - Demarcate: border is physically marked using some visible means
  - Administrate: procedure put in place to control and police border
- Physical borders
  - Follow natural features such as rivers or mountains
- Political borders
  - Korea
  - Post-Second World War
  - Line of latitude (38th)

14 Identity as a concept: Case study – Switzerland

 SYLLABUS LINK

Identity as a concept entails a variety of cultural factors including nationality, language, race, and religion.

By the end of this chapter, students will have studied:

◎ The historical development of Switzerland as a political entity on the physical and cultural landscape

◎ Swiss ethnicity (language and religion)

◎ Swiss culture

NOTE

This section should be allowed at least seven class periods (40 minutes).

CASE STUDY – SWITZERLAND

Introduction

14.1 Map of Switzerland

Located in central Europe, Switzerland covers an area of 41,277 km² – just over half the size of Ireland. It is a **landlocked** country with a 1,852 km border that it shares with five other countries: Austria, France, Italy, Liechtenstein and Germany.

Three-quarters of Switzerland's population, of over 7.5 million, live in urban centres. The capital, Bern,

has a population of over 300,000, although Zurich has a population of just over 1 million.

GEOTERMS

A **landlocked** country is completely surrounded by land, with no access to the sea.

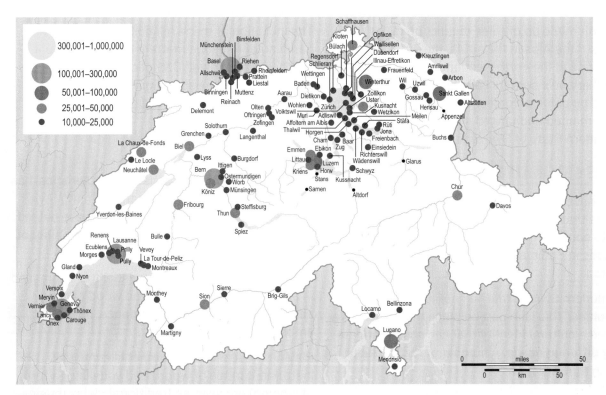

14.2 Switzerland's uneven population distribution

Due to physical factors (see Figure 14.4 on page 216), most of the population is located in the centre and north of the country.

Race, nationality and identity in a European region

When? The origins of Switzerland date back to **1291**, when three regions agreed to help defend each other. This Swiss Confederation was later joined by other regions.

In **1848** this confederation was replaced by a single unified government. **The modern country of Switzerland was established.**

14.3 The Swiss national flag

Why? The establishment of Switzerland as a European nation state was somewhat unusual. Although it had been in existence for hundreds of years, the Swiss Confederation was a strategically created area. Historically it was more like a miniature multicultural political entity where people of different identities came together for protection. There was no real sense of nation. A common culture and identity did not really exist.

Defensive concerns were the real unifying factors of the Swiss Confederation.

Today this historical lack of cultural unity and identity is reflected in the diversity of Switzerland's population.

- There are three significant ethnic groups – 65 per cent of the population is German, 18 per cent is French and 10 per cent is Italian.
- There are two dominant religions – Roman Catholic and Protestant.
- Unusually for a modern nation state, Switzerland has four national and official languages: German, French, Italian and Romansch (a language closely related to French).

Physical and political boundaries

The external borders of Switzerland developed over many centuries. The Swiss Confederation gradually grew from its original three **cantons** to 26 by 1848. These cantons in turn created Switzerland's border.

GEOTERM

Canton: how Switzerland is divided up for governmental purposes. In Ireland we use counties.

Although made up of three distinct physical regions – the Alps in the south, the Jura Mountains in the north-west and a central **plateau** – Switzerland's borders have been principally shaped by political forces. These external borders have remained unchanged since the creation of the modern State of Switzerland.

Swiss cultural identity

As we have already seen, **politically created borders that enclose different cultural groups can lead to conflict** – Nationalists in Northern Ireland, Basques in Spain and France and Kurds in Turkey and Iraq.

The modern Swiss State has not experienced such difficulties. This is in part because the Swiss have created a **cultural identity that can accommodate many differing needs**. A number of factors help explain this situation.

Religious tolerance

Christianity is the dominant religion. However, Switzerland has no official State Church. Religious matters are handled by the cantons.

Following the (religious) civil war of 1847, the subsequent Swiss Constitution, unlike the Irish Constitution, did not identify any religion as having special status. Instead equal rights were given to both the Protestant and Catholic faiths.

The inclusion of these religious rights, and the handling of religious matters by the individual cantons, has allowed Catholics and Protestants to peacefully co-exist. Religious conflict was therefore not an issue in the development of Switzerland after 1848.

Swiss characteristics

The creation of certain Swiss 'characteristics' has helped generate a **sense of nation** among Swiss people. These Swiss characteristics have helped **unite** the country and so **lessen the possibility of conflict**.

Folk art is one such characteristic. It is expressed in activities such as music and wood carving although it is also present in dance, poetry and embroidery.

Playing the alphorn (a trumpet-like musical instrument made of wood) and yodelling (a form of singing) are seen as traditional Swiss music forms. The decoration of everyday wooden objects and figure carving are seen as Swiss activities.

GEOTERMS

A **plateau** is a relatively flat area of high ground.

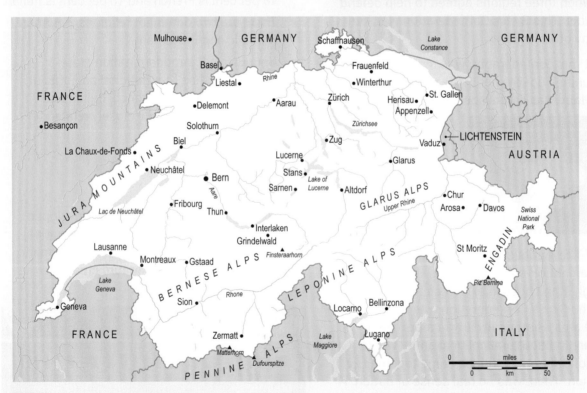

14.4 Physical map of Switzerland

14.5 An alphorn concert

Sport has also contributed. Much like Gaelic games in Ireland, mountain sports such as skiing and mountaineering are viewed as key ingredients of the Swiss identity.

The role of migration

Initially Switzerland was predominantly a country of emigrants. This changed in the nineteenth century with the industrialisation of the country. Instead immigration began to exceed emigration.

Since the Second World War, approximately two million people have immigrated to Switzerland or live there as the descendants of immigrants. Currently 22 per cent of Switzerland's population are classified as foreigners.

These foreign nationals have come from two main sources.

- Large numbers of (mostly Italian) **guest workers**, who arrived after the end of the Second World War.
- **Refugees:** up until the 1980s Switzerland accommodated refugees from various conflicts, including 14,000 from Hungary in 1956 and 12,000 Czechs and Slovaks in 1968. During the 1980s and 1990s the number of asylum applications, particularly from Turkey, Lebanon, Sri Lanka and the West Balkans, increased, peaking at 46,000 applications in 1999. In recent years the number of asylum applications has averaged at 16,000 a year. Currently there are 46,203 refugees residing in Switzerland.

Although migration to Switzerland has led to much debate within the country, non-Swiss nationals appear to integrate well. **Migration has not led to widespread racial conflict.**

Political culture in Switzerland

In 1847 there was a brief civil war in Switzerland. As a consequence of the civil war, Switzerland made a Constitution. The Constitution set up a federal government. This was done because of the internal diversity of the country. It was an attempt to accommodate the needs and demands of the different religious and linguistic groups within the State.

The federal government was given responsibility for defence, trade and certain legal matters. Each of the 26 cantons was given its own Constitution, parliament, government and courts.

Most modern nation states created strong central governments in order to help unify the nation. In Switzerland there is a lack of central government control. Instead significant power lies with the cantons. **This decentralisation of power has helped accommodate the needs of the different groups within Swiss society.**

14.6 The Swiss federal parliament building

GEOTERMS

Federal government: when the power of a government is divided between the national and local authorities. The national government usually takes control of matters such as foreign relations and the military.

Conclusion

Despite its cultural diversity and varied physical landscape, Switzerland is a healthy nation state. The establishment of modern Switzerland as a political entity has to date been successful for a number of different reasons.

- **Historical:** the very gradual assimilation of the different cantons between 1291 and 1848
- **Religious:** the early settling of religious conflict
- **Cultural:** the creation of a unifying Swiss culture
- **Social:** the migration and integration of non-nationals
- **Political:** the federalist structure of government that has ensured that all groups have a say in government affairs

QUICK QUESTIONS

1. When was the modern country of Switzerland established?
2. Briefly describe migration patterns to Switzerland after the Second World War.
3. Why can Switzerland be considered an unusual nation state?
4. 'Identity as a concept entails a variety of cultural factors.' Discuss this statement with reference to one case study of a European region that you have studied. (Timed activity: 10 min; 6/8 SRPs)

QUESTIONS

Higher Level – Long Questions
Culture and identity

1. 'Identity as a concept entails a variety of cultural factors, including nationality, language and religion.' Discuss.

   2015, Section 3, Q20, 80 marks

2. Identity as a concept entails a variety of cultural factors. Discuss this statement with reference to one case study of a European region that you have studied.

   2013, Section 3, Q21, 80 marks

The marking scheme for a question like this on a Higher Level paper is as follows:

3 aspects identified @ 4 m each	**12 marks**
Discussion: 8 SRPs @ 2 m each per aspect	**48 marks**
Overall coherence	**20 marks**
Total	**80 marks**
4 aspects identified @ 3 m each	**12 marks**
Discussion: 6 SRPs @ 2 m each per aspect	**48 marks**
Overall coherence	**20 marks**
Total	**80 marks**

Allow credit for up to two examples from SRPs (different examples and in different aspects).

Accept named region as one SRP once. Discussion must refer to at least three different factors.

EXAM HINTS

All questions are worth 80 marks and require an essay-style answer. Your answer should include:

- An introduction: lay out all the material that will be covered later in the essay.
- Three to four paragraphs: each should focus on a new aspect of the answer; there should be six to eight SRPs in each paragraph.
- A conclusion: draw together all the information that was discussed in the essay.

Mind map

Swiss cultural identity

- **Religious tolerance**
  - No official State Church
  - Equal rights – Protestant and Catholic faiths
  - Religious conflict not an issue
- **Swiss characteristics**
  - Helped generate a sense of nation among Swiss people
  - Folk art
  - Music
  - Sport
- **The role of migration**
  - Predominantly a country of emigrants
  - Nineteenth-century industrialisation – immigration began to exceed emigration
  - Non-Swiss nationals appear to integrate well
  - Migration has not led to widespread racial conflict
- **Political culture in Switzerland**
  - Federal government
  - Accommodates needs and demands of different religious and linguistic groups
  - Responsible for defence, trade, certain legal matters
  - Twenty-six cantons – own Constitution, parliament, government and courts
  - Decentralisation of power helped accommodate different groups' needs within Swiss society

Switzerland

Physical and political boundaries

- Originally three cantons
- Twenty-six by 1848
- Three distinct physical regions
- Borders shaped by political forces

Features

- Located in central Europe
- Landlocked country
- Shares border with five other countries
- Population located in centre and north of the country
- Swiss Confederation
- 1848 Switzerland
- Common culture and identity did not really exist
- Diverse population
- Two dominant religions
- Three significant ethnic groups
- Four national and official languages

Glossary

Aeration: introduction of air.

Affluent market: a wealthy market.

Age dependency ratio: the number of people in a region above the age 65 and below the age 15.

Agricultural Revolution: improvements in machinery and technology to increase output.

Alluvium/alluvial deposits: fertile material deposited by a river.

Apartheid: segregation of people according to their social standing or race.

Arable farming: involves growing crops.

Arranged marriage: someone other than the couple getting married chooses the people to be wed.

Aspect: the direction in which a slope faces.

Asylum seeker: someone who claims to be a refugee but whose claim has not yet been confirmed.

Autonomy: the power or right of self-government.

B

Biodiversity: the range of organisms present in a particular ecological community or biome.

Biome: a major world region that has its own unique climate, soil type, flora and fauna.

Birth rate: the number of babies born per 1,000 per year.

Braiding: when a river's channel is broken up into smaller channels called distributaries.

Brain drain: young, highly educated people leave an area in search of work.

Bridging point: a shallow area of a river where bridges can be built.

Brownfield site: derelict industrial or manufacturing site.

Bustee: shanty town, slum areas of poorly built huts with few services.

C

Calcification: an impermeable build-up of calcium on the ground, can lead to crop failure.

Canopy: the topmost layer of foliage in a forest.

Canton: how Switzerland is divided up for governmental purposes; in Ireland the equivalent are counties.

Capillary action: the upward movement of water.

Carbon cycle: uptake of carbon dioxide by plants, ingestion by animals and respiration and decay of the animals.

Carbon sink: environmental reservoir that absorbs and stores carbon.

Carrying capacity: the number of individuals that can be supported by a given area.

Cash crops: crops grown to make a profit.

CBD: central business district.

Celtic Tiger: a nickname for Ireland during the late 1990s and early to mid-2000s when the country experienced rapid economic growth.

Census: an official (government) count and survey of a population.

Cholera: waterborne disease; where basic healthcare is minimal, it can be fatal.

Civil rights: the rights of equality afforded to all citizens under the law in a democracy.

Climate: the average weather across a large area over a period of time, i.e. 35 years.

Climate change: unusual changes in a region's climate caused by increased CO_2 levels.

Colonialism: when one country is politically controlled and then economically exploited by another country.

Constitution: a set of general laws that are written down.

Conurbation: a large urban area formed when several towns and cities meet.

Core region: a well-developed, richer and more central region.

Counterurbanisation: when urban workers move to the countryside.

Course: the journey a river takes.

Crop rotation: changing the crops grown in an area to allow nutrients to regenerate.

Cyclones: very strong winds.

D

Death rate: mortality rate, the number of deaths per 1,000 per year.

Decolonisation: when former colonies gain political independence.

Deforestation: the removal of trees from an area of forest.

Delta: area of alluvium at the mouth of a river.

Demesne: land or an estate belonging to a manor.

Demographic transition model: a population model expressing the predictable patterns of death rate, birth rate and natural increase of a country as it becomes more developed.

Denudation: the collective name for weathering and erosion.

Dependent population: see *Age dependency ratio*.

Deranged drainage pattern: rivers have a chaotic appearance.

Desertification: the spreading of the deserts, caused by climate change and human activities.

Discriminate: to treat a person or group of people differently on grounds other than individual ability, particularly with regard to race, religion, sex or nationality.

Diurnal temperature change: the difference between the maximum and minimum temperature in one day.

Dormitory town: a residential area from where people commute to work.

Dublin Regulation/system: all migrants should be processed in the country in which they entered the EU.

Dynamic: very active or resourceful.

E

Economically active age group: people aged 16–64 years, the age group that earns money.

Economic interdependence: occurs when two countries rely on each other for trade.

EEA: European Economic Area.

Electric cars: cars powered by battery.

Emigrant: a person that leaves a country to settle in another.

Empty diagonal: an area in France that has low population density.

'Englishisation': a term used to describe the influence of modern American culture in an increasingly globalised world.

ERDF: European Regional Development Fund.

Ethnic cleansing: the forceful removal by slaughter, threat or terror of a minority group from an area.

Ethnic group: a group of people that have a common trait such as language, race or religion.

Ethnicity: a combination of race, language, religion and nationality.

F

Fallow: the stage in crop rotation when the land is not used to grow crops.

Federal-style government: there is a central government but regions within a country have control over their own internal affairs.

Fertility rate: the number of births per mother.

Fluvial: describing rivers.

Fossil fuels: fuels formed by natural processes, e.g. coal.

G

GDP: Gross domestic product.

Genetically modified (GM) foods: plants that have been altered to take on certain characteristics.

Gerrymandering: a way of distorting an election result by manipulating geographic boundaries so that one group will do better than another.

Ghetto: a rundown part of a city that is inhabited by minority groups.

Global warming: see Climate change.

Gradient/slope: the angle of a piece of land.

Green belt: an area of woodland or parks surrounding a community.

Green Revolution: research, development and technology programmes that increased agricultural output.

Greying: when a large percentage of the population is older.

Growth pattern: is the change in the population growth pattern over time.

Gully erosion: when fast-moving water concentrates on a small area and carves out channels.

H

Heritage: the monuments, documents, records, archaeological finds, flora, fauna and habitats of a region.

Hinterland: the edge of a city.

Horizon: layers in the soil.

Horticulture: market gardening.

Humus: dark brown sticky substance full of nutrients, formed from decaying plant matter.

Hybrid cars: cars that use two or more sources of power.

I

IDA: Industrial Development Authority.

Ideology: a body of ideas, usually political and/or economic, forming the basis of a national or sectarian society.

IFSC: International Financial Services Centre.

Igneous rocks: rocks formed when lava or magma cooled down and solidified.

Immigration: people moving into a country.

Indigenous people: native people of a country or region.

Industrialisation: government policy to develop industry by improving infrastructure and communications links and the labour force through education.

Industrial Revolution: improvements in machinery and technology to increase industrial output.

Infant mortality rate: the numbers of babies that die aged one year or less per 1,000 live births.

Inflated land prices: when land prices increase rapidly in a place because it is popular.

Integration: when different cultures live peacefully together and minority groups have access to the same opportunities as the majority group.

Intensive farming: produces as many crops or livestock as possible without exhausting the land.

Inward migration: people from another place move to and settle in an area.

Irrigation: the artificial watering of land.

K

Kyoto Protocol: an international agreement that aims to reduce global warming.

L

Laterites: soil type rich in iron and aluminium, formed in hot and wet tropical areas.

LDCs: less developed countries.

Leaching: washing minerals and nutrients out of reach of plant roots.

Lemass era: Seán Lemass was Taoiseach during a period of economic prosperity from 1959 to 1966.

Life expectancy: the average age a person is expected to live to in a region.

Lower emission cars: cars that emit lower levels of pollution.

M

Malnutrition: occurs when a person does not receive enough nutrients to stay healthy.

Market gardening: growing salad crops in greenhouses close to a large urban area.

Maternal death: the death of a woman during or shortly after pregnancy.

MDCs: more developed countries.

Mean: the average.

Melting pot: different cultural groups take on the cultures and traditions of a host country.

Metamorphic rocks: rocks that are created when igneous or sedimentary rocks come under great heat or pressure.

Migration balance: the difference between numbers of emigrants and immigrants in a country.

MNCs: Multinational corporations.

Monoculture: when the same crop is grown every year.

Monsoon: a seasonal wind created in the south-east Asia; heavy rain follows.

Monetary union: a trading bloc with a single market and a common currency.

Muslims: followers of Islam.

N

Nation: a population united by a common culture and identity.

Nation state: when people of of a similar culture and identity (a nation) decide to politically control a certain geographic area (a state).

Natural decrease: when the death rate of a region is higher than the birth rate.

Natural increase: when the birth rate of a region is higher than the death rate.

NDP: National Development Plan.

NICs: newly industrialised countries.

Niche holidays: alternative, specialised or adventure holidays.

Nutrient cycle: all the processes by which nutrients are transferred from one organism to another.

O

Optimum: the best or most favourable amount.

Outward migration: people leave their home place to settle elsewhere.

Overcropping: planting crops year after year and not allowing the minerals time to regenerate.

Overgrazing: too many animals eating the grass.

Overpopulation: too many people for the natural resources of a country to support.

Overspill: the proportion of the population that leaves a district.

P

Package holiday: an all-inclusive holiday arranged with a travel agent.

Parent rock: the bedrock of an area.

Pastoral farming: involves grazing animals such as sheep and cows.

Peripheral region: an underdeveloped, poorer and marginal region.

Plateau: a relatively flat area of high ground.

Population density: the amount of people per km².

Population distribution: the spread of people across an area.

Population explosion: a dramatic increase in the world's population.

Pore spaces: the spaces between the mineral particles in soil.

Porous: water can pass through it.

Poverty line: the lowest level of income needed to achieve an adequate standard of living in a country.

Prehistoric: time before anything was written down.

Prevailing wind: the most common wind in an area.

Primary economic activities: involve the removal of natural resources from the Earth.

Primate city: has more than twice the population of the next largest city in the country.

Propaganda: the spreading of information/ideas that may not be true to harm individuals or groups.

Pull factor: a reason that attracts a migrant to a region.

Push factor: a reason that pushes migrants from their homes.

R

Race: the categorisation of a person based upon physical characteristics such as skin colour.

Radial drainage pattern: rivers spread out from a central point.

Raindrop erosion: wearing away the exposed soil from the rain's direct impact.

Range: taking the lowest figure from the highest figure.

Rationalisation: older, less productive industries are closed down in favour of newer plants.

Reafforestation: the planting of trees in areas where deforestation has occurred in the past.

Refugee: a person that flees their country from safety reasons and moves to another country.

Region: an area of the Earth's surface that has certain boundaries or characteristics that set it apart from other areas.

Regolith: weathered pieces of rock, also called scree or talus.

Relief: the lie of the land.

Relief rainfall: when moisture-laden clouds have to rise over a mountain range.

Remittance: money sent home by migrants to help their families.

Resource: anything that can be used by humans; can be divided into renewable and non-renewable resources.

Rezone: to change land use, e.g. from industrial to residential.

Roll-on roll-off ferries: ferries designed to carry wheeled cargo that are driven on and off.

Route focus/nodal point: where the main transport routes are concentrated.

S

Salad bowl: concept that different cultural groups keep their own cultures and traditions when living in a host country.

Salinisation: a build-up of dissolved salts on the land, which are poisonous to plants.

Satellite towns: towns on the outskirts of a large urban area that have become part of it.

Savannah: mix of grasslands with sparse trees.

Scale: the ratio between a distance on a map and the actual distance on the ground.

Schengen Agreement: abolished all major checks at countries' borders within the EU excluding Ireland and Britain.

Secondary economic activities: when raw materials are processed or semi-processed materials are further developed; this usually takes place in an industry.

Sedimentary rocks: rocks created from the compressed remains of plants or animals.

Seed germination: growing seeds.

Senile stage: stage 5 of the demographic transition model, when the death rate is higher than the birth rate.

Shanty town: see *Bustee*.

Slash and burn: cutting trees and burning their stumps and the surrounding vegetation.

Smog: low-lying polluted air caused by smoke from factories, cars and homes.

Social stratification: the tendency of people of similar incomes and social backgrounds to live in the same area of a town/city.

Soil degradation: destruction caused to the quality of the soil.

Soil heaving: the upward thrust of the ground caused by the freezing of moist soil.

State: when people come together to rule an area.

Subsistence farming: only produces enough to feed the farmer's family.

T

Tariff: a tax levied by a government on imported or exported goods.

Tertiary economic activities: providing services.

Till: the unsorted material dropped by a glacier.

Topography: landscape.

Total fertility rate (TFR): the average number of babies born per mother.

Traffic bottleneck: the point at which traffic becomes congested, causing it to slow down or stop.

Trellised drainage pattern: tributaries join the main river at right angles.

Tsunami: a large wave created by an earthquake under the ocean.

Typhoid: waterborne disease of the digestive tract; where basic healthcare is minimal, it can be fatal.

Typhoon: violent tropical storm that occurs in the Western Pacific and Indian Oceans.

U

Underpopulation: the number of people living in a country cannot exploit the resources fully.

Urban fringe: the outskirts of a city.

Urban infill: the regeneration of an inner city area.

Urban regeneration: the improvement of an area through the creation of new facilities.

Urban renewal: the demolition of old buildings and their replacement with modern ones.

Urban sprawl: the uncontrolled growth of cities into the surrounding countryside.

W

Water stress: the need for more water than there is available.

Water table: the area underground beneath which the rock and soil are saturated with water.

Wattle and daub: building material using woven sticks and sticky wet soil, sand, dung and straw.

X

Xenophobia: hatred or fear of foreigners.

Z

Zone of ablation: area where snow melts.

Zone of accumulation: area where snow builds up.

Zone of saturation: area of soil or rock below the level of the water table where all the available spaces are filled with water.

Zoning: to designate land for a specific use.

Index